General Studies

An AS- and A-level Coursebook

SECOND EDITION

Colin Swatridge

Published by HarperCollinsPublishers Limited
77–85 Fulham Palace Road
Hammersmith
London
W6 8JB

www.CollinsEducation.com
Online support for schools and colleges

Reprinted 10 9 8 7 6 5 4 3 2 1

ISBN 0-00-712852-5

British Library Cataloguing in Publication Data
A Catalogue record for this publication is available from the British Library

Illustrations: Nigel Jordan except page 32, Mike Phillips
Page design: Jordan Publishing Design
Cover design: HartMcleod, Cambridge
Cover photograph: gettyimages
Commissioning editor: Thomas Allain-Chapman
Project management: Kate Haywood
Edited by Kate Haywood and Hugh Hillyard-Parker
Picture research: Kathy Lockley
Production: Katie Morris
Printed and bound by Imago, Thailand

You might also like to visit
www.fireandwater.co.uk
The book lover's website

Acknowledgements

The author would like to thank Helier Dreux, Head of General Studies at Reigate College, for all his help with 'Making a presentation', page 134ff.

The following permissions to reproduce material are gratefully acknowledged.

The Maths Gene: Why Everyone Has It But Most People Can't Use It extract by Kevin Devlin, published by Weidenfeld & Nicolson; *All Must Have Prizes* extract by Melanie Philips, published by Little, Brown & Co.; *Wisdom, Information and Wonder* extract by Mary Midgley, pubished by Routledge; *Issues and Debates* extract by Steve Taylor, 1999, © Macmillan, reproduced with permission of Palgrave; *Maybe One* extract © Bill McKibben, 1999. Extract from *Maybe One*, published by Transworld Publishers, a division of the Random House Group Ltd. All rights reserved. Used with permission; *Where Did We Go Wrong?* extract by Eric Roll from *The Gold Standard to Europe*, published by Faber & Faber Ltd; *The Hungry Spirit* extracts by Charles Handy, published by Hutchinson. Used by permission of the Random House Group Limited; *The World in 2000* extract by Iain Carson © The Economist Publications, London; *Hand to Brand Combat* extract by Katharine Viner from *The Guardian* © The Guardian. Used with permission; *Political Geography* extracts by Richard Muir, 1997, © Macmillan, reproduced with permission of Palgrave; *Political Ideologies* extract by Richard Jay, published by Routledge; *Power Without Responsibility* extract by James Curran and Jean Seaton, published by Routledge; *A Revolution in Progress* extract by Alastair Bruton, published by Little, Brown & Co.; *The Problems of Philosophy* extract by Bertrand Russell, first published by Oxford University Press 1912 Oxford University Press, reprinted by permission of Oxford University Press; *On the Death of a 3-month-old Girl* extract by Clare Dyer from *The Guardian* © The Guardian. Used with permission; *Godless Morality: Keeping Religion out of Ethics* extract by Richard Holloway, published in 1999 by Canongate Books, 14 High Street, Edinburgh; .*Concise Routledge Encyclopedia of Philosophy* extract by David Braddon-Mitchell and Frank Jackson, published by Routledge; *The Language Web* extract by Jean Atkinson, 1997, published by Cambridge University Press; 'We are Never Going to Score' extract from *The Daily Mail* © The Daily Mail. Reprinted by permission of Atlantic Syndications on behalf of *The Daily Mail*; 'You Won't Get Far' extract from an article by Janet Street-Porter, first published in *The Independent on Sunday*, 17 December 2000. Reprinted by permission of Independent Syndications; *Creative Britain* extract by Chris Smith, published by Faber & Faber Limited; 'Our Generation of Couch Potato Kids, Stuck in their Rooms and Glued to TV' extract from an article by Rhys Williams and Andrew Buncombe, first published in *The Independent*, 19 March 1999; *British Theatre Since the War* extracts by Dominic Shellard ©1999; *Television: A Media Student's Guide* extract by David McQueen, published by Arnold; *Earth Matters* extract © Friends of the Earth, 2000; 'Developers of Direct Sites to Get Tax Relief' extract from an article by Clayton Hurst, first published in *The Independent on Sunday*, 1 October 2000. Reprinted by permission of Independent Syndications; *Labour sympathizer takes over at BBC* extract by Joe Murphy, published in *The Sunday Telegraph* on 14 June 2000; *An Intelligent Person's Guide to Modern Culture* extract by Roger Scruton, published by Duckworth; *Civil Liberties* extract by Helen Fenwick, 2nd edn, 1998, London: Cavendish Publishing; *Hard shoulders to cry on* extract by John Vidal © The Guardian, 1993 www.guardian.co.uk

AKG London 22, 33r, 49, 74, 83, 105/Bianconero 34; Britstock-IFA/Alaska Stock 27/Erich-Bach 11a/Willmann/Bach 67; *Brookside* photograph reproduced by kind permission of Phil Redmond, creator of *Brookside* 117; Robert Harding Picture Library 11b, 47, 90, 103, 104/N. Francis 51; Hulton Archive 38, 94a, 94b; Courtesy of Intel 55; 20th Century Fox/Courtesy Kobal Collection 35; Nova Development Corporation 8; Novosti (London) 107; PA Photos 65, 71, 85; Photofusion/Colin Edwards 69b, 84/Crispin Hughes 33 l/Debbie Humphry 39a, 96; Science Photo Library/David Gifford 26/Laguna Design 28/Mehau Kulyk 14; Still Pictures/Dylan Garcia 69a/Hartmut Schwarzbach 53/Mike Schroder 77/Peter Frischmuth 39b/Robert Holmgren 29; © Tate London, 2001: *Equivalent VIII* 1966 © Carl André/VAGA, New York/DACS, London 2001, 115.

Contents

Introduction

Traditionally, General Studies has been a makeweight subject, a point-scoring subject, even an income-earning subject. It has been all subjects, and no subject at all.

Now, perhaps for the first time, we have the opportunity to make a real subject of it: one that has theoretical integrity as well as practical utility. The new specifications have been framed to match the Subject Criteria drawn up by the Qualifications and Curriculum Authority (QCA), with the help and support of the examining boards. They make it clear what General Studies is, and what a General Studies course should do. It is agreed that:

- it is about significant contemporary issues
- it should focus on these issues from a number of perspectives
- there are certain important concepts which should inform thinking about the issues
- among these concepts is the nature of knowledge and the evidence on which it is based
- we should understand what we mean when we speak of facts and opinions, values and beliefs.

In the past, General Studies has borrowed its reason-for-being from traditional school subjects. These have supplied the *what* of General Studies; but they have not contributed much *how* or *why*.

This book, like General Studies itself, has a new organizing principle: it is issues, or topics-based, as its predecessor was; but these topics have been set on a continuum of evidence that ranges from 'hard' to 'soft' – from mathematics to the arts; from the quantitative to the qualitative.

Hard evidence   Quantitative data

Mathematics
Physical sciences
Natural sciences
Social sciences
History
Economics
Politics
Philosophy
Religion
Arts

Soft evidence   Qualitative ideas

This is neither an ascent nor a descent: it is the range of ways in which we get knowledge of a more or less certain, more or less shared, kind.

The diagram is over-simplified, of course; and in some ways it would have been truer to life if the continuum was circular rather than linear, since there is much in present-day maths and science that borders on the aesthetic, not to say the visionary.

History	Economics
Social sciences	Politics
Natural sciences	Philosophy
Physical sciences	Religion
Mathematics	Arts
Hard evidence	Soft evidence

The topics are grouped in ten units, as shown on the previous page, with titles that are recognizable from the traditional subject curriculum.

Concepts (A–J) alternate with the issues (Units 1–10). These concepts include those already referred to: facts, knowledge, opinions, values and beliefs, together with others highlighted in the Subject Criteria: culture, ideology and criticism. These concepts are not discussed in the abstract: their meanings are hammered out on the anvil of further, quite concrete issues.

The key skills of Communication and Application of number run all the way through the book; and many opportunities for class discussion or group work (or Working with others) are suggested. In addition there is a skills section (pp. 122–139): Writing an essay, Solving a problem and Making a presentation (the latter being combined with information technology, thus combining two key skills). Essays continue to be the primary means by which the knowledge and understanding of students will be assessed, therefore the section Writing an essay is devoted to the all-important skill of writing essays, both short and long. Further key skills opportunities are provided in the Resource Pack, which includes 10 ready-to-run key skills assignments, all in agreement with the September 2001 changes. These assignments have been specifically designed to enable students to gain evidence for the first three key skills.

Questions of an open and closed kind are posed throughout the book, and answers to the closed questions are given at the end of the book. A good many suggestions are given, too, to show the direction that answers to the more open questions might take. These are not put forward as definitive answers, nor are they sufficiently developed. General Studies is no longer a subject that will make do with short answers to short questions of a factual kind. It has a new remit now: it is to be the framework within which students might develop key skills; reflect on what it means to be a citizen of the world; and gain confidence as critical thinkers.

The Coursebook and the specifications

Thinking and analytical skills	Coursebook
These skills are listed separately in the AQA/A specification; but they are taken from the Subject Criteria, and are subsumed in all the specifications for the subject.	
• Use of and distinctions between concepts of knowledge, truth and belief, understanding of what constitutes proof*. The possibilities and limitations of knowledge.	Knowledge pp.22, 23; Truth pp.82, 83, 87, 110 Belief pp.106, 107 Facts pp.10, 11 Ideology pp.58, 59
• Similarities and differences between arts, sciences and social sciences; methods, processes and limitations of different disciplines.	Physical sciences pp.14, 15; Natural sciences pp.26, 27 Social sciences pp.38, 39; The Arts pp.110–117 Introduction (p.i)
• Exploration of sources of knowledge and information, research methods.	Ideology pp.58, 59
Differences between facts and opinions, quantitative and qualitative data.	Facts pp.10, 11; Substance abuse and health pp.84, 85 Introduction (p.i)
• Assessment of the validity* and reliability of data and information.	
Objectivity and subjectivity and the recognition of bias.	Objectivity pp.34, 35
Understanding the nature of argument.	Argument pp.46, 47
The influence of values and judgement.	Values pp.94, 95; Criticism pp.118, 119
• Deductive and inductive reasoning.	Deductive reasoning pp.3, 10, 46; Inductive reasoning
Argument from cause, authority, and by analogy.	pp.10, 11; Authority pp.49, 80, 103; Analogy pp.47, 49
Fallacious and unsound reasoning*.	Ideology, pp.58, 59
Syllogisms; the effect of language on meaning.	Language and stereotyping pp.108, 109

* These items are further developed in the Resource Pack.

AQA/A

AQA/A	Coursebook
AS	
• religious and value systems; world religions	Values pp.94, 95; Faith and faiths pp.100, 101
• cultural values; nature and use of language;	Culture pp.70, 71; Language and stereotyping pp.108, 109
arts and society; participation; arts in education	The Arts pp.110, 111
• art forms; critical appreciation;	Mapping the Arts pp.112, 113; Criticism pp.118, 119
media and popular culture	Art as entertainment pp.116, 117
• universe theory*; energy; Earth's resources;	Forces p.15; Energy pp.16, 17; Resources pp.16, 17
life; human progress; the influence of science	Physical sciences pp.12, 13; Natural sciences pp.26, 27
• history of science; communications and transport;	The school curriculum p.24; Science past p.78;
scientific method	Electromagnetism pp.18, 19; Transport pp.12, 13;
	Scientific method pp.10, 11
• science and ethics	The sanctity of life pp.88, 89; see also pp.21, 29, 30, 31
• science and technology and the environment	Energy pp.16, 17; The atmosphere pp.20, 21
• mathematical reasoning	Mathematics pp.2, 3; Abstraction pp.4, 5
• society and the individual; freedom, rights and	Self and others pp.32, 33; see also pp.49, 82, 92
responsibilities; equality of opportunity	Rights and duties pp.90, 91; Equal opportunities pp.96, 97
• government and politics	Politics pp.62, 63; Government pp.64, 65
• human behaviour; crime*; the family, class,	Social sciences pp.38, 39; Families pp.40, 41; Social
gender; race, disability; education	Class pp.36, 37; Schools and life-chances pp.42, 43
• law, culture, and ethics	Law and justice pp.48, 49
business, commerce and industry; employment and	The market pp.54, 55
poverty; economic development	Wealth and poverty pp.52, 53
A2	
• religious and value systems; religious experience,	Religion pp.98, 99; Morals pp.102, 103
belief, and art;	A balance sheet pp.104, 105
beliefs and values in a multi-faith society;	Faith and faiths pp.100, 101; Values pp.94, 95
ethical philosophy	The sanctity of life pp.88, 89
• cultural differences and values;	Culture pp.70, 71; Europe pp.72, 73
English as a foreign language*	
creativity, art and design, and meaning;	The Arts pp.110, 111
critics, patrons, the state, and critical judgement;	The visual Arts pp.114, 115; Criticism pp.118, 119
artistic movements and forms	Art past, p.79; Mapping the Arts pp.112, 113
• media and communication;	The fourth estate pp.66, 67
popular culture and 'high' art; entertainment;	Art as entertainment pp.116, 117
media bias*, censorship*, and power	
• scientific hypothesis, theory, and law;	Physical sciences pp.14, 15; Natural sciences pp.26, 27
natural resources;	
biotechnology, food, drugs, and health	Genetic engineering pp.28, 29; Substance abuse and health pp.84, 85
• science history; ICT; transport;	Science past, p.78; Information technology pp.134-139;
scientific method and principles	Electromagnetism pp.18, 19
• science and ethics	The sanctity of life pp.88, 89; see also pp.21, 29, 30, 31
• science, technology, and the environment, and	Energy pp.16, 17; The atmosphere pp.20, 21
religious conflict	Genetic engineering pp.28, 29; Biodiversity and sustainability pp.30, 31
• spatial and mechanical relations	Measurement of space and time pp.6, 7
• freedom, rights and responsibilities, law and	Rights and duties pp.90, 91; see also pp.49, 82, 92;
religious belief	Belief pp.106, 107
• democracy and politics, national and international;	The people pp.68, 69; Nationalism and internationalism
news media	pp.60, 61; The fourth estate pp.66, 67
• sociological method; crime; the family, health and	Social sciences pp.38, 39; Families pp.40, 41; Wealth and
welfare; minorities	poverty pp.52, 53; Equal opportunities pp.96, 97
• law, culture, and ethics; international relations	Law and justice pp.48, 49; Nationalism and internationalism pp.60, 61; Ideology pp.58, 59
• business, commerce and industry	The market pp.54, 55; Globalization pp.56, 57
economic issues; creation and distribution of	Economics pp.50, 51
wealth; world problems	Population, p.44

* These items are further developed in the Resource Pack.

AQA/B

AQA/B	Coursebook
AS	
Conflict	
● Animal and human aggression*	Biodiversity and sustainability pp.30, 31; Self and others
Controversy in science and technology	pp.32, 33; see also pp.17, 20, 21, 28, 29
● Tensions in the modern family	Families pp.40, 41
Social class divisions	Social class pp.36, 37
● Mass and minority taste; stage and screen	Culture pp.70, 71; Art as entertainment pp.116, 117
● Business competition	The market pp.54, 55; Globalization pp.56, 57
Employment and unemployment	Social class pp.36, 37
● Stereotyping; the public and private	Language and stereotyping pp.108, 109; freedom pp.49, 82, 92
Power	
● The energy debate; physical fitness*	Energy pp.16, 17
● Education as empowerment; politics, voting	Schools and life-chances pp.42, 43; Politics pp.62, 63
● Media power; art and society	The fourth estate pp.66, 67; The Arts pp.110, 111
● Marketing and advertising; corporations	The market pp.54, 55; Globalization pp.56, 57
● Power in society; faith and faiths	Positions of power pp.80, 81; Faith and faiths pp.100, 101
Space	
● Atmosphere and climate change, personal space	The atmosphere pp.20, 21; Self and others pp.32, 33
● Housing, transport, migration	The built environment pp.128–133
● Architecture*, sculpture, global media*	
● Agribusiness, location of industry	Genetic engineering pp.28, 29; Globalization pp.56, 57
● Land ownership; environmentalism	Direct action pp.92, 93
A2	
Conflict-resolution	
● Public understanding of science and technology	Natural sciences pp.26, 27
Research; ecology, sustainability	Biodiversity and sustainability pp.30, 31
● Party politics, democracy	Politics pp.62, 63; The people pp.68, 69
Equal opportunities	Equal opportunities pp.96, 97
● Art-criticism; media bias*	The visual Arts pp.114, 115; Criticism pp.118, 119
Meaning and metaphor	Language and stereotyping p.109; Literature pp.121
● Market research; industrial relations; personal finance and credit*	Economics pp.50, 51; The market pp.56, 57
● Nationalism and internationalism	Nationalism and internationalism pp.60, 61
Rights and responsibilities	Rights and duties pp.90, 91
Religious controversy	Morals pp.102, 103; A balance sheet pp.104, 105
Power-resolution	
● 'Big science'; science and change	Energy pp.16, 17; Electromagnetism pp.18, 19
Regulation of science and technology	Genetic engineering pp.28, 29
● Pressure groups; democratic accountability; law enforcement	The people, p.68; Direct action pp.92, 93; Law and justice pp.48, 49
● Censorship*; the art market; media ownership	The visual Arts pp.114, 115; The fourth estate pp.66, 67
● Industry regulators; consumerism	Positions of power p.80; see pp.56, 57, 84, 85, 95
International trade	Globalization pp.56, 57
● Social justice; citizenship; decline in deference to authority	Law and justice p.48; see pp.68, 69, 90, 91; Positions of power pp.80, 81; Morals p.103
Space-time	
● Universe theory and research	Measurement of space and time pp.6, 7
Measurement of scale; progress in science and technology	Progress pp.76, 77
● Cultural diversity; social change; social and political reform	Culture pp.70, 71; Equal opportunities pp.96, 97; Government p.65
● Aesthetics; new media	The Arts pp.110, 111; Information technology pp.13–139;
Music* and literature	Literature pp.120, 121
● Heritage; ICT and work-patterns*	
Transport and tourism	Transport pp.12, 13; Tourism pp.122–127
● Historical fact and belief	History pp.74, 75
Cultural relativism, religion and secularism	Culture pp.70, 71; see also p.103; Religion p.99

*These items are further developed in the Resource Pack.

Edexcel

Edexcel	Coursebook
AS **Unit 1: Aspects of Culture**	
• cultures, western culture, popular culture, high culture, relationship between cultures	Culture pp.70, 71; The Arts pp.110, 111; Art as entertainment pp.116, 117
• the basis of moral reasoning, religious teaching, utilitarianism, social contract, moral problems	The sanctity of life pp.88, 89; Values pp.94, 95; Rights and duties pp.90, 91; Morals pp.102, 103
• religious belief and experience, religious symbolism, purpose in life	Religion pp.98, 99; Faith and faiths pp.100, 101
• development of artistic style, literary or musical form	Art past, p.79; The Arts pp.110, 111; The visual arts pp.114, 115; Literature p.120
• key elements in different styles of the arts	The fourth estate pp.66, 67
• media power and influence, media ownership, censorship	
Unit 2: Scientific Horizons	Physical sciences pp.14, 15; Natural sciences pp.26, 27;
• revolutions in different sciences*	Science past, p.78
• experimental procedures in physical sciences*	Facts pp.10, 11
• inductive science and creativity	The atmosphere pp.20, 21; Genetic engineering pp.28, 29
• ethical and environmental issues in technology	
• number statements and quantitative reasoning	Mathematics pp.2–9
• scientific progress; science and the media	Progress pp.74, 75
Unit 3: Social Perspectives	
• race, gender, age, and disability	Equal opportunities pp.96, 97
• government and politics: Britain and Europe	Politics pp.62, 63; Government pp.64, 65; Europe pp.72, 73
• work, leisure and unemployment	Social class pp.36, 37; Art as entertainment pp.116, 117
• crime*, deviance, and the legal system	Law and justice pp.48, 49
• family life	Families pp.40, 41
A2 **Unit 4: Cultural Expressions**	
• culture and society, 'high' and popular culture, government funding of the arts*	Culture pp.70, 71; The Arts pp.110, 111
• contemporary moral positions; genetic engineering, family, artistic freedom of expression	Morals pp.102, 103; Genetic engineering pp.28, 29 Families pp.40, 41; The visual Arts pp.114, 115
• religious belief; belief and behaviour; religion and science and morality; religious symbolism	Religion pp.98, 99; Belief pp.106, 107; Morals pp.102, 103; Faith and faiths pp.100, 101
• styles and forms of art as responses to social structures and traditions*	Art past p.79; The Arts pp.110, 111
• subjective and universal criteria of aesthetic evaluation	Subjectivity and objectivity pp.34, 35; Criticism pp.118, 119
• mass media; ownership; market forces; influence	The fourth estate pp.66, 67; Art as entertainment pp.116, 117
Unit 5: Modern Society	
• cultural value systems; multiculturalism, equal opportunities	Ideology pp.58, 59; Culture pp.70, 71; Values pp.94, 95; Equal opportunities pp.96, 97
• government and politics; electoral and legislative processes; devolution*	Politics pp.62, 63; Government pp.64, 65; The people pp.68, 69
• work, leisure, and unemployment; the nature of social sciences	Social class pp.36, 37; Social sciences pp.38, 39; Schools and life-chances pp.42, 43
• crime and law; punishment*	Law and justice pp.48, 49
• family life; economic and social change	Families pp.40, 41; Economics pp.50, 51; Globalization pp.56, 57
Unit 6: The Contemporary World	
• influence of technology on the arts; public understanding of science; science and religion	Mapping the Arts pp.112, 113
• aspects of cultural expression and society	Culture pp.70, 71; Language and stereotyping pp.108, 109
• the international nature of scientific endeavour; technology and quality of life; evidence in the sciences (inc. statistics)	The built environment pp.128–133 Evidence pp.14, 15; Vital statistics pp.8, 9

*These items are further developed in the Resource Pack.

OCR

OCR	Coursebook
AS **The Cultural Domain** ● knowledge, belief and unbelief ● the roles of instinct, indoctrination, personal experience, reason, faith, and revelation ● formative influences: family, friends, neighbourhood, school, workplace, media, leisure, travel, and literature ● matters of conscience and public morality, the limits of tolerance ● the culture of any minority group, whether determined by age, locality, race etc. ● evolving or conflicting cultures ● ways in which the media influence public opinion ● moral issues arising from the activity of the media ● current developments within the media and communications*	Knowledge pp.22, 23; Belief pp.106, 107 Self and others pp.32, 33 Faith and faiths pp.100, 101 Families pp.40, 41 Schools and life-chances pp.42, 43 Tourism pp.122–127 Morals pp.102, 103 Culture pp.70, 71 Europe pp.72, 73 The fourth estate pp.66, 67 Information technology pp.134–139
The Scientific Domain ● greenhouse gases and global warming, energy and transport, space exploration ● population dynamics, genetic engineering and biotechnology, health and fitness*, fertility control, organ transplantation ● conservation and environmental pollution ● induction and classification ● hypothesis testing and deduction, theory and law ● modelling, forecasting and reliability* ● experimental design* ● the role of time scale ● the layout of data sets ● amounts and sizes* ● scales and proportion ● statistics ● formula	The atmosphere pp.20, 21 Energy pp.16, 17; Transport pp.12, 13 Population pp.44, 45; Genetic engineering pp.28, 29 The sanctity of life pp.88, 89 The atmosphere pp.20, 21 Facts pp.10, 11 Mathematics p.3; Physical sciences p.15 Measurement of space and time pp.6, 7 Vital statistics pp.8, 9
The Social Domain ● political parties, leading political figures, areas of political controversy ● voting trends in the UK ● disagreements in the social sciences: facts, opinions, judgments ● education, housing, health ● work and leisure, unemployment* ● the division of wealth ● travel and transport	Politics pp.62, 63 Rights and duties pp.90, 91 The people pp.68 Social sciences pp.38, 39 Facts pp.10, 11; Opinion pp.82, 83 Schools and life-chances pp.42, 43; Substance abuse and health pp.84, 85 Wealth and poverty pp.52, 53 Tourism pp.122–127; Transport pp.12,13
A2 **The Cultural Domain** ● central tenets of any one religion ● substitutes for religion: humanism, rationalism, materialism, hedonism ● architecture* ● painting, photography, sculpture ● the state, the screen, and all kinds of music* ● aesthetic evaluation	Faith and faiths pp.100, 101 Nationalism and internationalism pp.60, 61 The built environment pp.128–133 Mapping the Arts pp.112, 113; The visual Arts pp.114, 115; Art as entertainment pp.116, 117 The Arts pp.110, 111; Criticism pp.118, 119

* These items are further developed in the Resource Pack.

OCR *continued*

OCR	Coursebook
The Scientific Domain	
● disease control and health*	
● gravitation motion; longitude	Physical sciences p.15
● the impact of information technology*	Information technology pp.134–139
● nuclear energy and fossil fuels	Energy pp.16, 17
● telecommunications	Electromagnetism pp.18, 19
● food supply and distribution	Population p.44
● herbicides, pesticides, and organic production	Biodiversity and sustainability p.31
● weapons and peace keeping	Nationalism and internationalism pp.61
● resource exploitation	Energy pp.16, 17
● sustainability and stewardship	Biodiversity and sustainability pp.31, 32
The Social Domain	
● important political ideologies and values	Ideology pp.58, 59; Values pp.94, 95
● important current social, economic and political issues	Social sciences pp.38, 39; Subjectivity and objectivity
● research methods used in the social sciences and their reliability	pp.34, 35 Self and others pp.32, 33; Positions of power pp.80, 81
● influences on human behaviour	Social class pp.36, 37
● community life and relationships	
● crime and law enforcement*	Law and justice pp.48, 49; The sanctity of life pp.88, 89;
● the law and important ethical and cultural dilemmas: secrecy, abortion, euthanasia, discrimination, drugs, animal rights	Equal opportunities pp.96, 97; Substance abuse and health pp.84, 85 Globalization p.57; The people pp.68, 69; Direct action
● obeying the law; pressure groups; different forms of dissent and protest	pp.92, 93

*These items are further developed in the Resource Pack.

Mathematics

This introduction to mathematics is designed to get you thinking about what mathematics is, and where and when it is used. It then moves on to explore what kind of knowledge mathematics is. There is something philosophical about this line of enquiry, but it is one with which you, as a student of General Studies, will need to be familiar.

The roots of mathematics

The word *mathematics* comes from the Greek root, *mathein*, to learn. *Mathetes* is the word used in the Greek New Testament for the disciples of Jesus: they were learners, or pupils. The root is preserved in the word *polymath*, meaning someone who is learned in many fields.

Mathematics has a clear historic connection with the idea of learning and study. Indeed, in Ancient Greece mathematics was studied for its own intrinsic beauty and for the training in logic. The study of mathematics made it possible to reason at higher levels of complexity and abstraction, as well as to solve everyday problems.

For **Pythagoras** (philosopher and mathematician, c.582–500 BCE), mathematics and philosophy were one and the same thing. For him, mathematics was the highest form of knowledge, underlying all other subjects and, in particular, music and astronomy. He thought of mathematics as the language of the gods.

The idea that numbers are a part of nature – that everything is based upon numbers – continued into the early modern period (the 1500s and 1600s). In Western thought, numbers were associated with order and plan – specifically, God's order and plan. **Sir Thomas Browne** (author and physician, 1605–82) wrote:

> All things began in order, so shall they end, and so shall they begin again; according to the ordainer of order and mystical mathematics of the city of heaven.
>
> Sir Thomas Browne *The Garden of Cyrus* 1658

Mathematics in three aspects

Although today mathematics is no longer thought of as mystical and spiritual, it does have different nuances of meaning – from the practical to the abstract. Mathematics touches many areas from the highly specialized academic study at university, to the subject studied in schools, to its use in science, to calculations made in everyday situations.

A useful way of looking at these meanings is to see mathematics in three aspects, as follows.

Aspect 1 – everyday maths

Mathematics is a sort of shorthand used for counting, adding, multiplying, working out simple ratios, and so on. In this sense

mathematics is as old as language – human beings have always had to have words for numbers:

> Adam is just two moons old.
>
> Three hunters left, but only one came back.
>
> We have just seven bushels of wheat left to last us till the next harvest.

On a day-to-day basis it is useful to be able to handle percentages and fractions, and basic weights and measures. It also helps to use the symbols for these, such as % and ¼, rather than laborious words and sentences.

Q1 Think of some examples of when this type of mathematics is used on a more or less daily basis.

Aspect 2 – the language of science

Mathematics is the language that scientists use to explore and express scientific ideas. As such it is just like everyday maths (Aspect 1) in that it is utilitarian or practical.

It is generally reckoned that the more mathematics there is in a science, the more certain or objectively true that science is. There is a great deal of mathematics in physics and chemistry, and there is quite a lot in biology. These subjects, particularly physics and chemistry, tend to be regarded as exact sciences and people expect mathematics to play a large part in them.

> The man who undertakes to solve a scientific question without the help of mathematics undertakes the impossible. We must measure what is measurable and make measurable what cannot be measured.
>
> Galileo Galilei (mathematician, astronomer and physicist, 1564–1642)

Aside from the traditional sciences, subjects such as engineering, economics and the social sciences also use mathematics. The social sciences of sociology and psychology in particular make frequent use of statistics.

Aspect 2 mathematics is the language of science – and, as a student of General Studies, you may come across some mathematics on this level.

Q2 Think of some examples of when you use Aspect 2 mathematics in your study of subjects other than maths.

Q3 When might calculations be made in biology, economics, sociology and psychology?

Q4 Does the fact that social sciences use maths mean that they are as factually objective as physics or chemistry? Give reasons for your answers.

Aspect 3 – academic study

This is the level at which maths, perhaps, does get a little mystical: it is the level on which mathematicians speak of constants (such as π and ε), infinity, Fermat's Last Theorem, symbolic logic and taking risks. It is what is sometimes called pure maths, or 'higher' maths.

Mathematics possesses not only truth, but supreme beauty – a beauty cold and austere, like that of sculpture.
Bertrand Russell (philosopher and mathematician, 1872–1970) *Mysticism and Logic* 1963

Some non-mathematicians can just about understand the fascination of some people with Mandelbrot fractals, but they are entitled to wonder whether there are not more important things for great minds to think about.

Q5 Does higher mathematics contribute to our understanding of the world?

Q6 Is maths so important that it should be on the curriculum right up to university entrance, as it is in most of the countries of Europe? If so, what sort of mathematics should be taught?

The building blocks of mathematics

Maths appears to be absolutely factual: a body of utterly irrefutable truth. You don't *believe* that $2 + 2 = 4$; you *know* it. Philosophically speaking, the fact that $2 + 2 = 4$ is a 'necessary truth'. What would be the point of trying to argue otherwise? Similarly, who would want to dispute the fact that the largest known prime number is $2^{756839} - 1$, a number having 227,832 digits (Dunham 1994)? Mathematics is either right or wrong. It is based on deductive reasoning.

Deductive reasoning

Deductive reasoning starts from 'necessary truths' – from facts that no one would dispute. The first (what is called the *major premiss*) is a general truth: for example, a triangle is a figure having three straight sides, and internal angles (a, b and c) that add up to 180°.

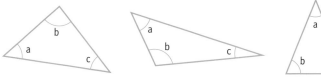

The second (the *minor premiss*) is a truth about a particular instance: for example, this figure has three straight sides and one of its internal angles is 90°.

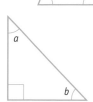

From these premises it can be concluded that the other two internal angles (*a* and *b*) in this triangle must add up to 90°.

This is the *conclusion*.

The strength of this kind of argument is that, if it is certain that the premises are true, it is certain that the conclusion is true. The weakness of deductive reasoning is that, outside mathematics and the exact sciences, there are rather few certain truths in the world.

For this reason, much of everyday reasoning – even in the sciences – is inductive (see Concept A: Facts).

Q7 Research and present some other examples of deductive reasoning, outside mathematics.

Is mathematics a sort of knowledge?

Mathematics is a sort of language – an artificial language with its own rules and conventions. It is a convention, for example, that:

- 0, 1, 2, 3 … are natural numbers
- 0, +/–1, +/–2, +/–3 … are integers
- $\frac{1}{2}, \frac{2}{3}, \frac{4}{5}$ … are rational numbers
- π and ε … are irrational numbers.

Mathematics is a closed system. Once you know the numbers, the rules (such as the four rules of arithmetic: addition, subtraction, multiplication, division) and the symbols for operations that mathematicians use, everything else follows.

Chess is another closed system. There are a certain number of pieces and moves, and a game is a process of deductive reasoning. There may be an infinite number of ways of winning or losing a game, but nobody would claim that chess is a sort of knowledge. It contributes nothing to our understanding of the world.

Nor does mathematics give us knowledge. It has been called 'a supreme achievement of the human intellect' (Gandy 1999), but then so is language. Mathematics is a language in which people express knowledge of a certain, absolute kind.

Absolute truth

Perhaps there is no such thing as absolute truth, even in mathematics. **Kurt Gödel** (mathematician, 1906–78) said that no one can prove an arithmetic truth by reference to any other arithmetic truth. In other words, a closed, formal system (such as arithmetic or chess) cannot be proved or refuted from within that system.

John Barrow (scientist and science writer), in his book *The Artful Universe*, makes the point succinctly:

There is no such thing as absolute truth in logic and maths. The best that one can do is talk of the truth of statements given a set of rules of reasoning. It is quite possible to have statements that are true in one logical system, but false in another.
John Barrow *The Artful Universe* 1995

Q8 If there is no such thing as absolute truth in logic and maths, can there be absolute truth anywhere?

Barrow, John D. (1995) *The Artful Universe: The Cosmic Source of Human Creativity* Oxford: OUP/Penguin

Dunham, William (1994) *The Mathematical Universe* London: John Wiley

Gandy, Robin in Allan Bullock and Stephen Trombley (eds) (1999) *The New Fontana Dictionary of Modern Thought* London: HarperCollinsPublishers

Part 1 Abstraction

What is abstraction?

Abstraction can be thought of as a removal from nature or reality. Abstract thinking is thinking, not about actual objects, but at a level one or more steps removed from them. Abstract art does not seek to represent nature in all its intricacy: rather, it concerns itself with pure form and pattern.

1

2

3

A closely-observed representation of a Norway spruce conifer
A semi-abstract representation of a 'Christmas tree'
An entirely abstract configuration of conifer branch-like shapes

The ability to recognize patterns

The human brain is able to recognize patterns because of its ability to work in the abstract. Humans understand generalized concepts because they can recognize common properties from specific examples. For example, a person's concept of the colour green comes from being presented with numerous objects all different except for the fact that they are green. They are told that all these objects are green and so disregard the differences between them and focus on what they have in common, namely the colour.

Mathematics has been called the 'science of patterns'. The mathematician **Keith Devlin** argues in *The Maths Gene* (2000) that the ability to learn and use mathematics, and the ability to learn and use language, are one and the same. He contends that the 'gene' for maths is the same 'gene' as for language. Both language and maths are by-products of human ability to recognize different *types* of things in the world. The human brain evolved – and grew hugely in size – in order to cope with the thinking involved in recognizing types. The cost of a brain that consumes 2% of the body's energy was paid for by the survival advantage that type-recognition gave humans over other animals.

For example, in studies of language acquisition and use, **Noam Chomsky** (1928–) and other linguisticians, have asserted that a 'deep structure' of language – a basic noun-verb framework – is genetically programmed into the human brain. Linguistic science represents this as a 'tree'. In its simplest form, the tree has just two branches:

S(entence)

N(oun) **P**(hrase)   **V**(erb) **P**(hrase)

The presence of this 'language gene' would explain why children are able to recognize the linguistic patterns within sentences, namely the noun phrase and verb phrase patterns. It would also explain:

- how children learn language as fast as they do
- why all languages have the same fundamental structure.

Just as language structure has been described as *innate* (in-born), so too has the human approach to number. Babies only a few days or weeks old can recognize the difference between one, two and three objects: 'oneness', 'twoness' and 'threeness' appear to be innate.

There is further evidence that this recognition of one, two and three objects is natural to humans. All early systems of numeration consisted of I, II, or III strokes or dots, vertically or horizontally. The ancient Indian system used horizontal lines. As these symbols were written down and the pen was not lifted from the paper, they became stylized as shown in the diagram:

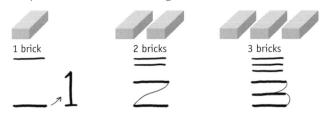

1 brick   2 bricks   3 bricks

Q1 Evidence of how fundamental 1, 2 and 3 are is offered by all the words that we have for oneness, twoness and threeness (far more than we have for, say, fourness, fiveness and so on). Examples are 'single', 'double', 'triple'. Think of other examples.

Levels of abstraction in humans and other animals

Devlin speaks of four levels of abstraction:

- **Level 1 abstraction**: thought or observation of real objects – though these objects may not be in the direct line of sight. Many species of animal are capable of this.

- **Level 2 abstraction**: thought about objects that are not physically present in the environment. Higher primates are capable of this.

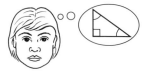

- **Level 3 abstraction**: thought about objects that have never been physically encountered by the thinker. Only humans seem to be capable of this.

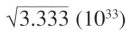

- **Level 4 abstraction**: thought about symbols that have no relation to anything existing in the real world. All humans are capable of this.

$$\sqrt{3.333}\ (10^{33})$$

Q2 Certain sets of numbers are highly significant for all of us (dates, telephone numbers, etc.). What numbers are particularly significant for you?

Advanced vs elementary mathematics

Humans have an innate ability to handle symbols (words and numbers) of the sort that they learn and use in the first two years of their life. Thereafter, what we call 'simple' arithmetic is actually quite hard. In Devlin's words:

Arabic notation makes basic arithmetic so mindless that in the days before cheap hand-held calculators, elementary arithmetic was one of the least popular classes in schools … Arithmetic is a dull and mindless task which our creative intellect has found ways to automate.

Keith Devlin (2000)

Devlin makes a claim that may surprise non-mathematicians: "Advanced mathematics is generally much easier than elementary mathematics." Consider the following passage from Devlin:

Millions of years of evolution have equipped us with a brain that has particular survival skills. Part of that endowment is that our minds are very good at recognizing patterns, seeing connections, and making rapid judgements and inferences. All of these modes of thinking are essentially 'fuzzy'. Although the term 'fuzzy thinking' is often used pejoratively, to mean sloppy and inadequate thinking, that is not my intended meaning here. Rather, I am referring to our ability to make sensible decisions rapidly from relatively little information. This is a powerful ability well beyond our biggest and fastest computers. Our brains are not at all suited to the kinds of precise manipulations of information that arise in arithmetic – they did not evolve to do arithmetic.

s an example of advanced mathematics, Devlin cites **Euclid** (mathematician, c.300 BCE) and his proof that there is an infinite number of prime numbers.

Euclid supposed that there was a largest prime number: P.

He imagined multiplying all the prime numbers up to P:
$2 \times 3 \times 5 \times 7 \times 11 \times 13 \ldots \times P$

He said: let the product be N.

But N + 1 would also be a prime. (This is because it would be divisible neither by 2 – and therefore any even number – nor by any multiple of 3, 5, 7, etc. Therefore, it would not be divisible by any number at all less than itself.)

If $2 \times 3 \times 5 \times 7 \times 11 \times 13 \ldots \times P = N$, then N + 1 divided by any of the prime numbers would leave a remainder of 1.

Therefore N + 1 is a prime number bigger than P.

Therefore there can be no P. There will always be another, bigger prime.

This (the *Fundamental Theorem of Arithmetic*) is concise, even 'elegant'.

It is highly abstract, but no more 'difficult' than, say, 9×6, 8×7 or 9×7.

The more concrete a problem is, the more confident we are in our attempt to find a solution. Consider this problem, called the Wason Test.

There are four cards on a table.

Each card has a number on one side, and a letter on the other. If there is a vowel on one side, there is an even number on the other.

Q3 What is the smallest number of cards you need to turn over to be sure that the rule holds? Which cards are they?

Devlin makes the problem more concrete by putting it into an everyday context:

Four young people in a pub have their student cards on the table next to their drinks. Two cards are face up, two are face down. Of the students whose cards are face down, one is drinking beer, the other Coke. Of the students whose cards are face up, one is over-age, the other is under-age; but both are drinking what might be vodka or 7-Up.

Q4 You are the publican. What do you do to check that no one is breaking the law?

Q5 Explain in your own words why Devlin believes that "advanced mathematics is generally much easier than elementary mathematics". Say why you do or do not agree with him.

Are innate abilities being forgotten?

Not everyone agrees that advanced mathematics is easier than elementary mathematics. Many people feel daunted by advanced mathematics. Why should this be the case if, as Devlin argues, mathematics is built on pattern recognition and this one of the most natural things for the human mind to cope with? Consider the following by Melanie Philips in her book *All Must Have Prizes* about problems in the British education system:

An authoritative report in 1995 by the London Mathematical Society and others identified three main problems: a serious lack of ability to undertake numerical and algebraic calculation with fluency and accuracy; a marked decline in analytical powers when faced with simple problems requiring more than one step; and a changed perception of what mathematics was, particularly the place of precision and proof.

The emphasis on the practical application of maths and the obsession with presenting problems 'in context' – in other words, relating them to real life situations – had denigrated the primary importance of maths as a training for the mind … Children were no longer being taught properly arithmetic, fractions, ratios, algebraic technique and basic geometry. Instead, they were much more dependent on calculators and computers.

Melanie Philips (1996)

Q6 Summarize Philips' concerns regarding the teaching of mathematics.

Q7 In what way does Philips appear to contradict Devlin?

Q8 Do you agree with either, both or neither points of view?

Devlin, Keith (2000) *The Maths Gene* London: Weidenfeld and Nicolson

Phillips, Melanie (1996) *All Must Have Prizes* London: Little, Brown & Co.

Part 2 Measurement of space and time

Ancient measurements

It may be natural to regard space and time as two separate concepts, but in fact they have always been very closely linked. "How far is it to X?" is a question otherwise expressed as: "How long does it take to get there?" Thus, a 'journey' was a distance that could typically be covered in one day (as in the French, *un jour, une journée*).

Measuring space and time (and everything else) has always meant dividing a large amount into smaller units. The problem has always been to decide on how many units, how many groups of units and what to take as a base.

The Babylonians (1894–1158 BCE) chose 60 as their base. They observed (or they thought they observed) that there were 360 days from one equinox to the next. The full circle of their year took 360 days, and a year was divisible into months, each of $\frac{60}{2}$ = 30 days. Each day was divisible into hours, each hour into (60) minutes, and each minute into (60) seconds.

Early spring-driven clocks of the 1500s could only show the hour, then halves and quarters. A smaller division of time was called (in Latin) a *minuta*, or 'little one'. A still smaller division was called a *minuta secunda*, or 'second little one'.

Just as the circle of the year was divided into 360 days, so the geometrical circle was divided into 360 degrees (°); each degree was divided into 60 minutes (1° = 60') and each minute into 60 seconds (1' = 60").

Other bases have been adopted at different times by different peoples. The *heptad* (a group of seven things) was significant for both the Babylonians and Jews.

Q1 What significant heptads can you think of, particularly in the ancient world?

At some point in time and place, the numbers 2, 5, 10, 12 (10 + 2), 20 have all been bases for measurement.

Q2 What *duodecades* (groups of 12 things) can you think of that have had significance in the past?

Q3 Where is base 12 still used?

Q4 What advantage does base 12 have?

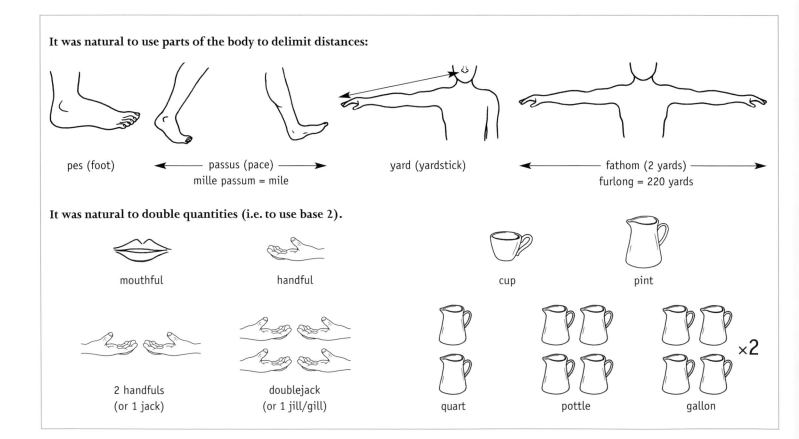

It was natural to use parts of the body to delimit distances:

pes (foot)

← passus (pace) →
mille passum = mile

yard (yardstick)

← fathom (2 yards) →
furlong = 220 yards

It was natural to double quantities (i.e. to use base 2).

mouthful

handful

cup

pint

2 handfuls
(or 1 jack)

doublejack
(or 1 jill/gill)

quart

pottle

gallon

×2

Base 10: the metric system

Base 10 was chosen by the French Academy Weights and Measures Committee in 1791. Careful measurements were made of the polar quadrant of the Earth through Paris (that is, one quarter of the Earth's circumference) and the standard length was defined as one ten millionth (10^{-7}) of this arc. This standard length was to be the metre (from Greek *metron*, a measure).

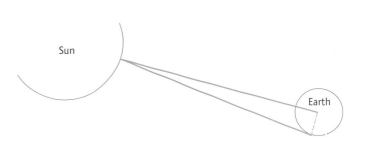

The metric system of weight was then determined by measuring the amount of water in a cube whose sides measured one hundredth of this metre (that is, one centimetre). This unit of weight or mass was called a gramme.

At this time the new system of measurement was called the centimetre/gramme/second (or *cgs*) metric system. The *cgs* system has been replaced in the *Système International* (SI) by metre/kilogram/second (or *mks*), which is now the international standard.

Universally accepted prefixes

Terametre (Tm) = 10^{12}m	Millimetre (mm) = 10^{-3}m
Gigametre (Gm) = 10^{9}m	Micrometre (µm) = 10^{-6}m
Megametre (Mm) = 10^{6}m	Nanometre (nm) = 10^{-9}m
Kilometre (km) = 10^{3}m	Picometre (pm) = 10^{-12}m

Q5 A kilometre is one thousand (1000) metres. Write out the value in metres of one terametre, in words and digits.

Q6 A millimetre is one thousandth ($\frac{1}{1000}$) of a metre. Write out the value in metres of one picometre, in words and digits.

From microcosmic to cosmic

It has been calculated that a chromosome is about 10^{-6} m long (1nm). The diameter of the Earth from pole to pole is known to be 1.2714×10^{7} m. The height of Everest was measured a century before it was climbed. How is it known that the distance from the Earth to the Sun is 1.49×10^{11} m? How were these measurements made?

This is where trigonometry – the measurement of triangles – is used.

In a right-angled triangle, if the length of one side and one angle other than the right angle are known, the lengths of the other two sides can be calculated.

$$\tan \alpha = \frac{\text{opposite side}}{\text{adjacent side}} = \frac{a}{b}$$

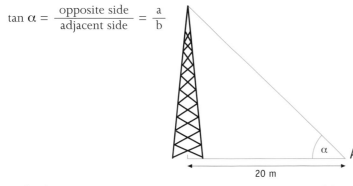

20 m

In the diagram, the angle (α) between point A and the top of the radio mast is 44°. The distance between Point A and the mast is 20m.

Q7 Work out the height of the radio mast (using the *tan* button on a calculator).

Klein, Herbert A. (1988) *The Science of Measurement: A historical survey* New York: Dover Publications Inc.

Sun

Earth

Giovanni Cassini (1625–1712) used trigonometry to calculate the Sun's distance from the Earth at 22 000 times the radius of the Earth. This radius was known to be about 6378 km. This gave him one side of a triangle and he knew that one angle must be very nearly 90 degrees, so he calculated that the sun was just over 140 316 000 km away. Considering the telescopes of the time and the possibilities of error, Cassini's calculation was remarkably close to the actual distance (149 million km).

Of the three SI units – metre, kilogram and second – the Babylonian second is the most standard and reproducible of all. Formerly, the second was defined as the $\frac{1}{86\,400}$ part of the solar day. In 1956, this was adjusted to $\frac{1}{31\,556\,925.974\,7}$ of the seasonal year 1900.

However, the irregularities of the geometry and behaviour of the Earth disqualify it as a timekeeper. Thus, in 1967, the second was defined in terms of radiation emitted from atoms of the element Caesium under specified conditions. This matches, as closely as possible, the astronomical second. We now take as the definition of the astronomical (solar) year:

365.2422 days or 8765.812 hours

Herbert Klein (1998)

Q8 How many (astronomical) seconds are there in a year?

Q9 What prevents us from metricating the year, the day or the hour?

Part 3 Vital statistics

There are three kinds of lies: lies, damned lies and statistics.
Benjamin Disraeli (Conservative politician and Prime Minister, 1804–1881)

Politicians use statistics in the same way that a drunk uses lampposts – for support rather than illumination.
Andrew Lang (poet, historian and folklorist, 1844–1912)

■ Statistics and data

The word *statistics* is derived from the root of the words, *state* and *status*. Statistics were originally data relating to facts of state – often they still are. As a branch of applied mathematics, statistics ought to be facts beyond dispute. However, data* are not found – they are made. They are selected and presented for a purpose. How they are selected and presented needs to be examined carefully. Statistics, like photographs, may not be lies, but they may not be the objective facts that they appear to be.

* *data* is today often used as a singular noun, although properly it is plural and means 'things given'

■ Statistical facts or fictions?

A America says yes to pet cloning

The story was syndicated in all the big regional newspapers, and it went out on CNN, and so was picked up around the world: Texas billionaire Paul Rosario is paying geneticists at Bellevue University to clone his German Shepherd dog 'Bullet'. The local radio station in Huntsville, Alabama, ran a telephone poll on the regular Tuesday morning 'Pet Shop' programme to sound out opinion on the issue: 11 listeners rang in to say they disapproved, but 38 listeners said that, if it was affordable, they'd certainly want their pets cloned. That's 77.5 per cent of the sample. If three-quarters of Americans would like their pets cloned, Mr Rosario might have started something, and the boffins at Bellevue might soon be very busy indeed.

Q1 Why might the sample referred to not be very representative?

Q2 Why might it be unsafe to speak of "three-quarters of Americans" wanting their pets cloned?

B Rank order of problems identified by householders in their area

Problem	% of householders who perceive this as a problem
Crime	68
Vandalism & hooliganism	55
Litter & rubbish	41
Dogs & dog-fouling	34
Graffiti	29
Noise	24
Neighbours	14

Source: Survey of English housing 1997/8

Q3 The statistics in the table were quoted in a government report, so we can assume that the sample was sizeable and representative, but what question or questions might have been asked to gain these responses? Would it make any difference to the outcome whether or not the seven problems were suggested to respondents?

Q4 In this type of survey, it is sometimes difficult to ensure that the separate items are indeed separate. Are these seven problems clearly distinguishable, or is there some overlap?

C Severity of casualties for road users 1999

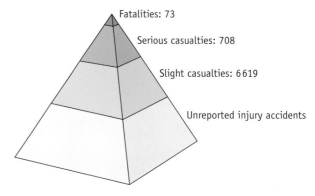

Fatalities: 73
Serious casualties: 708
Slight casualties: 6 619
Unreported injury accidents

Source: Surrey County Council, June 2000

According to the Surrey survey, most accidents result in only slight injuries, but in the accidents reported throughout the county in 1999, 11 per cent of casualties sustained fatal or serious injuries. When looking at the severity of injury of road-user groups classed as 'vulnerable' (e.g. pedestrians), it is clear that they suffer more serious or fatal injuries than less vulnerable road users. However, more than half of all fatal and serious casualties were car occupants. Studies have indicated that perhaps 60 per cent of all injury accidents are not reported to the police.

Q5 Is this a helpful way of presenting the statistics? How else might they have been presented?

Q6 *Average* might mean one of three things: mean, median or mode. Explain each of these terms in the context of the weekly-income figures below.

D These are the figures for the weekly income of six households:

£150   £175   £210   £210   £250   £985

The mean weekly income is £330.
The median weekly income is £210.
The mode weekly income is £210.

The highest figure raises the mean, and this gives a false impression of what five-sixths of the population actually earn.

Below the poverty line*

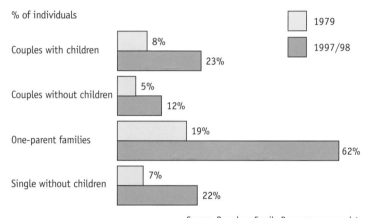

% of individuals

- 1979
- 1997/98

Couples with children — 8% / 23%

Couples without children — 5% / 12%

One-parent families — 19% / 62%

Single without children — 7% / 22%

Source: Based on Family Resources survey data

* *Poverty line defined as income below half that of the national average.*

Q7 It is not known here whether the percentage of individuals has been calculated from knowing the *mean* average or the *median* average of national income. What conclusion would be drawn about the 'growth of poverty' in Britain if it was one rather than the other?

E This graph represents the exchange rate of the Euro against the dollar over a two-month period in 2000. Things do not look at all good for the Euro – indeed the Euro weakened steadily against the dollar throughout 2000.

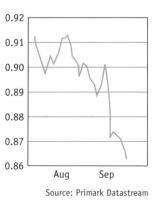

Source: Primark Datastream

Notice that the fall is accentuated in two ways:

- the vertical axis does not start at zero
- the horizontal (time) axis has been set quite narrow.

Q8 What would the graph look like if the vertical axis started at 0 rather than 0.86, and the horizontal axis was stretched?

F Why new cars go downhill faster

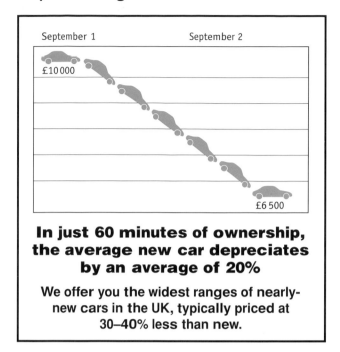

September 1   September 2

£10 000

£6 500

In just 60 minutes of ownership, the average new car depreciates by an average of 20%

We offer you the widest ranges of nearly-new cars in the UK, typically priced at 30–40% less than new.

Source: *Observer* 17 September 2000

G Percentage price depreciation of a range of 'nearly new' cars initially priced at c.£10 000

Citroen Saxo	22%
Fiat Punto	37%
Ford Fiesta	35%
Nissan Micra	39%
Peugeot 206	11%
Renault Clio	35%
Rover 25	40%
Skoda Fabia	21%
Suzuki Swift	36%
Toyota Yaris	32%
Vauxhall Corsa	42%
Volkswagen Polo	35%

Source: *What Car?* July 2000
Teddington: Haymarket Magazines Ltd

Q9 Source F is from an advertisement for a dot.com car sales company. In what respect(s) might the graphic be misleading?

Q10 Does the information in Source G confirm or contradict the information in Source F?

Facts

fact n. *thing certainly known to have occurred, or be true; a state of affairs; the reality of a situation; that which is (Latin factum, from verb facere – make, or do)*

Nothing in education is so astonishing as the amount of ignorance it accumulates in the form of inert facts.

Henry Brooks Adams (historian, essayist and novelist, 1838–1918)

Now what I want is Facts … Facts alone are wanted in life.

Gradgrind in Charles Dickens' *Hard Times* 1854

Science is built up of facts as a house is built of stones; but an accumulation of facts is no more a science than a heap of stones is a house.

Jules Henri Poincaré (mathematician and philosopher of science, 1854–1912) *Science and Hypothesis* 1905

Comment is free, but facts are sacred.

C.P. Scott (newspaper editor, 1872–1932) *The Manchester Guardian* 1921

Nature, so far as it is the object of scientific research, is a collection of facts governed by laws; our knowledge of nature is our knowledge of laws.

William Whewell (scientist and philosopher, 1794–1866)

The aim of education is the knowledge not of facts, but of values.

William Ralph Inge (Dean of St Paul's, 1860–1954)

Facts are generally over-esteemed. For most practical purposes, a thing is what men think it is.

John Updike (author, 1932–) *Buchanan Dying* 1974

Q1 How far do you agree with the thoughts on facts expressed above?

Facts and knowledge

It was suggested in the Introduction to this book that knowledge might be thought of as a continuum running between 'hard' and 'soft' evidence. At the hard end are the sorts of closed questions that expect hard facts for answers. At the soft end are open questions to which there may never be certain answers. For example, 'How can we reduce crime?' is an open question. There are many 'answers' to it. Evidence for these answers will not be based on hard facts alone. The evidence will be at least partly 'soft'. It will be open to debate because it will be based on how people behave and on what values they hold – on what is important to them. People are not as predictable as rocks, plants and other substances that make up the physical world; and even where the facts are not in dispute, they may attach different values to them.

There must be some facts, even at the soft end of the continuum, if there is to be such a thing as *knowledge*.

Deductive reasoning and facts

Facts might be described as 'what are known to be the case'.

One way of illustrating this statement is to look at mathematics. Statements in mathematics are 'facts'. For example, 2 squared equals 4 ($2^2 = 4$) is about as 'hard' a fact as it is possible to establish. However, this is a *deductive fact* – the 'truth' of this fact is only known because it is established from within a closed system of mathematical rules (see Unit 1, introduction). Given certain rules, it is possible to deduce certain applications of those rules: given that 2 multiplied by 3 equals 6 ($2 \times 3 = 6$), 6 divided by 2 must equal 3 ($6 \div 2 = 3$).

Weights and measures, the calendar, chess and other formal games are further examples of closed systems.

Q2 Think, in a group, of as many deductive facts as you can – facts that *are* facts because they are deduced from the rules of a particular system.

Q3 Now think of some facts, equally beyond dispute, that are not deduced from rules set by humans, but that have nevertheless been *found* to be the case.

Inductive reasoning and facts

Francis Bacon (philosopher and politician, 1561–1626) believed that people should not be content to reason things out in their heads. He suggested that people should find things out for themselves by observing a certain number of things and using those observations to draw general conclusions about them. This method of proceeding from the particular to the general is called *inductive reasoning*.

Scientific study is founded principally on inductive reasoning. Science (which might be described as 'knowledge methodically acquired') begins with a 'state of affairs' and a theory as to how that state of affairs came to be. If the theory stands up to repeated observation and/or experiment, the finding is a *fact* – and if it is a very hard *fact* indeed, it may be the basis for a law.

Facts begin life as *particular* observations. Look at Examples 1 and 2.

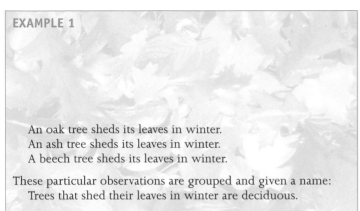

EXAMPLE 1

An oak tree sheds its leaves in winter.
An ash tree sheds its leaves in winter.
A beech tree sheds its leaves in winter.

These particular observations are grouped and given a name:
Trees that shed their leaves in winter are deciduous.

The observations are repeated and become a commonplace – a fact or law.
Deciduous trees are those that shed their leaves in winter.

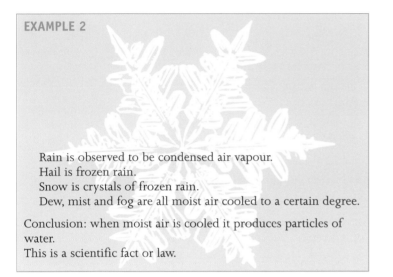

EXAMPLE 2

Rain is observed to be condensed air vapour.
Hail is frozen rain.
Snow is crystals of frozen rain.
Dew, mist and fog are all moist air cooled to a certain degree.

Conclusion: when moist air is cooled it produces particles of water.
This is a scientific fact or law.

Q4 Think of another, similar, inductive process, either individually or in groups. Test it in class discussion.

The difference between inductive and deductive reasoning

Inductive and deductive reasoning appear to be quite different. Deductive reasoning proceeds from a general truth to particular instances or consequences, whilst inductive reasoning proceeds from particular instances to generalizations. But they are only as different as the two sides of one coin.

Only when a general conclusion is reached can anything be deduced from it about the behaviour of any particular thing. Induction must precede deduction. What, for example, can be deduced from the inductive fact about the condensation of air? By knowing that when moist air is cooled water droplets are formed, it can be deduced that when a bottle of wine is taken from the fridge, warm air will cool on the bottle and form particles of water.

Q5 What deductions can you make from the inductive argument(s) that you put forward for question 4?

Facts in context

It is not enough to make observations, form conclusions and arrive at facts – facts need to be seen in context. The next section, entitled 'Transport', looks at a number of statistical facts relevant to the question: 'What are the problems that face passenger transport in Britain at the beginning of the 21st century?'

There are many facts that can be gathered about transport in Britain. Here are two at random:

Fact 1 The 5 202 412th – and last – Ford Escort was driven off the production line on 21 July 2000.

Fact 2 Modernization of the West Coast main line from London to Glasgow is costing £5.6 billion.

Interesting though they may be in themselves, these facts are like those Henry Brooks Adams called *inert* – they are meaningless out of context.

The sets of facts in the following section on transport were published by the Office for National Statistics (ONS) in *Social Trends*, an annual publication which collects together selected data on aspects of life in present-day Britain. A further selection has been made of ten data-sets relevant to passenger transport in Britain. The ONS has no political bias or hidden agenda: the statistics that it publishes are neutral in themselves, although, it has to be said, any selection from a wide choice of possible facts must be based on a principle of some sort.

Facts are essential – but they are not sufficient on their own. (This is the mistake that Mr Gradgrind made in the quotation from *Hard Times* at the start of this section.) There is more to knowledge than just facts.

Q6 facts + *x* = knowledge
What would you say is the missing ingredient (*x*) in this equation?

Q7 There is a distinction between fact and fiction. A fact is something made or done in the 'real world'; fiction is a product of the imagination. Yet, in a library, there is a distinction not between fact and fiction, but between:

◀ **FICTION**   **NON-FICTION** ▶

How would you account for this?

Transport

What are the problems that face passenger transport in Britain at the beginning of the 21st century?

Most people will think they know what the problems are because they read the newspapers, watch the television and see for themselves the 'facts on the ground'. The problems are being increasingly well aired. In order to reach an understanding of the problems and to find solutions, certain facts have to be established first.

Note: all figures in the following sources are for Great Britain.

A Growth in car-ownership over a period of 40 years

- In 1961, 3 out of 10 British households had a car.
- In 1998, 7 out of 10 British households had at least one car.

B Ownership of cars in rural and urban areas

Households with one or more cars by type of area, 1996–98

	Percentage
London borough	61
Metropolitan built-up area	59
Large urban area	69
Medium urban area	70
Small urban area	78
Rural	83
All areas	70

Q1 What type of average of the six percentages does the 'all areas' figure represent:
(a) the mean
(b) the mode
(c) the median?

Q2 What is the range of these figures (from top to bottom)? Is it bigger or smaller than you might have expected?

C Engine capacity of cars

- In 1989, 53% of cars had an engine capacity greater than 1300 cc.
- In 1998, 73% of cars had an engine capacity greater than 1300 cc.

Q3 What might be inferred from these figures?
Q4 What might some of the reasons be for the increase?

D Distances travelled by vehicle (in kilometres)

- In 1951, Britons travelled 53 billion vehicle kilometres.
- In 1998, Britons travelled 455 billion vehicle km.
- In 2001, Britons were expected to travel 478 billion vehicle km.
- In 2006, Britons are expected to travel 524 billion vehicle km.

Q5 Are the figures for 2001 and 2006 facts? If not, what are they?

E Average daily flows of motor vehicles by class of road

	Thousands			
	1981	1991	1996	1998
Motorways	30.4	53.8	62.4	67.1
Major roads	7.9	11.2	11.7	12.0
Minor roads	1.0	1.4	1.4	1.4

Q6 Work out the percentage increase in the use of motorways:
(a) from 1981 to 1991
(b) from 1981 to 1998.

F Journeys undertaken on foot

Average total distance walked each year

	Kilometres	
	1985/6	1996/8
Males	388	309
Females	396	312

Q7 What is the percentage drop for distances walked by males and females from 1985–86 to 1996–98?

Q8 How might this drop be accounted for?

G Journeys undertaken by children

- In 1985–86, 35% of all children's journeys were as passengers in a private vehicle.
- In 1996–98, 50% of all children's journeys were as passengers in a private vehicle.
- The proportion of children's journeys undertaken on foot fell from 47% to 37% between 1985 and 1998.

Q9 Why might children be walking less (to school and elsewhere) than they did in the mid-1980s?

H Journeys by rail

Rail journeys	Millions					
	1981/2	1991/2	1993/4	1996/7	1997/8	1998/9
All main line	719	792	740	801	846	892
All underground (London and Glasgow)	552	765	749	786	846	881
All light railways and trams	14	49	58	74	79	85
All journeys by rail	1 285	1 605	1 547	1 661	1 771	1 858

Q10 Construct a line graph, with millions of journeys on the vertical axis and years on the horizontal axis, for all four sets of figures.

Q11 What is the percentage increase for all journeys by rail, between 1981–82 and 1998–99? What might account for this change?

Problems that face passenger transport in Britain in the 21st century

I Journeys by different modes of transport

Journeys per person, per year, by main mode of transport, 1996–98

	Car	Walk	Bus/coach/rail	Other	All modes
Number of journeys per person	643	288	79	41	1 051

Q12 Work out the proportion of journeys undertaken:
(a) by car
(b) by public transport
(c) on foot.

Analyzing the facts

When faced with information like this, the observer has to decide whether, or how, these facts constitute a problem. One way of doing this is to attach a positive or a negative value to each of the 10 sets of data (in other words, decide whether a trend is 'good' or 'bad').

You may conclude that some trends are good for some people and bad for others. What is good for the individual may be bad for society, and vice versa. The crucial question is who wins and who loses in the context of any problem, and in the context of any solution.

Q13 Go through each data set and make a list of groups that:
(a) might benefit from the trends (are 'winners')
(b) might be disadvantaged by them (are 'losers').

Q14 Write a paragraph in which you explain who is likely to experience the most serious problems over all, and why. (Pedestrians? Children? Motorists? Businesses? Old people? Commuters?).

J Vehicle emissions

- In the period 1971–97, CO_2 emissions from road vehicles almost doubled in the UK.
- In 1997, road transport accounted for three-quarters of all CO_2 emissions.
- The Department of Health calculated that deaths of 12 000 to 24 000 Britons each year are hastened by short-term exposure to air pollution.

All data from the Office for National Statistics (2000) *Social Trends* 30 London: The Stationery Office

Physical sciences

Subatomic particles

Defining science

There is *science* and there are *The Sciences*. The former is used to refer to knowledge acquired in a certain methodical way. **Herbert Spencer** (1820–1903), a Victorian free-thinker, put it succinctly:

> *Science is organized knowledge.*   Education 1861

By this definition, all academic study and the knowledge acquired through formal, methodical, academic study is scientific. Thus, economics, politics, history, and even theology, are all sciences – there is such a thing as political science, after all, and theology used to be called the 'Queen of the Sciences'.

Thomas Henry Huxley (1825–95), another Victorian free-thinker (the first man to call himself a religious agnostic), friend and spokesman of Charles Darwin, wrote in an essay:

> *Science is nothing but trained and organised common sense, differing from the latter only as a veteran may differ from a raw recruit: and its methods differ from those of common sense only as far as the guardsman's cut and thrust differ from the manner in which a savage wields his club.*
>
>   Collected Essays 1893–4

Huxley did not want to make a hard-and-fast distinction between 'science' and 'common sense', let alone between 'science' and all other academic subjects. He accepted Spencer's definition of science as organized knowledge; both men would have known the Latin origin of the word:

> *scientia* (n.) knowledge, intelligence, science
>
> *scio, scire (v.)* to know, understand, perceive, have knowledge of, be skilled in

Q1 What do you make of this definition of science? How is science defined today? Is it defined too narrowly? Did Spencer and Huxley define it too broadly?

It does seem as if Spencer and Huxley were typical of their time. A famous contemporary of theirs, **Louis Pasteur** (chemist and microbiologist, 1822–95), said in an address in 1872:

> *There are no such things as applied sciences, only applications of science.*

In contrast to these nineteenth-century definitions, people today refer to 'the sciences' as if they are set apart from other branches of knowledge. An economist, historian or philosopher would not normally be called a 'scientist' nowadays. The modern idea of a scientist is someone who works at laboratory benches or at computer screens, carrying out research and making advances of which most people stand in awe. After all, science has been successful in helping people to come to an understanding of the world and to take control of it.

Q2 What do you think of this following definition of science?

> *Man is the interpreter of nature, science the right interpretation.*
>
>   **William Whewell** (scientist and philosopher, 1794–1866) *Philosophy of the Inductive Sciences* 1840

What makes a science?

Many attempts have been made, then, to distinguish between science and all other knowledge – however methodically this other knowledge may be acquired. Equally, it is possible to make distinctions *within* science: that is, between one science and another. We tend, for example, to divide science into three: physical science(s), natural science(s) and social science(s).

Hard and soft evidence

The convention of dividing science into three areas is adopted in this General Studies course. Knowledge is acquired in a methodical way in all the sciences, but knowledge is based on evidence, and this evidence can be thought of as 'hard' or 'soft'. Of all the sciences, physics is reckoned to be based on the hardest evidence of all. This is because it is the study of *inorganic matter* and the behaviour of matter. The evidence is about as exact, fixed or hard as evidence can be. This evidence is obtained by experiment, observation and fine measurement.

In contrast, social sciences are based on 'soft' evidence. Here, people are the subject matter and there are limits to how far you can experiment on people. Social scientists observe people, but the observers are people, too, so they cannot be as objective as physicists.

Some definitions of physics

Q3 **Sir Ernest Rutherford** (Nobel prize-winning physicist, 1871–1937) once said 'All science is either physics or stamp collecting'. By this he meant that physics is the only mathematically-certain science, while other sciences are merely involved with classification. Was Rutherford being as objective as a physicist should be?

Q4 Do you agree or disagree with the following two statements? Give reasons for your answer.

> *The problem of physics is how the actual phenomena, as observed with the help of our sense organs aided by instruments, can be reduced to simple notions which are suited for precise measurement and used for the formulation of quantitative laws.*
>
> **Max Born** (physicist, 1882–1970) Experiment and Theory in Physics 1943

> *A Muslim, a Copt, a Druse and a Buddhist disagree on many things, but if they have thought about the matter at all, they agree about the laws of physics.*
>
> **Roger Scruton** (philosopher, 1944–) Modern Philosophy 1994

Q5 Do your answers to questions 3 and 4 confirm or deny that physics can be seen as an exact science based on hard evidence?

Scientific laws

Physicists have successfully devised theories about the nature and behaviour of matter, tested those theories, replicated their tests, and stated *laws*. These laws seem to give us knowledge based on very solid or 'hard' evidence.

The same can be said of chemistry. For example, there are the Gas Laws of **Robert Boyle** (1627–91), the periodic law of **Dmitri Mendeleyev** (1834–1907), and others.

There are four fundamental forces in nature that physical scientists have been concerned with:

- *gravitational force* – the weakest force, but the one that has the longest range of effects and that dominates the behaviour of large bodies, from footballs to planets

- *electromagnetic force* – a much stronger force than gravitation, and especially important in atomic physics

- *weak nuclear force* – the force which causes unstable elementary particles to decay

- *strong nuclear force* – the strongest force known; it is an attractive force at short distances, binding elementary particles together.

The first two of these forces were the great discoveries of classical physics. By the end of the 19th century, some physicists felt that they had discovered all there was to discover about the forces of nature. There was something satisfyingly final about, for example, the equations of the physicist **James Clerk Maxwell** (1831–79).

The high profile of mathematics in physics is one of the marks of this hard science. It is something that practitioners of the softer sciences have sometimes envied. However, is physics as exact or hard as might be assumed?

Questioning the hardness of the evidence

Physics at the end of the 19th century was about to be shaken up. Along came **Einstein**, **Planck**, **Bohr**, **Schrödinger** and **Heisenberg**, and much that had seemed certain was rendered highly uncertain in just a few years.

Q6 Look up each of the above in a biographical dictionary. What contribution did each make to the new uncertainty in physics?

What had once seemed to be pleasingly concrete grew increasingly abstract, to the point where even the business of what Max Born (see question 4) called 'precise measurement' seemed to be at risk. Some would have said precise measurement was what physical science was all about – now, in his Uncertainty Principle of 1927, **Werner Heisenberg** (1901–76) was suggesting that the states and paths of elementary particles were inherently indeterminate. Hence, **Stephen Hawking** (physicist, 1942–) wrote:

> *In effect we have redefined the task of science to be the discovery of laws that will enable us to predict events up to the limits set by the uncertainty principle.*
>
> A Brief History of Time 1988

Just as physics had to contend with uncertainty, so it had to contend with controversy. There had always been some controversy in the physical sciences, but in the 20th century, that controversy was political.

Q7 What controversies did physicists become involved in that still have repercussions today?

Hawking, Stephen (1988) *A Brief History of Time* London: Bantam Books

Scruton, Roger (1994) *Modern Philosophy* London: Sinclair Stevenson

Part 1 Energy

Solar energy

The Sun supplies the Earth with 99.98 per cent of its energy. It arrives mostly as visible and ultraviolet radiation and its energy rating is 1.7×10^{17} watts, or 170 thousand million million joules per second (1 watt = 1 joule per second). The remaining 0.02 per cent of the Earth's energy is geothermal energy (approximately 30×10^{12} watts) which transfers from the Earth's core by conduction through rocks or by convection through hot springs and volcanoes.

The diagram below shows how a small fraction of the Sun's radiant energy can be harnessed for human use.

The global energy budget

Incoming solar radiation
(1.7×10^{17} W)

Sun

Moon

30% scattered
(short-wave)

[contained within
the 30% scattered]

26% reflected by
clouds and water
particles

4% reflected back
from Earth's surface

19% absorbed
and stored in
clouds, lakes,
rivers and
water vapour

Gravitational
potential
energy of
Moon
supplying
tidal energy

Earth

51% absorbed by the
Earth's surface (much
of this short-wave
energy is re-radiated
back into space at
night, as infrared or
long-wave radiation)

0.2% (370×10^{12} W)
Kinetic energy powering
convection currents in
oceans, winds and waves

0.2% absorbed by
plants by
photosynthesis

0.02% of Earth's
energy (30×10^{12} W)
Geothermal energy

food

fossil fuels
(stored for
over 600
million years)

Uranium-235
atoms mined from
the Earth can be
split to release
heat energy and
nuclear radiation.

Fossil fuels

Fossil fuels – non-renewable energy sources such as coal, oil and natural gas – were formed from the fossilized remains of plants living hundreds of millions of years ago. As such, they represent the result of past solar energy. The potential chemical energy from this past solar energy is 40×10^{12} watts.

The contribution made by these fuels to the UK's generating capacity changed markedly in the 1990s as the two pie charts show.

Burning these three fuels releases carbon dioxide (CO_2) into the atmosphere.

Fuel	kg of CO_2 per gigajoule (GJ) of heat
Coal	120
Oil	75
Gas	50

$1 \text{ GJ} = 1 \times 10^9 \text{ J}$

Source: Annual Energy Statistics 2000

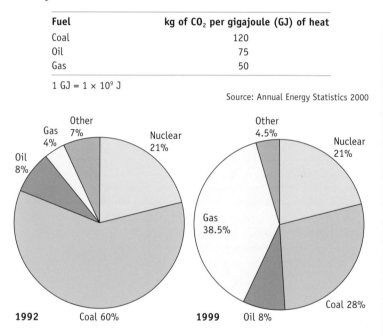

1992

Oil 8%
Gas 4%
Other 7%
Nuclear 21%
Coal 60%

1999

Other 4.5%
Nuclear 21%
Gas 38.5%
Coal 28%
Oil 8%

Q1 Convert the fuel/kg of CO_2 table above into a pie chart showing the percentage contributions that different fossil fuels make to the release of CO_2.

There are two big problems with fossil fuels:

● There is a finite supply of them, so at some point in the future there will be no more coal, oil and gas to extract.

● The carbon dioxide that is released when they are burned is a greenhouse gas, contributing to global warming (see Unit 2, part 3).

These problems are encouraging experimentation with alternative, renewable, non-CO_2-emitting fuels.

Q2 What lay behind the rise in the use of gas and the decline in the use of coal in the 1990s?

Q3 'Given a serious commitment to energy conservation around the world, the need for new supplies of whatever sort would obviously be lessened' (Elliott 1997). In other words, if less energy is used now, there will be more energy available in the future. Is this politically possible, in your view?

Nuclear energy

Uranium-235 atoms mined from the Earth can be split to release heat energy and nuclear radiation. This process is called *nuclear fission*. The energy released from the inner core or nucleus of the atom when it is split is used to generate electricity. This method has been in use since the 1950s.

Whether *nuclear fusion* (the combining of nuclear atoms) to produce energy is feasible, remains to be proved. Fusion is the same process that powers the Sun. Energy is released when hydrogen nuclei bond together to form helium. There is a limitless supply of hydrogen, and helium is a non-polluting gas. Fusion is, in theory therefore, a 'perfect' power source .

Nuclear reactors ... provide a way of generating electricity without producing CO_2 (or SO_2 [sulphur dioxide]).

50 years after very large investment around the world, [nuclear power] still only provides under six per cent of the world's primary energy and the cost of the electricity produced remains high.

It takes around 25 000 years for the activity in plutonium to fall by a half, the so-called 'half life'. It would take even longer for the activity levels to fall off to negligible levels.

Q4 What did advocates find so attractive about nuclear power in its early days?

Q5 Today, there is fresh interest in nuclear power. This is due in part to:
- a desire to move away from fossil fuels and their impact on global warming
- the fact that there is a limited contribution of renewable energy in the near future.

Are these good arguments for keeping faith with nuclear power?

Renewable fuels

The long-term technical potential for on-land wind power is usually put at up to 20 per cent of UK electricity requirements, with basic siting constraints perhaps reducing this to 10 per cent.

According to the UK government's Energy Technology Support Unit, between 100 and 150 TW h [1 terawatt hour = 1×10^{12} W h] per annum could, in theory, be obtained from sites in shallow water off East Anglia (i.e. up to 50 per cent of mid-1990s UK electricity requirements).

Around 20 per cent of the world's electricity already comes from conventional hydroelectric dams.

Hydroelectric power can be harvested in so-called 'micro-hydro' projects in rivers and streams.

The potential geothermal resource is thought to be quite large, representing, if fully developed, perhaps 10 per cent of UK energy requirements.

Current predictions suggest that if a major commitment were made to developing renewable energy technology, it would take between 50 and 100 years before renewables could supply half of the nation's energy.

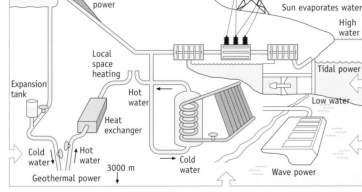

The proposed 11-mile long 8.6 GW ebb generation Severn tidal barrage would generate 17 TW h per annum in total, around six per cent of annual UK electricity requirements.

The problem facing the UK [tidal] barrages was finance and the relatively short-term economic perspective that prevailed in the industry following the privatisation of the UK electricity sector.

Typical energy densities at good sites (e.g. 100 miles or so off the NW of Scotland) are on average around 50 kW h per metre of wave-front ... equivalent to 10 per cent of the UK's current installed generation capacity.

Given its Atlantic positioning, the UK has most of the best sites and about one-third of the total European wave-energy resource.

Photovoltaic cells convert sunlight directly into electricity. They are already to be found in some outlying rural areas where there is no grid electricity.

There is interest in using photovoltaic cells to substitute for roof or fascia cladding on buildings, thus saving on the cost of conventional roofing or wall materials and offsetting the cost of the photovoltaic cells.

Q6 The following questions can usefully be asked of any source of energy.
(a) Is the energy renewable?
(b) How long will it last?
(c) How much energy can be produced?
(d) Will there be adverse effects on the environment?
(e) What is the time-scale of research and development?
(f) What is the likely cost of research and development?
(g) What is the likely cost of the energy produced?
(h) Is there a risk of political controversy?

Consider these questions for each of the 10 energy sources mentioned on these two pages. Make a personal value judgement about each answer using the scale below.

5 = Very positive 4 = Positive 3 = Neutral
2 = Negative 1 = Very negative

All quotations from David Elliott (1997) *Energy, Society and Environment* London: Routledge

Part 2 Electromagnetism

▌ What is electromagnetism?

Electromagnetism is the branch of physics that focuses on the relation of electricity to magnetism. It is a relation that has been exploited in the development of wireless communications (mobile phones, radio and satellites), electric motors and generators, and electric power distribution.

Foundations of electromagnetism

A succession of discoveries over a 50-year period resulted in what is termed *electromagnetic theory*. Important scientists associated with this branch of science are listed in the table.

Hans Oersted (1777–1851)	Discovered that a compass needle could be deflected if it was brought close to an electric current flowing in a wire.
André Ampère (1775–1836)	Concluded that an electric current is capable of generating a magnetic field, and that the direction of the electrical current determines the direction of a magnetic field.
Michael Faraday (1791–1867)	Demonstrated that changes in the electric field were proportional to the rate of change in the magnetic field.
James Clerk Maxwell (1831–79)	Concluded that light is an electromagnetic phenomenon (i.e. he explained light in terms of electromagnetic waves) and suggested there might be a much wider spectrum of electromagnetic radiation than could be observed as visible light.
Heinrich Hertz (1857–94)	Proved Maxwell's theories by producing waves outside the visible spectrum, thereby demonstrating a wide spectrum of electromagnetic radiation.

▌ Electromagnetic radiation

Electromagnetic radiation is the propagation of energy through space by means of electric and magnetic fields. The energy travels in waves of varying lengths.

The electric and magnetic fields in an electromagnetic wave travel in the same direction and are at right angles to each other. This fact is important: if the electric field changes, it causes a change in the magnetic field; similarly, as the magnetic field varies, so too does the electric field. This means that electromagnetic waves have a wide variety of applications.

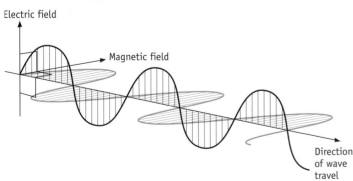

Electric field

Magnetic field

Direction of wave travel

Electromagnetic waves travel in various mediums (including space, water and air). The names of these waves are familiar: radio waves, microwaves and gamma waves, for example.

▌ The electromagnetic spectrum

The electromagnetic spectrum is the distribution of electromagnetic waves according to their *wavelength* (measured in metres) or *frequency* (the number of wave cycles per second, measured in Hertz).

In a vacuum, all electromagnetic waves travel at the speed of light (299 793 km/s), but frequency and length vary according to the source of radiation and the medium through which it passes.

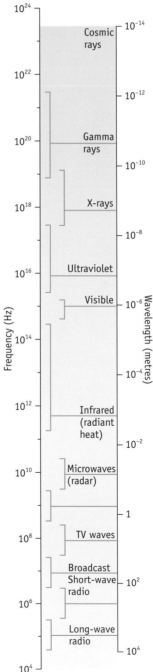

Cosmic rays are extremely high-energy particles: atomic nuclei, protons (nuclei of hydrogen atoms) and electrons, which are probably the result of distant supernova explosions (explosions occurring at the end of stars' lives). They produce the radioactive isotope Carbon 14, whose decay in terrestrial matter enables scientists, by 'carbon-dating', to establish the age of natural and manufactured objects.

Gamma rays are similar in nature to X-rays, but of shorter wavelength. They are emitted from certain radioactive substances. They have important medical applications: for example, in radiotherapy and to sterilize materials and kill bacteria.

X-rays are highly penetrating and have a variety of applications. In medicine, they can be used to examine internal body tissues. Other applications include studying the atomic and molecular structure of crystalline substances, and examining substances such as DNA. They are also used for security at airports.

Ultraviolet radiation is very powerful. It produces sunburn, but also causes vitamin D to form in the skin. It is used in lighting and security systems.

Visible light is made up of the following:

Violet 4×10^{-7} m
Indigo
Blue
Green 5.5×10^{-7} (550 nm) The peak of the curve of visual perception (towards the yellow end of green)
Yellow
Orange
Red

Display screens make use of the visible light spectrum.

Infrared radiation has a wide range of applications, including heating, remote control (e.g. for televisions), police and fire brigade cameras to detect humans (e.g. at night, in collapsed buildings). Aluminium blankets used to prevent hypothermia work because they reflect the infrared radiation, which would otherwise be lost from the body.

Microwaves are used in radar, radio broadcasting, heating and cooking.

Radio and broadcast waves are used in communications.

Band	Application
Extremely high (EHF)	Radar and satellite communications
Super high (SHF)	Radar
Ultra high (UHF)	TV, short-range mobile communications, radar
Very high (VHF)	Short-range mobile communications and navigation
High (HF)	Long-range mobile communications
Medium (MF)	Radio broadcasts, short-range navigation
Low (LF)	Radio broadcasts, short-range navigation
Very low (VLF)	Long-range navigation

Q1 List the wave bands and frequencies of any radio programmes you listen to.

Satellites

Satellites use electromagnetic radiation for a variety of purposes. Communications is one area, but there are many others, including taking detailed images, assessing crops, surveying for oil, monitoring for pollution, mapping the ozone layer and monitoring the weather.

Geostationary satellites appear stationary above the equator and are used to relay communications around the globe. Images from geostationary satellites give complete coverage of the Earth, if not in the detail needed for mapping.

Polar and **low orbit satellites** can be used to assess the type and quality of vegetation by analyzing the electromagnetic waves reflected and emitted by these surfaces.

Satellites that only receive electromagnetic waves from the Earth are called **passive satellites**. Those that also emit electromagnetic waves are called **active satellites**.

This diagram shows the application of electromagnetic radiation for communications.

Q2 If 300 kHz is equal to 3×10^5 Hz, express the lower and upper limits of each of the five remaining wavebands (above Low Frequency – LF) in the same way.

Q3 In your own words, briefly define the following:
- an artificial satellite
- a microwave signal
- a waveband
- the wavelength of a signal.

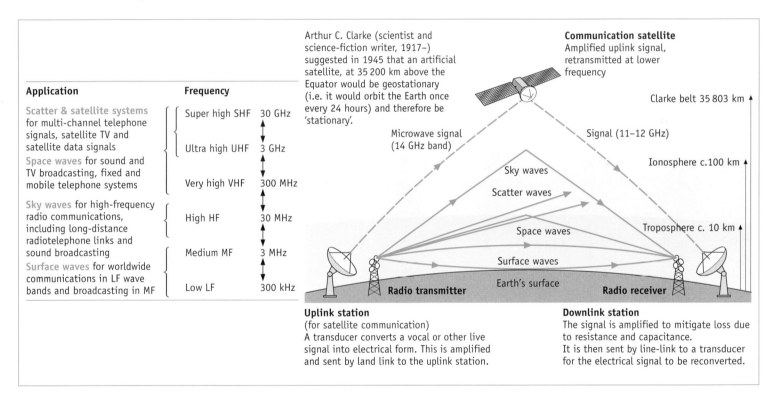

Application		Frequency	
Scatter & satellite systems for multi-channel telephone signals, satellite TV and satellite data signals	Super high SHF	30 GHz	
	Ultra high UHF	3 GHz	
Space waves for sound and TV broadcasting, fixed and mobile telephone systems	Very high VHF	300 MHz	
Sky waves for high-frequency radio communications, including long-distance radiotelephone links and sound broadcasting	High HF	30 MHz	
	Medium MF	3 MHz	
Surface waves for worldwide communications in LF wave bands and broadcasting in MF	Low LF	300 kHz	

Arthur C. Clarke (scientist and science-fiction writer, 1917–) suggested in 1945 that an artificial satellite, at 35 200 km above the Equator would be geostationary (i.e. it would orbit the Earth once every 24 hours) and therefore be 'stationary'.

Communication satellite
Amplified uplink signal, retransmitted at lower frequency

Clarke belt 35 803 km

Signal (11–12 GHz)

Microwave signal (14 GHz band)

Ionosphere c.100 km

Sky waves

Scatter waves

Space waves

Troposphere c. 10 km

Surface waves

Earth's surface

Radio transmitter

Radio receiver

Uplink station
(for satellite communication)
A transducer converts a vocal or other live signal into electrical form. This is amplified and sent by land link to the uplink station.

Downlink station
The signal is amplified to mitigate loss due to resistance and capacitance.
It is then sent by line-link to a transducer for the electrical signal to be reconverted.

Other applications of electromagnetism

Electric motors

In terms of the contribution that it has made to society and modern economies, the electric motor is as important as the steam engine and internal combustion engine.

An electric motor converts electricity into *mechanical energy*. If a wire carrying a current is placed in a magnetic field, the wire will experience a force. In simple terms, this causes a rotary motion, which works the motor. This has many applications, many of which are in the home.

Q4 Where would you find electric motors in the home?

Generating electricity

Electrical energy can be generated by a process that is the reverse of the electric motor. This process is called *electromagnetic induction*. Instead of supplying a current to produce motion (as in the motor), the motion of a wire in a magnetic field produces a current. This is called a generator.

Examples range from a bicycle dynamo to power stations generating electricity for entire communities.

Q5 In its basic form, a bicycle dynamo consists of a conductor (usually a coil of wire) which rotates between the poles of a magnet. The mechanical energy from the movement of the bicycle wheel moves the coil and generates electricity.

Bearing in mind the need for mechanical movement, which renewable energy sources can be used by power stations to generate electricity by electromagnetic induction?

Part 3 The atmosphere

The atmosphere: climate and weather

The atmosphere is the theatre of weather and climate events. The *weather* changes locally on a daily and weekly basis. *Climate* is a word we normally use to cover changes over wider geographical areas and over longer periods of time. Weather changes are interesting, but scarcely a major issue; climate change, however, is.

Global warming

The globe has been warming. Since the last ice age (some 10 000 years ago), the world's mean temperature has risen by about 4 °C. It has risen by about 0.5 °C in the last 100 years. It is thought likely that it will rise by another 1.5 °C in the next 50 years.

Some scientists attribute this global warming to perfectly natural cyclical change; most blame the fact that certain gases — the product of human activity on Earth — are trapping outgoing thermal radiation in the atmosphere, which would normally escape into space.

Gases naturally occurring in atmosphere (%)

Oxygen 20.94%
Nitrogen 78.04%
Carbon dioxide 0.03%
Argon 0.93%
Neon, Helium, Ozone, Hydrogen, Krypton, Xenon, Methane 0.06%

Greenhouse gases

Halocarbons 14%
Tropospheric ozone 12%
Nitrous oxide 6%
Sulphur dioxide 50%
Methane 18%

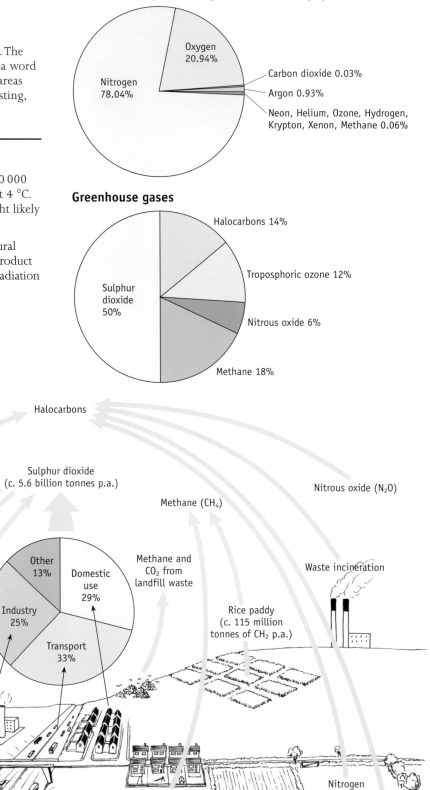

30% short-wave radiation scattered

19% absorbed by clouds and water

SOLAR RADIATION (100%)

51% absorbed by Earth's surface and reradiated as long-wave radiation. Greenhouse gases delay the escape of this radiation. The denser the gases, the longer the delay — and the warmer the surface of the Earth.

Refrigerants
Aerosol spray
Propellants
Foam packaging

Halocarbons

Sulphur dioxide (c. 5.6 billion tonnes p.a.)

Methane (CH_4)

Nitrous oxide (N_2O)

Some absorption of CO_2 by oceans and forests

Termites feeding on dead trees emit CH_2

Methane and CO_2 from landfill waste

Waste incineration

Deforestation (1–2.5 billion tonnes of CO_2)

Consumption of fossil fuel energy

Other 13%
Domestic use 29%
Industry 25%
Transport 33%

Rice paddy (c. 115 million tonnes of CH_2 p.a.)

Cattle (c. 73 million tonnes of CH_2 p.a.)

Nitrogen fertilizer

Conversion of land to agriculture

It had been thought that the oceans would absorb *anthropogenic* (human-made) sulphur dioxide (SO_2). In 1957, it was shown that the *biosphere* (the part of the Earth's surface and atmosphere inhabited by living things) could not absorb all the excess CO_2, and that levels of this gas in the atmosphere would inevitably rise.

Of further concern, methane and the halocarbons (including chlorofluorocarbons – CFCs) are far more potent as greenhouse gases than CO_2. Methane is produced when organic matter breaks down under *anaerobic* conditions (that is, when there is no oxygen present) and when the tundra melts. (The tundra is a vast treeless zone between the ice cap and the timberline of North America and Eurasia, and has a permanently frozen subsoil.)

Deforestation contributes to the amount of CO_2 in the atmosphere for several reasons. When forests are being cleared, they are often burned and CO_2 is released. In addition, by eliminating trees, a natural CO_2 sink is destroyed because plants absorb CO_2 in *photosynthesis*. Also, the cleared land adds to cattle pasture and provides a suitable environment for termites.

Q1 In what ways is global warming anthropogenic?

Q2 Find a recent news article that accepts that global warming will occur and one that casts doubt upon it. What scientific evidence does each article rely on? Which presents the more convincing argument?

What are the likely consequences of global warming?

Much of the controversy that now surrounds the issue of global warming is not whether global warming will occur, but just how sensitive the climate is to increases in carbon dioxide levels …

If global warming is to come then these are the challenges that we face, not just the temperature and precipitation changes, but also our perception of them and our reactions to them as a society.

Frances Drake (2000)

These are the likely consequences (randomly ordered) of a rise in surface temperature of, say, 1.5–4.5 °C:

1   Sea levels would rise, and low-lying islands (for example, the Maldives, the Florida Keys) and atolls (coral islands) might be flooded.

2   There would be much coastal erosion and sea defences would have to be strengthened at great cost (for example, the Netherlands, much of the US Atlantic coast).

3   Freshwater wetlands and river estuaries would be contaminated by salt water and farmland would be rendered infertile.

4   There would be a shortage of fresh water, particularly in developing countries, and a possible increase of water-borne diseases.

5   Land areas would warm more than the oceans, particularly in high northern latitudes. This warming would lead to the melting of ice and of tundra land, releasing more methane into the atmosphere from hydrates in the tundra and in the mud on the continental shelf.

6   The melting of sea-ice would mean that the sea (which is 'darker' than ice) would absorb more solar radiation.

7   The clearing of forests and the desertification of grasslands would raise further the reflectivity (*albedo*) of the Earth's surface, and so its temperature.

8   The rise in temperature would be too fast for much plant-life to adapt in time. Much forest and many plant species would be lost.

9   Some animal species would migrate; others would compete for space with humans.

10 Communicable diseases associated with the tropics (such as malaria, plague and typhus) once familiar in more temperate zones, would migrate northwards.

Who is responsible?

The contribution of different countries/regions to CO_2 emissions

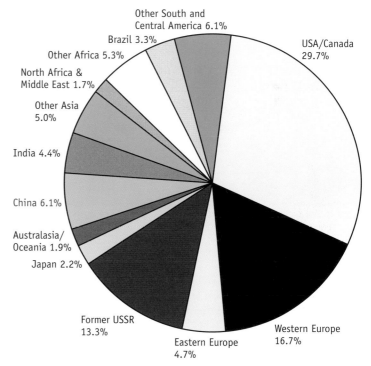

Q3 Present the information in this pie chart in the form of a bar graph (perhaps amalgamating certain of the slices).

Q4 What is the contribution to CO_2 of 'developed' countries relative to 'developing' countries?

Q5 Which countries/regions are likely to make an increasing contribution in the future? Why?

Q6 "We all consume energy, we all use transport, we are all part of the problem. It's not just industry and power generators that need to change their ways … Global warming is often too large an issue for the individual to respond to and therefore nothing can be done." Drake 2000.

Do you agree with Drake's comment?

Drake, Frances (2000) *Global Warming: The Science of Climate Change* London: Arnold

Knowledge

Facts and knowledge

The term *epistemology* is used to refer to theories of knowledge. This section examines – in the context of the history of Western thought – changing ideas of what knowledge is, its value and how it might be achieved. In 'Facts' (Concept A) it was acknowledged that facts are necessary to knowledge, but that they are not sufficient on their own.

Quest for knowledge

Adam and Eve in the Garden of Eden

Early writers were very suspicious about man's quest for knowledge. They associated it with arrogance. In the Old Testament, Adam disobeyed God and was expelled from the Garden of Eden for eating fruit from the tree of knowledge; men built the tower of Babel to reach heaven, and God knocked it down. In Greek mythology, Prometheus stole fire from the gods, who punished him by tying him to a rock, where an eagle fed each day on his liver:

> *Of the tree of knowledge of good and evil, you shall not eat of it; for on the day that you eat of it you will surely die.*
>
> Genesis 2:17

> *He who increases knowledge, increases sorrow.*
>
> Ecclesiastes 1:18

> *Knowledge is proud of itself, but love enlightens.*
>
> I Corinthians 8:1

At first, knowledge was forbidden fruit; over time, biblical writers dismissed it as not worth having. Even after the Renaissance of the fifteenth century, when the thought of the ancient Greeks and Romans was rediscovered, the church viewed 'worldly' knowledge with disapproval.

Empiricism versus rationalism

The great scholarly debates in philosophy in Europe from the 16th century onwards have been based upon two different schools of thought: *empiricism* and *rationalism*.

Empiricism

The humanist and scholar-politician, **Francis Bacon** (1561–1626), reached out for the fruit of the tree of knowledge:

> *All knowledge and wonder (which is the seed of knowledge) is an impression of pleasure in itself.*
>
> Advancement of Learning 1605

Wonder (or curiosity) came first; then, according to Bacon's *inductive* method (see Concept A, Facts) came the gathering of relevant *facts* – and knowledge followed. Bacon's method is described as *empirical*. As a definition in philosophy, this refers to the idea that individuals gain knowledge from their experience of the material world.

Rationalism

The approach of the philosopher, **René Descartes** (1596–1650), was very different: lying in bed contemplating spiders' webs, or sitting by a warm stove thinking, were his preferred ways of acquiring knowledge. Descartes reasoned that everyone's experience of the world is unique, and so empirical knowledge cannot be true knowledge. Reasoning was the way to knowledge, which involved step-by-step analysis and rational argument. This was how Descartes claimed people should know what was worth knowing. In philosophy, this approach is referred to as *rationalism*.

Expanding the debate – the British empiricists

John Locke (philosopher, 1632–1704) was more impressed by Bacon's empiricism than by Descartes' rationalism. He took the following view:

> *No man's knowledge here (that is, of this world) can go beyond his experience.*
>
> Essay on Human Understanding 1690

For British empirical philosophers, *experience* was the seed of knowledge – above all, sense-experience: that is, experience of the world gained by seeing it, hearing it, smelling it, touching it and tasting it.

> **Q** Is it your view that you can know things by thinking about them – by reasoning – as Descartes suggested? Or do you believe that you can only know things if you have direct or indirect sense-experience of them?

Of course, people's senses can deceive them. Locke was careful, therefore, to acknowledge that they give *probability*, rather than knowledge. Nevertheless, they do give 'an assurance that deserves the name of knowledge' (Locke 1690).

Scottish philosopher **David Hume** (1711–76) was still more of a sceptic – that is, he was even less sure that anyone could ever really know anything. Reason cannot tell anyone that a flame is hot; only a live sense-impression of heat can do this. We feel the heat of a flame on one occasion, and subsequent occasions confirm the impression. Flame and hot are ideas whose 'constant conjunction', or association, gives us a passable basis for knowledge. We can really only believe in the heat of the flame when we come close to it; we have no irrefutable reason for believing that it is hot when the flame is in the next room. We can only fill in the gaps between successive sense-impressions by using our imagination and by appealing to custom. What we think of as knowledge, said Hume, was really only making an informed guess.

John Stuart Mill (philosopher, 1806–73) was such a dedicated empiricist that he believed that people's knowledge of mathematics derived from a sense-experience of quantities of things and their relationships. People know that 2 + 3 = 5, abstractly, only because they have had direct sense-experience of two things, and three things, and five things. To this extent there is no difference between how people know geometrical truths and how they know geographical truths.

Alfred Jules Ayer (philosopher, 1910–89) was an empiricist, too. For him, most knowledge is the product of experience and experiment – *scientific* knowledge; what Ayer called *synthetic* knowledge. Knowledge of maths and logic, though, are the product of reasoning from first principles, and this Ayer called *analytic* knowledge.

Q2 Which seems to you more likely: that you know that 2 + 3 = 5 because you experience this arithmetic relationship, or that you come to know mathematical truths by thinking – by logical analysis?

Empiricism cannot give certainty – indeed, it may induce a thoroughgoing scepticism. Empiricism is inductive: it depends upon particular facts. But just as people's senses may deceive them, so associations of particular facts may deceive them. **Bertrand Russell** (philosopher, 1872–1970), yet another empiricist, explained the 'problem of induction' in this way:

> *A horse, which has been often driven along a certain road, resists the attempt to drive him in a different direction. Domestic animals expect food when they see the person who usually feeds them. We know that all these rather crude expectations of uniformity are liable to be misleading. The man who has fed the chicken every day throughout its life at last wrings its neck instead …*
>
> *The most we can hope is that the oftener things are found together, the more probable it becomes that they will be found together another time, and that if they have been found together often enough, the probability will amount almost to certainty.*
>
> The Problems of Philosophy 1912

Q3 What do you understand to be the 'problem of induction'?

The limits of philosophy

Philosophers have always striven for certainty – for some absolute basis for knowledge – and there are those among them who strive for it still. The philosopher **Richard Rorty** thinks this is still the driving force of philosophy, but that it is misguided.

> *Philosophy as a discipline sees itself as the attempt to underwrite or debunk claims to knowledge made by science, morality, art, or religion. It purports to do this on the basis of its special understanding of the nature of knowledge and of mind. Philosophy can be foundational in respect to the rest of culture because culture is the assemblage of claims to knowledge, and philosophy adjudicates such claims. It can do so because it understands the foundations of knowledge, and it finds these foundations in a study of man-as-knower, of the 'mental processes' or the 'activity of representation' which makes knowledge possible. To know is to represent accurately what is outside the mind. So to understand the possibility and nature of knowledge is to understand the way in which the mind is able to construct such representations.*
>
> Richard Rorty (1980)

Q4 What rather grand claims do philosophers make for themselves, according to Rorty?

Q5 'Culture is the assemblage of claims to knowledge.' What do you think about this?

Rorty denies that 'philosophers have a special kind of knowledge about knowledge', and so does the philosopher **Mary Midgley**.

> *The question raised by Descartes and others, 'How do you know that you know?', has perhaps as little sense as 'How do you know that you offer?' or 'How do you know that you thank?' The meaning of the word 'know', like that of other words, is its use. This word is not the name of a peculiar mental state or process because, like very many other words, it is not a name at all. Its work is not the work of referring or corresponding to some set object, but of helping people to distinguish between the more reliable and the less reliable parts of the world around them.*
>
> Mary Midgley (1991)

Q6 Find out how knowledge is defined in a dictionary. What does Midgley mean when she says the meaning of this word is 'its use'?

Q7 The diagram below shows one way of thinking about knowledge; not as 'scientific', 'historical' or 'philosophical', but just more or less 'reliable', more or less certain, more or less securely based on evidence, hard or soft. Do you think this approach is helpful? If not, suggest alternatives.

CERTAINTY

Knowledge		Uncertainty
Fact	Belief	Opinion
	Impression	
Law	Theory	Conjecture
	Hunch	

Midgley, Mary (1991) *Wisdom, Information and Wonder: What is Knowledge For?* London: Routledge

Rorty, Richard (1980) *Philosophy and the Mirror of Nature* Oxford: Blackwell

Russell, Bertrand (1912) *The Problems of Philosophy* Oxford: OUP

The curriculum

Knowledge in the West has been divided up in many ways. It all started with philosophy – the pursuit of wisdom. There has always been debate about which areas of knowledge should be pursued. **Herbert Spencer** (Victorian free-thinker, 1820–1903), for example, asked: "What knowledge is of most worth?"

The school curriculum in Britain has broadly represented the division of knowledge into subjects that, at various times, have been considered to be 'of most worth'. No new school subject has been inspired by one person only, but the following were pioneers who took learning along important new paths.

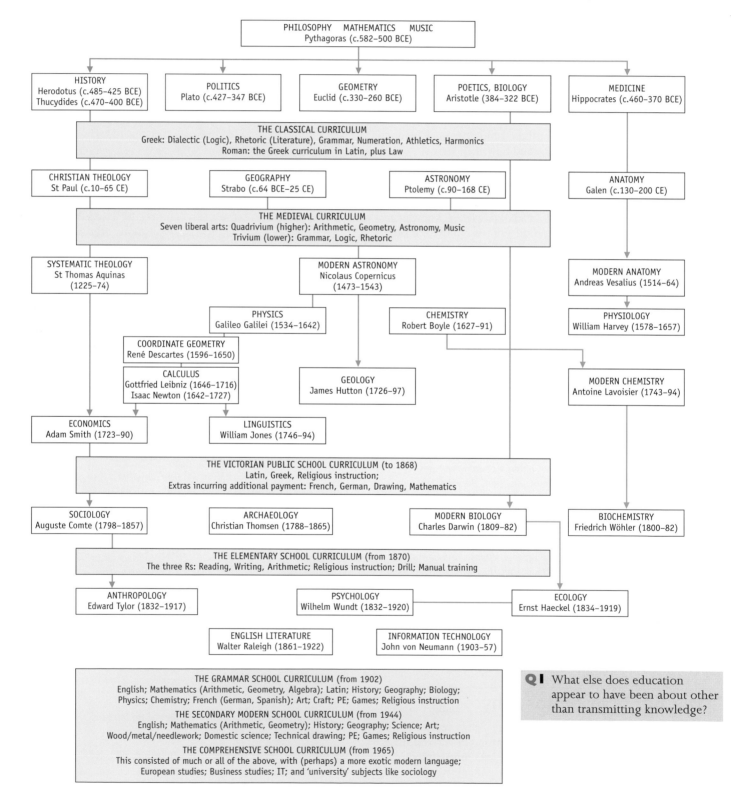

PHILOSOPHY   MATHEMATICS   MUSIC
Pythagoras (c.582–500 BCE)

HISTORY
Herodotus (c.485–425 BCE)
Thucydides (c.470–400 BCE)

POLITICS
Plato (c.427–347 BCE)

GEOMETRY
Euclid (c.330–260 BCE)

POETICS, BIOLOGY
Aristotle (384–322 BCE)

MEDICINE
Hippocrates (c.460–370 BCE)

THE CLASSICAL CURRICULUM
Greek: Dialectic (Logic), Rhetoric (Literature), Grammar, Numeration, Athletics, Harmonics
Roman: the Greek curriculum in Latin, plus Law

CHRISTIAN THEOLOGY
St Paul (c.10–65 CE)

GEOGRAPHY
Strabo (c.64 BCE–25 CE)

ASTRONOMY
Ptolemy (c.90–168 CE)

ANATOMY
Galen (c.130–200 CE)

THE MEDIEVAL CURRICULUM
Seven liberal arts: Quadrivium (higher): Arithmetic, Geometry, Astronomy, Music
Trivium (lower): Grammar, Logic, Rhetoric

SYSTEMATIC THEOLOGY
St Thomas Aquinas
(1225–74)

MODERN ASTRONOMY
Nicolaus Copernicus
(1473–1543)

MODERN ANATOMY
Andreas Vesalius (1514–64)

PHYSICS
Galileo Galilei (1534–1642)

CHEMISTRY
Robert Boyle (1627–91)

PHYSIOLOGY
William Harvey (1578–1657)

COORDINATE GEOMETRY
René Descartes (1596–1650)

CALCULUS
Gottfried Leibniz (1646–1716)
Isaac Newton (1642–1727)

GEOLOGY
James Hutton (1726–97)

MODERN CHEMISTRY
Antoine Lavoisier (1743–94)

ECONOMICS
Adam Smith (1723–90)

LINGUISTICS
William Jones (1746–94)

THE VICTORIAN PUBLIC SCHOOL CURRICULUM (to 1868)
Latin, Greek, Religious instruction;
Extras incurring additional payment: French, German, Drawing, Mathematics

SOCIOLOGY
Auguste Comte (1798–1857)

ARCHAEOLOGY
Christian Thomsen (1788–1865)

MODERN BIOLOGY
Charles Darwin (1809–82)

BIOCHEMISTRY
Friedrich Wöhler (1800–82)

THE ELEMENTARY SCHOOL CURRICULUM (from 1870)
The three Rs: Reading, Writing, Arithmetic; Religious instruction; Drill; Manual training

ANTHROPOLOGY
Edward Tylor (1832–1917)

PSYCHOLOGY
Wilhelm Wundt (1832–1920)

ECOLOGY
Ernst Haeckel (1834–1919)

ENGLISH LITERATURE
Walter Raleigh (1861–1922)

INFORMATION TECHNOLOGY
John von Neumann (1903–57)

THE GRAMMAR SCHOOL CURRICULUM (from 1902)
English; Mathematics (Arithmetic, Geometry, Algebra); Latin; History; Geography; Biology;
Physics; Chemistry; French (German, Spanish); Art; Craft; PE; Games; Religious instruction

THE SECONDARY MODERN SCHOOL CURRICULUM (from 1944)
English; Mathematics (Arithmetic, Geometry); History; Geography; Science; Art;
Wood/metal/needlework; Domestic science; Technical drawing; PE; Games; Religious instruction

THE COMPREHENSIVE SCHOOL CURRICULUM (from 1965)
This consisted of much or all of the above, with (perhaps) a more exotic modern language;
European studies; Business studies; IT; and 'university' subjects like sociology

Q1 What else does education appear to have been about other than transmitting knowledge?

A two-tier system

It might be helpful to consider the way in which education has been divided in Britain on social-class lines.

education	training
theory	practice
academic	vocational
pure	applied

Grammar schools offered an *academic* education for the fortunate minority who passed the Eleven Plus exam. This would, in most cases, lead to the General Certificate of Education (GCE) in preparation for further education or the professions.

Secondary modern schools were non-selective and took students who had failed their Eleven Plus exam. Secondary moderns offered a *vocational* education – preparation for the 'world of work'. At these schools (after 1961) it was possible to take the Certificate of Secondary Education (CSE).

Since the 1970s, most grammar and secondary modern schools have been replaced by comprehensive schools, which in the main do not select on ability. (For further discussion of the education system and associated legislation, see Unit 4, part 2.)

Recent curriculum changes

In 1989, the National Curriculum 5–16 was introduced for all, leading to the General Certificate of Secondary Education (GCSE).

CORE AND OTHER FOUNDATION SUBJECTS

Core subjects	Other foundation subjects
mathematics	history
English	geography
science	technology (including design)
Welsh*	music
	art
	PE
	modern foreign language
	Welsh*

A modern foreign language is obligatory only in Key Stages 3 and 4.

Every school must also make provision for religious education.

All ten subjects are foundation subjects: three of them are described in the Education Reform Act (ERA) as core subjects, and the Secretary of State is obliged to introduce these first.

* In Wales, Welsh will be a core subject in schools where it is the medium of instruction; in the remaining schools it will be a foundation subject.

An Introduction to the National Curriculum (1989) York: The National Curriculum Council

Q2 To what extent is there still a first-class and second-class knowledge defined here?

Q3 What do we infer about subjects that are not 'foundation' subjects?

Q4 Citizenship is now a foundation subject in the curriculum. What does its inclusion suggest about the aims of the present-day curriculum?

A curriculum for the future

The Guardian ran a series of articles, in October 2000, about 'dumbing down'. Here is an extract from one of these articles:

Have exams got easier?

'Today's standards in basic education are lower than they were 55 years ago.' No, not the latest swipe against rising numbers of top grades in GCSEs, A-levels, or degrees. The complaint dates from 30 years ago. The then respected academic, Cyril Burt, set off a media frenzy with new research concluding that exam standards were not as good as they had been before the first world war. The 'research' was later found to have been fabricated.

Educational standards, it seems, have always been better in the past. National debates over falling standards are now an annual event ... Studies will be commissioned. All will end inconclusively. The claims are impossible to prove one way or the other.

The tragedy of this yearly obsession is that it obscures the real question that needs to be discussed: what knowledge, skills and values do we want to bequeath to our next generation? The answer shifts over time, reflecting how we change as a society ...

What do exams in 1951, 1977, and 2000 tell us about how our lives have changed over the last half-century? We have become more socially inclusive, less authoritarian and more liberal-minded. We now allow the young to think and argue for themselves, rather than adhere to accepted views. We let them apply knowledge rather than memorise it. Science and technology have transformed the world.

And at the dawn of the new millennium, the education system faces perhaps its toughest dilemma yet: is it still possible to transmit a core set of common values for the multi-cultural citizenry of the future?

Lee Elliott-Major *The Guardian* 28 October 2000

Q5 Why might it be a problem to draw up such a "core set of common values"?

Q6 Devise a curriculum – a set of subjects – that would include the "knowledge, skills and values" that you believe we should "bequeath to our next generation".

Unit 3 Natural sciences

Unit 3 moves on from the study of physical sciences, the subject of Unit 2, to look at *natural sciences* – or the study of *animate* or living organisms. There is inevitably some overlap between these areas of science and the issues that were relevant to Unit 2 – about the nature of scientific evidence, for example – will be equally relevant to this unit.

Scientific theory and scientific law

The introduction to Unit 2 discusses how the physical sciences had to live with a degree of uncertainty after 1927 (**Heisenberg**'s Uncertainty Principle). The hardness of evidence, on which scientific laws had previously been based was questioned, and physical sciences moved into the realm of the theoretical.

Chemistry (and its offshoots: electrochemistry, biochemistry and so on) was perhaps less subject to this uncertainty principle than physics – except in theoretical chemistry which is concerned with the application in chemistry of quantum mechanics (the branch of mechanics used for interpreting the behaviour of elementary particles).

However, for practical purposes, most of the findings of classical physics remain intact. It is only at speeds above the speed of light, and at wavelengths below the quantum, that it is safer to talk about *theory* than it is about *laws*. Certain theories – about superstrings, wormholes and catastrophe, for example – may be beyond possibility and resources to test, and so turn into laws. These types of theories belong to post-modern science or 'ironic science', as science-writer John Horgan calls it:

> *Practitioners of ironic science can be divided into two types: naïfs who believe, or at least hope, they are discovering objective truths about nature ... and sophisticates, who realize that they are, in fact, practising something more akin to art or literary criticism.*
>
> The End of Science 1996

Jacob Bronowski (physicist and broadcaster, 1908–74) wrote in the book accompanying one of his television series:

> *The essence of science: ask an impertinent question, and you are on the way to a pertinent answer.*
>
> The Ascent of Man 1973

One such impertinent question was asked by the schoolteacher **John Dalton** (1766–1844): why are the amounts of oxygen and hydrogen in a molecule of water always the same? The pertinent answer was his theory that atoms were the smallest parts of matter.

In his book, boldly entitled *The End of Science*, Horgan presses the point convincingly that scientists are running out of pertinent questions to ask.

> **Q1** Does it seem possible that science will come to an end? Will human beings run out of things to find out about – or that that they *can* find out about?

The appeal of natural sciences

If the 'hard' sciences have gone soft at the extremes, what of the natural sciences, where the study of inorganic matter and organic substances gives way to the study of living (animate) organisms?

There has always been less maths in biology (and in zoology and botany) than in physics and chemistry. Biology has generally been the first of the sciences to be introduced into the school curriculum and it is often the last that a non-scientist will drop. Few of us can make a lot of sense of **Einstein**'s Special and General Theories of Relativity, but most of us know something about Charles Darwin's Theory of Evolution. Darwin's book *On the Origin of Species by Means of Natural Selection* sold out on the first day of publication in 1859 and its readers were not all biologists.

> **Q2** What do you know about the Theory of Evolution? Pool ideas in a group, and then present your understanding of the theory to others.

Can natural sciences be based on hard evidence?

There is arguably some certainty and 'hardness' in the natural sciences. For example, the stages in the life cycle of a unicellular (single-cell) organism are basically known, and all there is to be known about the body-parts of dung beetles is pretty much understood. Even an understanding of the anatomy and physiology of 'higher' species may be close to complete, leaving aside fine brain processes for the moment. But there are at least two reasons why there will always be limits to the extent to which real 'hardness' in natural sciences can be achieved. In fact, perhaps they are connected. **Alfred North Whitehead** (philosopher and mathematician, 1861–1947) gives one reason:

Science can find no individual enjoyment in Nature; science can find no aim in Nature; science can find no creativity in Nature; it finds mere rules of succession.

Nature and Life 1934

Whitehead appears to have been warning natural scientists against the arrogance of believing that they would understand life just because they thought they could know something about the structure and function of certain parts of various living things. He was anxious about the so-called *reductiveness* of science: the way it seems to reduce life as it dissects it. (He would certainly have had doubts about the claims of the bolder genetic engineers of today.)

Werner Heisenberg (1901–76), physicist and author of the Uncertainty Principle, provides the second reason why there are limits to 'hardness' in natural sciences:

Natural science does not simply describe and explain nature, it is part of the interplay between nature and ourselves.

Physics and Philosophy 1958

Q3 What do you understand Heisenberg to mean when he says the natural sciences cannot describe and explain nature, bearing in mind that the physical sciences claim they can do this?

Reference was made earlier to the Theory of Evolution: Darwinism is still a theory, but in alliance with what is now known about genetics, Neo-Darwinism ('new' Darwinism) is close to being law-like. And yet, it is still not known how many species share this Earth with us. Neither is it known how many species become extinct as humans destroy their habitats. Indeed, there is no definition, universally accepted among biologists, of what a species is.

There have been some lavish television documentaries and press feature-articles about the abundance of life on Earth. Perhaps these 'biodramas' created a false impression that everything in the garden is lovely. Environmentalists have been quick to warn of the consequences of 'paving over the garden' to the extent of 'creating a sense of global anxiety' (Jeffries 1997).

David Attenborough's *Life on Earth* from the 1970s was one such television documentary. In the book that accompanied the series, he devoted his last chapter to the human race, coming to an end on this balancing note:

This last chapter has been devoted to only one species, ourselves. This may have given the impression that somehow man is the ultimate triumph of evolution, that all these millions of years of development have had no purpose other than to put him on earth. There is no scientific evidence whatever to support such a view and no reason to suppose that our stay here will be any more permanent than that of the dinosaur. The processes of evolution are still going on among plants and birds, insects and mammals. So it is more than likely that if men were to disappear from the face of the earth, for whatever reason, there is a modest, unobtrusive creature somewhere that would develop into a new form and take our place.

But although denying that we have a special position in the natural world might seem becomingly modest in the eye of eternity, it might also be used as an excuse for evading our responsibilities. The fact is that no species has ever had such wholesale control over everything on earth, living or dead, as we now have. That lays upon us, whether we like it or not, an awesome responsibility. In our hands now lies not only our own future, but that of all other living creatures with whom we share the earth.

Q4 'The real challenge of natural science is to learn more about the psychology of human beings.' How far do you agree with this statement?

Q5 What is there about current research in the natural sciences that could be called controversial?

Attenborough, David (1980) *Life on Earth* London: William Collins and the BBC

Horgan, John (1977) *The End of Science* Helix Books

Jeffries, Michael J. (1997) *Biodiversity and Conservation* London: Routledge

Part 1 Genetic engineering

Although the majority of people have heard of genetic engineering or biotechnology, fewer than a quarter of us can give any sort of adequate account of what these terms mean. Similarly, most people are unable to explain the meaning of such essential words as 'DNA' or 'gene', nor are they able to identify more than one or two, if that, uses or potential uses of the new technologies.

Michael J. Reiss and Roger Straughan (1996)

There are something like 10 million million, or 10^{13}, cells in the adult human body. In the nucleus of each cell there are 46 *chromosomes*. Each chromosome consists of two strands of *deoxyribonucleic acid*, or DNA. These strands form a ladder-like structure wound spirally to form what is called a *double helix*, resembling a spiral staircase. The DNA is very tightly packed in a human cell, as the diagram shows.

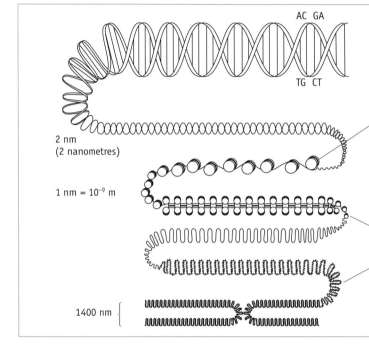

2 nm
(2 nanometres)

1 nm = 10^{-9} m

1400 nm

The rods represent chemical bases of alternating sugars and phosphates (or *nucleotides*).
Attached to each sugar is a nitrogenous base – adenine (A) bonding with thymine (T) and cytosine (C) bonding with guanine (G).

The DNA is coiled round *proteins*. Each protein consists of one or more *polypeptides* (or chains of amino acids, the subunits of proteins).
Each polypeptide chain is the product of a *gene*.
 The sequence of the four nucleotides ACGT constitutes the individual *genetic code* determining which proteins are produced.
 The DNA molecule in a single cell contains about three billion base-pairs.

The proteins are packed together into a long thread which is folded and re-folded densely in the chromosome, pictured here during cell division.

The total amount of DNA in one human cell weighs about 6 × 10–9 mg or 0.000000006 mg.

(Adapted from figures in Reiss and Straughan and elsewhere)

Playing God?

Research done into the mapping of the human *genome* (gene + chromosome), or genetic material, identifies the location and function of genes. The aim of such work is to find out the possibility of re-engineering the sequence.

A single gene *mutation* may be a cause of disease: thus, one adenine base instead of a thymine base, inherited from both parents, can lead to sickle-cell anaemia. Huntington's disease can be inherited from just one parent. Because of work done with the mapping of genes, it is now possible to counter these diseases.

Reengineering the human genome is like playing God.

Q1 Are contraception, abortion and slaughtering animals 'playing God'?

Q2 Does the charge 'playing God' have any relevance for an atheist?

Replacing one 'bad' gene is the top of a very slippery slope.

Q3 The 'slippery slope' is a powerful metaphor. How would you respond to someone who argued against genetic engineering in this way?

Genetic engineering: benefits vs drawbacks

Gene mutation, although it may cause disease, is the engine of evolution. The animal and plant species of today are the product of a long series of species-changing events. Very few such events take place in fewer than 5 000 years. Genetic engineering reduces this timescale to just a few years or months. The technology involves risks, but then so does any medical intervention.

Here are some typical arguments given in a discussion about the benefits and drawbacks of genetic engineering.

John Habgood (scientist and former Archbishop of York) suggested these six 'rules':
1 Human beings are more than their genes … We are more than a set of instructions.
2 Remember the valuable diversity of human nature.
3 Look for justice in the dealings of human beings with one another and for fairness in the use of resources.
4 Respect privacy and autonomy.
5 Accept the presumption that diseases should be cured when it's possible to do so.
6 Be very suspicious about improving human nature; and be even more suspicious of those who think they know what improvements ought to be made.

University of York, 1 February 1995

Benefits	Drawbacks
1 One-third of all agricultural production worldwide is lost to pests. Viruses can be engineered which will contain toxins to kill pests or inhibit their reproduction.	These supposedly insect-specific viruses could be toxic or otherwise harmful to insects that are not pests.
2 Ninety to ninety-five per cent of land for crops is treated with herbicide. Crops engineered to be herbicide-resistant would enable farmers to use the least expensive and least powerful herbicides.	There is a danger that herbicide-resistance would escape into weeds. Also, seed companies that patent their engineered seeds might charge prices that farmers in poor countries could not afford.
3 An anti-freeze protein found in flounders (a fish) has been inserted into potatoes, enabling South American farmers to grow potatoes at higher, colder altitudes.	Are such potatoes animal or vegetable? Can vegetarians eat them? Can anyone eat them knowing that they are safe?
4 The genetic integrity of many plants was compromised long ago. The engineered tomato is firmer and has a longer shelf life than its 'natural' forebears.	Food that is given a longer shelf life loses some of its nutritional value. Besides, there is the danger that we shall reduce biodiversity by such interference.
5 The gene that creates a protein to treat emphysema has been inserted into the mammary glands of sheep. The protein can then be extracted from their milk.	Such a procedure means animals are being used purely instrumentally, as means to humans' ends. The biological integrity of such animals is violated.
6 Many people die each year because of a lack of organs for donation. The organs of pigs can be coated with human protein so that they will not be rejected by recipients' immune response.	There will be those who object to receiving pigs' organs on religious and other grounds.
7 Some diseases are caused by gene mutations in bone-marrow cells. A sound copy of the gene can be inserted so as to ensure the health of blood cells.	Gene insertion in humans is still a hit-and-miss affair. A gene cannot be located with precision in a human chromosome.
8 Genetically engineered microorganisms can be used to synthesize insulin and the human growth hormone.	Should smallness be thought of as a defect? Besides, few conditions are purely genetic; environmental factors are significant, too.

Part 2 Biodiversity and sustainability

Definitions of biodiversity and sustainability

Two words that crop up with increasing frequency in discussions about the ecology and future of planet Earth are *biodiversity* and *sustainability*.

The word biodiversity was coined in the mid 1980s to capture the essence of research into the variety and richness of life on Earth ... [It is] increasingly used as a conceptual focus for conservation policy and practice in response to one of the strongest themes underpinning the founding work on biological diversity, species extinction and ecosystem loss.

Michael Jeffries (1997)

The Brundtland Commission (1982) defined sustainability in human terms as "development that meets the needs of the present generation without compromising the ability of future generations to meet their own needs."

Q1 In what ways might there be a tension between biodiversity and sustainability?

Why are species so diverse?

The Earth is about 4550 billion years old. The first life forms emerged 3.5 billion years ago. This is quite time enough for cells to divide or combine, and for their progeny to mutate, create new species and adapt to altered ecosystems, several million times – and this is why there is such diversity in the world.

Some ecosystems are more favourable to biodiversity and do more to promote it than others.

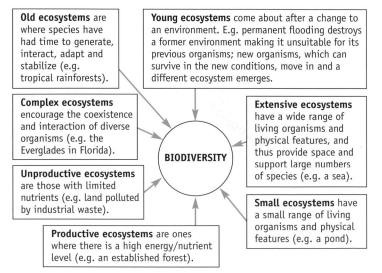

Old ecosystems are where species have had time to generate, interact, adapt and stabilize (e.g. tropical rainforests).

Young ecosystems come about after a change to an environment. E.g. permanent flooding destroys a former environment making it unsuitable for its previous organisms; new organisms, which can survive in the new conditions, move in and a different ecosystem emerges.

Complex ecosystems encourage the coexistence and interaction of diverse organisms (e.g. the Everglades in Florida).

Extensive ecosystems have a wide range of living organisms and physical features, and thus provide space and support large numbers of species (e.g. a sea).

BIODIVERSITY

Unproductive ecosystems are those with limited nutrients (e.g. land polluted by industrial waste).

Small ecosystems have a small range of living organisms and physical features (e.g. a pond).

Productive ecosystems are ones where there is a high energy/nutrient level (e.g. an established forest).

Note: the ecosystems in the diagram are not mutually exclusive. E.g. a tropical rainforest is an old, as well as an extensive, ecosystem.

Q2 Tropical rainforests are where species are at their most diverse. Why do you think this is? Where can rainforests be found?

Interaction between species

Interactions between species can promote or destroy local diversity in the short term but are a major force for evolutionary diversification.

Michael Jeffries (1997)

A basic food chain consists of three levels:

1　Primary producers trap solar energy and store it as chemical energy (e.g. grass).
2　Primary consumers eat the primary producers. They are usually herbivores (e.g. rabbits).
3　Secondary consumers eat the primary consumers. They may be predators (e.g. foxes).

A food web is more complex:

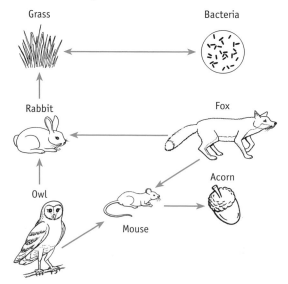

Grass　　Bacteria

Rabbit　　Fox

Owl　　Mouse　　Acorn

The longer a food chain or web is, the more unstable it becomes. This is partly because some energy is burned up at each level, but is mainly because a collapse at one level may destabilize all levels, with predators at the top being most vulnerable. Foxes, for example, were reduced in number when rabbits died from an epidemic of myxomatosis in the 1950s.

Does it pay to be primitive? The following facts suggest it may:

> *For 3.1 billion years, 80 per cent of the history of life, biodiversity was dominated by bacteria.*
>
> *Of the 1.75 million species so far identified, more than half are insects.*
>
> Michael Jeffries (1997)

Q3 Has anything been said, so far, that might strengthen the case for vegetarianism?

Extinction

> *Animal diversity is no more than one outcome from a mass of permutations ... The fate of the dinosaurs has forced a revision of our idea of extinction, once so firmly tied to ideas of inferiority and obsolescence. The danger may be less one of bad genes than of bad luck.*
>
> *The history of life is as much about extinction and loss as diversification and creation, but extinction and environmental change today are widely seen as symptoms of a problem, not a natural process.*
>
> Michael Jeffries (1997)

More than 95 per cent of all species that have ever lived have become extinct – many millions in catastrophes such as an ice age or meteorite impact, and millions more over time. Since 1600, 611 animal species and 654 plant species are known to have become extinct (Schoon 1996). Human beings had something to do with these 'modern' extinctions.

What are the threats to biodiversity?

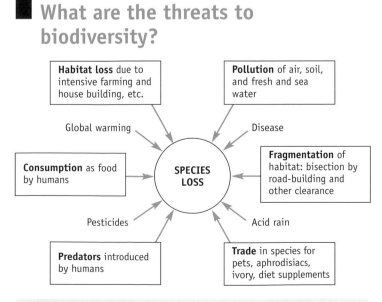

Q4 Give an example of each of the threats in the boxes, whether global or local.

What are the figures?

Groups Endangered	No. of species	Critically recorded endangered	Vulnerable	
		Numbers of threatened species		
Mammals	4 307	612	315	169
Birds	9 700	714	235	168
Reptiles	6 550	153	59	41
Amphibians	4 000	57	31	18
Fishes	28 000	443	134	157
Invertebrates	1 160 000	1 128	405	358
Plants	270 000	8 000	6 019	–

Adapted from tables in Schoon (1996)

Q5 What percentage of the total number of species recorded in each group is at some risk?

The percentages may seem small, but it is the rate at which extinctions are now occurring that is significant. Current estimates of loss rates suggest that 50 per cent of terrestrial vertebrates alive today may be extinct within 200 to 500 years.

Should action be taken?

Arguments for trying to preserve biodiversity and to reduce destructive human activity include the following:

- Humans have a moral responsibility for non-human species.
- It is important to preserve a diversity of food sources.
- Genetic diversity is an insurance against inbreeding and monoculture collapse. (If a society is dependent upon one crop, for instance, and that crop suffers catastrophic failure, there is no fall back. The collapse is when one crop or species, owing to disease or another catastrophe, fails.)
- Plants are highly valued for their pharmaceutical uses – actual and potential.
- Plants stabilize soil against erosion and perform other vital functions.
- Forests absorb carbon dioxide.
- Many indigenous peoples depend on biodiversity for their survival.

Q6 Why might developed and developing countries have different views about conservation of biodiversity?

Q7 "The UN Environment Programme reckons there are 13.63 million species in the world. The fittest will survive, as they always have." Discuss.

Jeffries, Michael J. (1997) *Biodiversity and Conservation* London: Routledge

Schoon, Nicholas (1996) *Going, going, gone* London: WWF-UK

Part 3 Self and others

The biological legacy

In 1859, **Charles Darwin** (naturalist, 1809–82) explained how species evolved by adapting to changes in the ecosystem. He could not explain how physical characteristics – let alone aspects of behaviour – were passed from one generation to the next.

It was **Gregor Mendel** (biologist, 1822–84) who, in 1865, showed how characteristics could be inherited. Every cell in the human body contains 46 chromosomes (see Unit 3, part 1): 23 of these derive from one parent and 23 from the other. The genes, packed tightly together in these chromosomes, are a chemical 'blueprint' passed from parents to their offspring.

All human beings are individuals, therefore, but all carry the characteristics both of the species as a whole and of one family in particular.

Human needs and drives

All animals have needs and drives crucial to their functioning. Humans have needs and drives that reach far beyond those of other species – some of them physical, some psychological. **Abraham Maslow** (psychologist, 1908–70) arranged these human needs in a hierarchy having seven levels.

Seven needs
(Maslow's *Hierarchy of Needs* 1954)

SELF-ACTUALIZATION Realizing one's full potential	
AESTHETIC NEEDS Love of beauty; need for order and form	Intellectual needs
COGNITIVE NEEDS Exploration and understanding of the habitat	
ESTEEM NEEDS Desire for respect of others; self-respect through competence	
LOVE & BELONGING Giving and receiving affection; wishing to be accepted	Emotional needs
SECURITY NEEDS Freedom from physical and mental threat	
PHYSIOLOGICAL NEEDS Air, food, drink, warmth, health	Physical needs

Q1 Aesthetic needs are highly individual. How are your own aesthetic needs most fully or most often met?

Psychologists now recognize eight drives, six of which match certain of the needs identified by Maslow.

Eight drives

Achievement drive – for success, goal-fulfilment

Self-esteem and ego-identity drive – for respect for oneself as an individual

Dominance drive – for others' acceptance of one's leadership

Aggression drive* – for assertion of self over others

Affiliation drive – for social integration and affection

Dependency drive – for protection and guidance

Sex drive – for intimate social interaction

Biological drive – for bodily comforts

The aggression drive* is innate; but it is only activated in response to attack, or when needs or inclinations are frustrated. Like all animals, the human animal responds to the unexpected in one of two ways: fight or flight.

The individual

Psychologists distinguish seven emotions that are innate in humans. The facial expressions that accompany these emotions are common to more or less all humans everywhere.

Happiness   Fear   Anger

Disgust   Sadness

Surprise   Interest

But these facial expressions are just one of a battery of ways in which the individual signals feelings in interpersonal encounters. Others are: how close to others one stands; bodily posture and contact; direction of gaze; movement of the head and hands; timing of speech and speech errors; emotional tone of speech; linguistic register of speech (e.g. formal or casual).

The family

The ways in which human babies express their emotions and their appetites are inborn, but these ways are only fully realized or actualized in the daily exchange of behaviours and responses in the family.

It is in the family that a child's behaviour is first approved or disapproved of. The behaviour provokes (more or less consistent) responses that serve as *feedback* to the child. Some behaviours are reinforced ("Good!"); some are corrected ("No!"); and some are redirected ("Let's play!"). Like the seven emotions earlier, much communication is *nonverbal* – some of it innate and some of it learned. As children develop, language comes to have increasing importance as the means by which they learn from the culture – the world beyond the family.

The culture

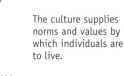

LANGUAGE

The culture rewards good behaviour and punishes antisocial behaviour.	The culture supplies norms and values by which individuals are to live.

THE INDIVIDUAL

In the early work on socialization, major emphasis was placed on the control of motivation by systems of rewards and punishments, with special reference to critical stress points in development: early bowel-training, control of aggression, the transition into adolescent sexuality. More recent studies have been more concerned with the process whereby children learn underlying rules and properties of the culture.

Jerome Bruner in Bullock & Trombley 1999

Q2 What rewards does the culture offer for good behaviour?

Q3 What 'norms' or 'underlying rules' can you think of that the culture transmits to the young?

Construction of the self

Sigmund Freud

Perhaps the longest-running debate in psychology has been between those who look to *nature* (or biology) for an explanation of human behaviour, and those who look to *nurture* (or upbringing). **Sigmund Freud** (physician and psychoanalyst, 1856–1939) revolutionized the popular view of human nature when he laid emphasis on the *unconscious* mind. He examined the psychosexual development of the individual (through the oral, anal and phallic phases) and the conflict within the individual between the *id* (the source of psychosexual energy), the *ego* (the self in the real world) and the *superego* (the mechanism of self-control, or conscience).

Freudian theory is not subject to conventional scientific investigation, however, and it attaches too little importance to influences on the individual of other individuals and groups.

> *Relationships with others are one of the main sources of happiness, but when things go wrong they produce very great distress and are one of the roots of mental disorder.*
>
> *The self-image is largely constructed out of the relations of others, and this leads to self-presentation behaviour designed to elicit appropriate responses in later social situations.*
>
> *The main origin of self-image and self-esteem is probably the reactions of others – we come to see ourselves as others categorize us. This has been called the theory of the "looking-glass" self.*
>
> Michael Argyle (1983)

Q4 Why might Freudian theory be considered unscientific?

Q5 Argyle refers to "self-presentation behaviour". How do people present themselves to others in such a way as to elicit the responses that they want?

Q6 How convincing do you find the theory of 'the "looking-glass" self'?

Argyle, Michael (1983) *The Psychology of Interpersonal Behaviour* (4th edn) London: Penguin Books

Bullock, Alan and Stephen Trombley (eds) (1999) *The New Fontana Dictionary of Modern Thought* (3rd edn) London: HarperCollinsPublishers

Subjectivity and objectivity

From the point of view of an individual, there is the *self* (the subject) and there is the *world* (the object). The subject/self sees the object/world, explores it, learns about it, and comes to terms with it. This is such a fundamental notion that it shapes human language:

SUBJECT	→ VERB →	OBJECT
I	eat	breakfast
We	shut	the car doors
People	mistrust	politicians

Subjective and objective opinions

If a person, or subject, observes a rainbow and says, "That is the archway over the door to paradise", the observation will be *subjective*. In other words, it is a personal opinion: it is one-sided, introspective and comes from an individual's own consciousness.

Picasso at work

The word *subjective* can be used in a negative way, to imply that the subject is prejudiced or is taking too narrow a view, as in "Picasso was a mere caricaturist".

The above view about the rainbow is neither true nor false: it is a judgment, not a statement of fact. It should still be called subjective even if many other people agreed with it. An *objective* statement, on the other hand, is one with which everyone would be bound to agree. It is based on matters of *fact*.

Q1 What objective statements might be made about a rainbow?

Q2 What objective statements might be made about the paintings of Picasso?

Put very simply, it could be said that a subjective judgement depends on the subject or person making it, and it may have little to do with the object. Likewise, it could be said that an objective statement is all about the object and its properties, and it makes no difference who utters it.

Consider the utterance: "Girls do better than boys in exams". If a boy said this, it might sound to a girl like an objective statement. If a girl said it, it might sound to a boy more like a subjective judgement. Which is it?

It would be simpler if all statements could be divided into two classes:

Objective statements	Subjective judgements
Facts about the material world, mathematics, physics and so on, that are either true or false	Opinions about art, religion, literature and so on, that are neither true nor false

But life is not this simple: it is complex and interesting, and can be divided into many more classes than two.

Q3 Consider the utterance: "The Millennium Dome was widely acknowledged to be an embarrassing failure." Is this a subjective judgement or an objective statement? Or is it both? What would determine whether it was more one than the other?

Scientific fact and objectivity

The distinction between subjective and objective is a relatively modern one. Pre-literate humans did not see the world as something *other*. The world was a phenomenon of which they were a part. They could explain phenomena such as thunder in human terms. Scientific understanding has enabled their descendants to explain it objectively.

Archaeologist **Henri Frankfort** (1897–1954) explains:

The basic distinction of modern thought is that between subjective *and* objective. *On this distinction scientific thought has based a critical and analytical procedure by which it progressively reduces the individual phenomena to typical events subject to universal laws ...*

We see the sun rise and set, but we think of the earth as moving round the sun. We see colours, but we describe them as wavelengths. We dream of a dead relative, but we think of that distinct vision as a product of our own subconscious minds. Even if we individually are unable to prove these almost unbelievable scientific views to be true, we accept them, because we know that they can be proved to possess a greater degree of objectivity than our sense-impressions ...

Primitive man [however] cannot withdraw from the presence of the phenomena because they reveal themselves to him in the manner we have described. Hence the distinction between subjectivity and objective knowledge is meaningless to him.

Henri Frankfort *et al.* (1949)

Q4 What do you suppose "primitive" humans thought (or felt) when they:

(a) saw the sun rise and set
(b) saw colours
(c) dreamed of a dead relative?

Making judgments

It's possible to be objective about *how* to split an atomic nucleus, but is it possible to be objective about whether it is *right* to do it, and for what purpose? Everybody can be objective about the nuisance of air pollution, but can they be equally objective about what individuals should do to minimize it? Could it be that there is no *absolute* distinction between a subjective judgement and an objective statement, but that the difference between them is one of degree?

Sound is objective, whilst *noise* is subjective. Sound can be measured with precision, in terms of the pressure of a sound wave, whereas noise is a subjective experience. Though people have tried to devise an index of noise, they have not been very successful. The diagram attempts to represent sound/noise on a continuum from objective fact to subjective opinion.

Mobile telephone bleeper

Objective

A In a concert hall during a quiet passage of a favourite piano piece

B In a railway carriage for the use of non-mobile-phone users

C In a restaurant where there is music and laughter

D In a street where there is much traffic-noise and bustle

Subjective

In case A, the vast majority would agree that the noise of the bleeper was an intrusion, whereas it would be very unlikely for people to object to the noise in case D.

It is an objective fact that diamonds are made of carbon; it is a subjective opinion that (as Marilyn Monroe sang in *Gentlemen Prefer Blondes*) "Diamonds are a girl's best friend".

Q5 Think of two observations that fit between the objective fact and the subjective opinion.

Marilyn Monroe in Gentlemen Prefer Blondes

Is objectivity possible in all sciences?

It is easy to be 'objective' in mathematics and physics.

A **Mathematics**

Pi (π) can be expressed to three decimal places (3.142) or to 30 places (3.14159265358979323846264383279). Both are objective statements. It is an objective fact that pi was expressed to 2 billion places in 1992. The excitement of certain mathematicians at the time was subjective.

B **Physics**

It is an objective fact that the boiling point of water can be expressed as 80° Réamur, 212° Fahrenheit, 100° Celsius, or 373.16 Kelvin. There is something subjective about the preference of Americans for the Fahrenheit over the Celsius scale in the context of weather forecasting.

Evidence in the physical sciences is 'hard' inasmuch as it is usually expressed in mathematical quantities, and the scientists who interpret the evidence may not be affected by it. Evidence in the social sciences is relatively 'soft' inasmuch as it is about human societies, and the scientists themselves are human. Historians of Nazi Germany, for example, cannot remain unaffected by evidence of the death camps. The 'problem' of objectivity and the nature of evidence will be explored further in Unit 4, Social sciences.

Frankfort, Henri *et al.* (1949) *Before Philosophy: The Intellectual Adventure of Ancient Man* London: Penguin Books

Social class

Classification

One step on the path towards understanding certain things is to *classify* them — to divide them up into classes. For example, there is a lot of stone in the world. It is impossible to make sense of all the particular examples of stone and it is unhelpful to speak of stone in general. So, in order to learn something about stone, and to make use of it, it is necessary to classify it. Stone can be classified in terms of its:

● geological origins and age

● weathering properties as a building material

● suitability for carving/sculpting for decorative and artistic purposes.

> **Q1** Identify some of the classifications made by:
> (a) mathematicians
> (b) physicists
> (c) chemists
> (d) biologists.
>
> **Q2** What other classifications do other subject specialists make?

Classifying people

There are a lot of people in the United Kingdom. It would be nice if everybody could be treated as individuals all the time, but this is impossible in practice. On the other hand, bracketing the population together as 'British' serves to identify nationality, but little else.

> **Q3**
> (a) Who might need to classify the people of the United Kingdom?
> (b) What are the benefits of identifying different groups within the population?

Karl Marx (philosopher, economist and social theorist, 1818–83) divided society into two groups:

● the bourgeoisie — owners of land or machinery

● the proletariat — owners only of their own labour.

Max Weber (sociologist, 1864–1920) believed this was too simple: he recognized the importance of small employers (often of family labour) — what he called the *petit*, or *petty bourgeoisie* — and of the difference between *white-collar* and *blue-collar* employees:

1 upper class — owners of land or machinery (or capital)

2 petty bourgeoisie — small employers

3 middle class — white-collar employees (in offices and shops)

4 working class — blue-collar employees (in factories, mines, etc.).

From 1921 to 1990, the Registrar General (formerly responsible for the 10-yearly census) divided the population into six classes, according to the occupation of the 'head of the household'.

The Registrar General's Scale (RGS)

I
Higher professional/ managerial

II
Lower professional/ managerial

IIIN
Supervisory (over manual workers) and lower routine non-manual

IIIM
Skilled manual

IV
Semiskilled manual

V
Unskilled manual, agricultural workers

This scale excluded, at the top, the 'idle' rich, and at the bottom, the unemployed poor. Market researchers relabelled the groups A, B, C1, C2, and D (D combined RGS classes IV and V: semiskilled and unskilled manual in industry, and agricultural workers), and added class E. This relabelling was called the Social Grading Scale (SGS).

E
Unemployed pensioners, housewives, permanently sick and disabled

> **Q4** The RGS and the market researchers' SGS are both *occupational* scales. What might be the drawbacks of basing a social classification on the occupation of the 'head of the household'?
>
> **Q5** What criteria, apart from occupation, might be used to classify people?

The central problem of any social classification is that it assumes a certain fixedness: it implies that people will stay in the class to which they are assigned by their job or by the income that goes with it. In fact, society has been changing over the past 50 years in ways which cannot easily be captured in pyramid diagrams. Consider these pie charts:

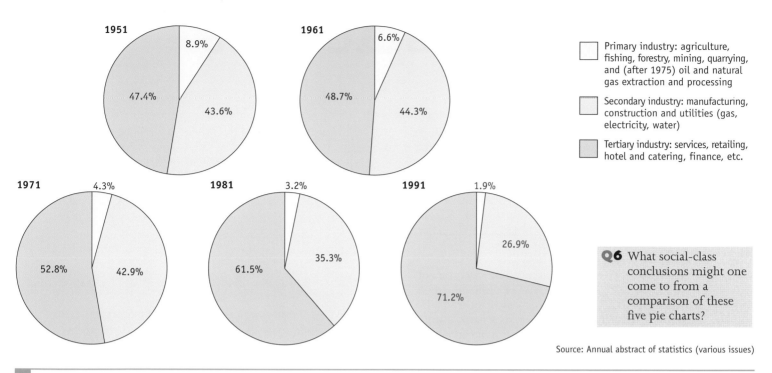

Primary industry: agriculture, fishing, forestry, mining, quarrying, and (after 1975) oil and natural gas extraction and processing

Secondary industry: manufacturing, construction and utilities (gas, electricity, water)

Tertiary industry: services, retailing, hotel and catering, finance, etc.

Q6 What social-class conclusions might one come to from a comparison of these five pie charts?

Source: Annual abstract of statistics (various issues)

Changing classifications

Earlier occupational scales could not express changing social patterns and, in particular, *social mobility* – that is the extent to which the members of classes moved up or down the pyramid. It was this mobility that interested **John Goldthorpe** in the 1970s. It was clear to him, apart from anything else, that the IIIN/C1 class of the RGS and SGS, respectively, would have to be divided further. The Standard Occupational Classification (SOC), which replaced the RGS for official purposes in 1990, is very similar to the Goldthorpe scale, but it is subdivided still further.

These are more sophisticated scales than those that preceded them, but they are still based on (largely male) occupations and there are still quite a lot of people excluded.

Q7 Which groups of people seem to you to be unaccounted for on the Goldthorpe Scale and the SOC?

Another question is whether people nowadays can be defined simply by their work. It need not determine where they live; it might not say much about their income or their lifestyle; and it may have little to do with how much power they have and with how they vote.

Q8 Is social class still important today? Is everyone middle class nowadays?

Q9 If people are not to be classified by occupation, how might they be classified?

Q10 Can any social classification be truly *objective*, or must any division of the population into classes be a 'point of view' and, therefore, *subjective*?

Service class	Higher professional, administrative and managerial	I	1	Managers and senior officials
	Lower administrative, higher technical and supervisory	II	2	Professional occupations
			3	Associate professional and technical occupations
Intermediate class	Routine non-manual	III	4	Administrative and secretarial occupations
	Small proprietors and self-employed	IV	5	Skilled trades occupations
	Foremen and lower-grade technicians	V	6	Personal service occupations
Working class	Skilled manual	VI	7	Sales and customer service occupations
	Semiskilled and unskilled manual in industry and agriculture	VII	8	Process, plant and machine operatives
			9	Elementary occupations

Goldthorpe scale (1980)   **Standard Occupational Classification (1990)**

This is the third unit that examines what are broadly known as *the sciences*. Unit 2 was about the *physical* sciences, while Unit 3 looked at *natural* sciences. This unit moves on to consider the *social* sciences and, continuing the theme of the nature of evidence, ponders the question whether social sciences are truly sciences in the same sense as physical or natural sciences are.

Studying people

Natural scientists (biologists, neurologists, psychologists) cannot be as *objective* – that is, as factual, dispassionate or disinterested – as physical scientists. This is not a fault or weakness. Evidence in the natural sciences is still quite hard, but it is not rock hard. Natural scientists might find it quite easy to be objective about anopheles mosquitoes, many of which carry malarial parasites; it is less easy to be objective about chimpanzees.

Social scientists, whose study is people, might be thought less objective still, because they are people themselves. Some would say that for this reason they are not 'real' scientists. In the 1980s, for example, Keith Joseph, a cabinet minister, caused what had been called the Social Science Research Council – the SSRC – to be renamed the Economic and Social Research Council – ESRC. Research by people about people could not be 'scientific', he supposed. This is rather unfortunate; it is not *what* people study that defines them as 'scientists'; it is *how* they study it.

Sociology

The simplest definition of sociology is that it is the study of human societies. It stresses the interdependence of different parts of societies and attempts to go beyond the description of specific events by establishing generalizations. For example, we all know that there are hundreds of different occupations but rather than trying to classify them all, some sociologists have argued that groups of people who do much the same type of job and earn roughly the same amounts of money may be generalized as constituting distinct 'social classes'. Sociologists also attempt to be systematic in the ways they study societies. Rather than just snatching at 'facts' which happen to support a particular point of view, they try to collect evidence in a more consistent way. For example, sociologists interested in health and illness could look at rates of illness between different social classes and this may then allow them to make further generalizations about the relationship between health and society.

However, defining sociology as the systematic study of societies does not take us far enough, because there are other academic subjects – anthropology, economics, politics and psychology, for example – which also attempt to make systematic generalizations about social behaviour. So, as sociology cannot be defined either in terms of what *it studies (people living in families, going to work, getting ill and so on) or in terms of* how *it studies them (making generalizations, interpreting statistics, asking questions and so on), how is it distinguishable from the other social*

sciences? The answer to this is to be found in the questions *that sociologists ask about social life. Sociology begins by asking how societies are possible. The fact that social life is a problem to be explained rather than a natural condition makes sociology* the *social science. It is first and foremost a particular way of thinking about societies. It involves being curious about the very fact of social order, about how it changes and, above all, about how our lives as individuals are shaped by the societies in which we live.*

Steve Taylor (1999)

Q1 According to Steve Taylor, what characteristics of sociology qualify it to be called a *science*?

Q2 What is your assessment of his claim that it is *the* social science?

Different thoughts on society

That 'society' can be defined in different ways is one of the splendours, and one of the difficulties, of social science. The way in which we use the word has changed over time: thus, Oscar Wilde's character Ernest (from *The Importance of Being Ernest*) could correct his friend:

Never speak disrespectfully of society, Algernon. Only people who can't get into it do that.

What a person thinks of society may depend on whether they are an optimist or pessimist, a philanthrope (someone who loves people) or misanthrope (someone who hates people). Optimists will think kindly of society:

Man seeketh in society comfort, use, and protection.

> Francis Bacon (philosopher, politician and writer, 1561–1626)

Man was formed for society.

> William Blackstone (Judge and writer on law, 1723–80)

Pessimists will think sourly of any society but their own or will view society as an overbearing, negative force that suppresses individuality:

Society than solitude is worse
And man to man is still the greatest curse.

> Anna Laetitia Barbauld (poet, 1743–1825)

Society everywhere is in conspiracy against the manhood of every one of its members.

> Ralph Waldo Emerson (philosopher, essayist and poet, 1803–82)

We have got three distinct terms, Barbarians, Philistines, Populace, to denote roughly the three great classes in which society is divided.

> Matthew Arnold (poet and critic, 1822–88)

Three was even a crowd for the robust American writer **Henry David Thoreau** (1817–1862), who claimed to have just three chairs in his house: one for solitude, two for friendship, and three for society (*Walden* 1854).

Q3 Do you agree that people's attitudes to society are determined by their character? Which of the quotations above do you most identify with? Which of them would you disagree most strongly with?

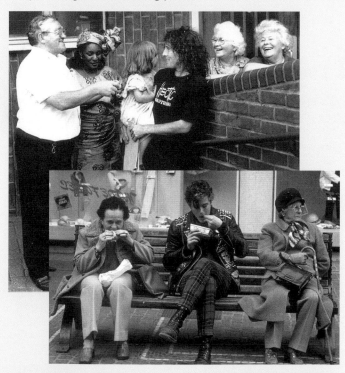

Q4 "Man is a social animal," said Aristotle; "There is no such thing as society," said Margaret Thatcher. Explain briefly what you think was meant by these comments.

How would you define society?

■ The sociologist and society

It is no wonder that no human can be thoroughly objective about human society, but there is another more subtle limit to objectivity in social scientists' motives for asking the questions that they do about society. Geologists may be curious – even passionate – about the rocks they examine, but they cannot have much effect on those rocks. Nor can the rocks have much effect on them. Biologists may have the power of life and death over the rats in their laboratory, but the rats are instrumental to their purpose. This purpose is more powerful than the rats. Sociologists, however, for all that they might take natural science as their guide, are involved *personally* in the research that they do: they are part of the very object they are studying.

While it is impossible for a social scientist to maintain an objective position, this does not invalidate their research, as Steve Taylor explains:

> *While sociological research can never be proved to be universally 'true', neither can we lapse into a relativism where one account is as good as any other. Research can show that one theory is better than another in given circumstances. Although complete objectivity is impossible to practise, it can still serve as a goal to which good research should aspire …*
>
> *[The] continuing ambition of most sociologists [is] to explain how societies work and change in the hope of contributing, in some way or other, to their improvement.*

It is this attempt to explain and improve society that caused some Thatcherite thinkers of the 1980s to view sociology with suspicion. It seemed to them that university departments of sociology were hotbeds of left-wing activism in academic disguise, and that sociologists were class-warriors with degrees.

Q5 How might a sociologist hope to improve society by explaining how it works and changes?

Q6 Does Taylor give grounds for concern that sociologists might have a hidden agenda?

Q7 Are the social sciences different in this respect from any other sciences? Might medical science, for example, have a hidden agenda?

Taylor, Steve (ed.) *Sociology: Issues and Debates* Basingstoke: Macmillan 1999

Part 1 Families

Can 'the family' be defined?

Socialization is the process by which individuals learn to get on with others – when they learn that others have needs, too. It is the process whereby the 'selfish gene' (the idea that individuals are genetically driven to pass on as many of their genes as possible to future generations) learns a little *altruism* – that is, learns to help others without necessarily expecting any reward.

Primary *socialization* takes place in the family. But what is a family?

> **Q1** Attempt a working definition of the family. Do this on your own first, then compare your definition with someone else's.

You might well have used words like:

> nuclear family – *to denote one or more parents and one or more children*
>
> extended family – *to denote a network of relatives living elsewhere than in the family home*

Social scientists might now use a word like:

> household – *to denote those who live in a shared space they might refer to (affectionately or not) as 'home'*

Social scientists are more likely to talk of 'families' than 'the family', because there is no one single thing as 'the family'. Politicians and moralists have been inclined to idealize 'the family', and to worry about what is happening to 'the family', and to recommend ways in which 'the family' might be saved from extinction. They speak of 'the family' as the building block of society, as if, like bricks, families are all the same. The truth is that they never have been the same as each other.

As a child, **Flora Thompson** (writer, 1876–1947) lived in an Oxfordshire hamlet in the 1880s. It was a cloistered sort of life, but family life in the hamlet was varied. Here are vignettes of two families living a stone's throw from each other:

> *When the men came home from work they would find the table spread with a clean whitey-brown cloth, upon which would be knives and two-pronged steel forks with buckhorn handles. The vegetables would be turned out into big round yellow crockery dishes and the bacon cut into dice, with much the largest cube upon Father's plate, and the whole family would sit down to the chief meal of the day. True, it was seldom that all could find places at the central table; but some of the smaller children could sit upon stools with the seat of a chair for a table, or on the door-step with the plates on their laps. Good manners prevailed. The children were given their share of the food, there was no picking and choosing, and they were expected to eat in silence. "Please" and "Thank you" were permitted, but nothing more. Father and*

> *Mother might talk if they wanted to; but usually they were content to concentrate upon their enjoyment of the meal. Father might shovel green peas into his mouth with his knife, Mother might drink her tea from her saucer, and some of the children might lick their plates when the food was devoured; but who could eat peas with a two-pronged fork, or wait for tea to cool after the heat and flurry of cooking? And licking their plates passed as a graceful compliment to Mother's good dinner ...*

> *Their mother would often tell the children about the Rectory and her own home in the churchyard, and how the choir, in which her father played the violin, would bring their instruments and practise there in the evening. But she liked better to tell of that other rectory where she had been nurse to the children. The living was small and the Rector was poor, but three maids had been possible in those days, a cook-general, a young housemaid, and Nurse Emma. They must have been needed in that large, rambling old house, in which lived the Rector and his wife, their nine children, three maids, and often three or four young men pupils. They had all such jolly, happy times, she said; all of them, family and maids and pupils, singing glees and part-songs in the drawing room in the evening.*

> Lark Rise to Candleford 1945

> **Q2** List the most obvious differences between the composition and life of (typical) families of the late 19th century, and those of today.

Looking at the statistics

A standard description of a family might start with talk of a couple getting married and then 'starting' a family, as if a couple (or single parent) with one child is only an incomplete family. A new family begins with a marriage. Estate agents advertise 'family houses' and car salesmen sell 'family saloons', as if every family will need three bedrooms and three passenger seats, respectively.

The typical family of two parents, one male and one female, and two (or 1.8) children, one boy and one girl (in that order), was a product of the advertisers' imagination for the manufacturers of breakfast cereals.

Perhaps the single most worrying fact about the family is the growing number of marriages that end in divorce. In 1971, the number was 74 000; in 1998, it was 145 000, an increase of 96% – almost a doubling in 27 years. The number of children under 16 in families affected by divorce rose over the same period from 82 000 to 150 000 (Social Trends 30, 2000).

It is safest not to make judgments (and not merely for feminist or politically correct reasons) about what the 'best' sort of family is. The word 'household' is the word used by statisticians – as in the following table:

Households: by type of households and family

Great Britain			Percentages (%)		
	1961	1971	1981	1991	1998/9
One person: under pensionable age	4	6	8	11	14
over pensionable age	7	12	14	16	15
Two or more unrelated adults	5	4	5	3	2
One-family households:					
Couple: no children	26	27	26	28	30
1–2 dependent children	30	26	25	20	19
3 or more dependent children	8	9	6	5	4
non-dependent children only	10	8	8	8	6
Lone parent: dependent children	2	3	5	6	7
non-dependent children only	4	4	4	4	3
Multi-family household	3	1	1	1	1
All households (100%) (millions)	16.3	18.6	20.2	22.4	–

Source: Social Trends 30, 2000

Q3 What appear to be the most obvious trends here?

Q4 What has been the percentage decrease over the period 1961 to 1998/99 in households consisting of couples having one or more dependent children?

Q5 What would you judge to be the most likely trends into the 21st century?

Q6 *"Discontent with marriage seems to be experienced as disillusionment with a particular relationship, rather than with the institution."* **Stevi Jackson** *in Steve Taylor 1999*

Statistics only tell us arithmetical truths about the state of the family in Britain. How far do you agree that as long as people continue to marry, or to cohabit, there is no need to worry for the future of 'the family'?

■ The family as social construct

Sociologists would say that the concept of the family is a *social construct*, that is, each culture in time and place will have its own ideas about what a family is, and – perhaps – what a family should be.

In 1998/99, according to the table above, 29 per cent of households in Britain consisted of just one person but most of these individuals will have been married at some time and had children, and/or had siblings who married and had children. Everybody moves in and out of families of different sorts throughout their lives.

Taylor, Steve (ed.) *Sociology: Issues and Debates* Basingstoke: Macmillan 1999

How many *families* are there in your *family*?

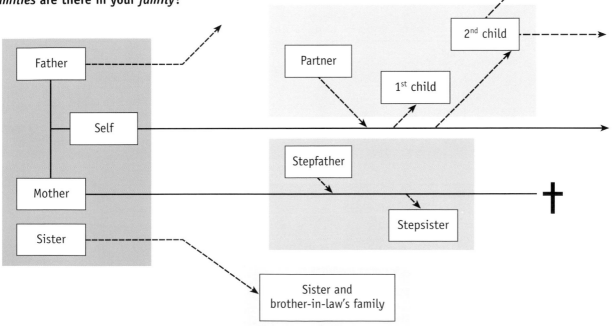

Part 2 Schools and life-chances

What is school for?

If families are the main setting for primary socialization, schools are normally the place where secondary socialization takes place. Schools are where children learn to live with each other and where 'society' transmits its prevailing norms and values to the next generation of citizens.

Just as social scientists classify, so they themselves can be classified. For example, each 'school' of sociologists looks at schools from a particular point of view:

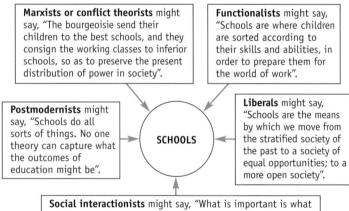

Marxists or conflict theorists might say, "The bourgeoisie send their children to the best schools, and they consign the working classes to inferior schools, so as to preserve the present distribution of power in society".

Functionalists might say, "Schools are where children are sorted according to their skills and abilities, in order to prepare them for the world of work".

Postmodernists might say, "Schools do all sorts of things. No one theory can capture what the outcomes of education might be".

SCHOOLS

Liberals might say, "Schools are the means by which we move from the stratified society of the past to a society of equal opportunities; to a more open society".

Social interactionists might say, "What is important is what actually goes on in schools and classrooms, and how teachers and students play the roles that are assigned to them".

Q1 Which of these approaches seems to be the most reasonable to you?

The big change: equality of opportunity?

1944 was a turning point in British education as it introduced a system of universal secondary education. Before 1944, the upper and middle classes had gone to public* and grammar schools. For the rest, education was provided up to the age of 14 in elementary schools and in 'central' schools in urban areas. The 1944 Education Act of Conservative minister **Richard Austen Butler** (1902–82) introduced the Eleven Plus examination. All primary school children would take this test. Those who passed went to grammar schools, which, after 1944, no longer charged fees. Children deemed to be 'good with their hands' went to technical schools (though, in practice, there were few of these), while the rest (about 75 per cent) went to secondary modern schools. This was called the 'tripartite' ('three-part') system (see below).

This meant that all children had a secondary education of some sort and, in theory, all children had an equal chance of going to a grammar school.

* private independent fee-paying schools.

Q2 In theory all children had an equal chance of passing the Eleven Plus examination. Why might they not have had an equal chance in practice?

Q3 What do you suppose were the essential differences between grammar schools and secondary modern schools?

The 1944 tripartite system

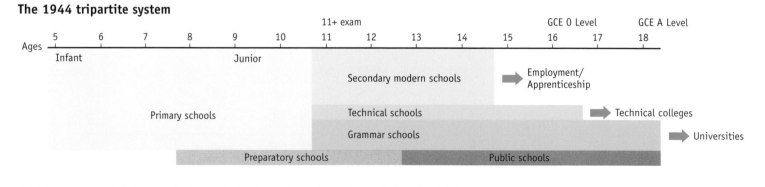

Going comprehensive

Some sociologists took an interest in who was selected for grammar (and to a lesser extent technical) schools at Eleven Plus. They asked these questions:

- Was Britain a genuine *meritocracy*, where talent and intelligence counted, rather than background?
- What was the fate of 'late-developers' – that is, children whose learning skills improve only after the age of 11?

- How did those working-class children who passed the Eleven Plus fare at grammar school?
- Did the Eleven Plus provide a genuine ladder of opportunity, as had been claimed?

Over time, the Labour Party committed itself to what came to be called the *comprehensive school*. This was to be for all children irrespective of their ability.

In 1965, **Anthony Crosland** (1918–77), the Education Secretary in Harold Wilson's Labour government (1964–70), asked local authorities to make plans for 'going comprehensive'. Certain Conservative authorities held out against the reforms, so grammar and secondary modern schools survived in some areas. (By 1986, 85 per cent of secondary-school students attended comprehensives.)

At the beginning of this 1965 reform, the school-leaving age was 15; it was raised to 16 in 1972.

Q4 Why do you suppose the Labour Party favoured the introduction of comprehensive schools?

Q5 Who might have opposed the abolition of the Eleven Plus exam, and why?

Some comprehensive schools ran mixed-ability classes, although most 'streamed' all or the majority of classes – that is, organized children into classes according to their ability. Sociologists were principally interested in whether the new schools increased equality of opportunity and how far they reallocated life-chances. On the whole, they found that middle-class children thrived at GCE O(rdinary) Level exams, and went on into the sixth form, whilst working-class children scored a few of the less-highly regarded CSE (Certificate of Secondary Education) grades, or left school without taking any exams.

Q6 What do you suppose were the advantages and disadvantages of streaming children?

Q7 Why did working-class children still not 'make the grade' in comprehensive schools?

The 1965 comprehensive system

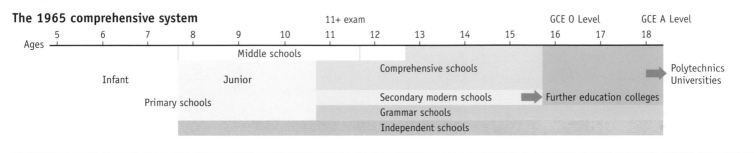

The National Curriculum

In 1988, the Conservative Education Secretary, **Kenneth Baker** (1934–), introduced the Education Reform Act (ERA), coinciding with the first year of the new GCSE courses. It introduced a National Curriculum, Key Stage tests, and grant-maintained (GM)

status for schools that chose to 'opt out' from local-authority control and be maintained by central government.

The 1997 New Labour government abolished GM schools, but allowed a number of variations on the basic comprehensive model.

The 1988/97 specialist comprehensive system

Education in crisis?

In recent years, the emphasis of governments has been on: standards and testing, particularly in basic literacy and numeracy; the creation of specialist schools; the use of 'league tables' to encourage market-style competition; parental choice of school, and involvement in its governance.

These measures have been introduced to raise standards. The worry is that too many young people still leave school with poor qualifications, and lack the skills that are needed in an increasingly competitive world. In spite of all the testing and the consistent improvement in test and exam results, there is a perception that standards are slipping and that schools are 'failing'.

The evidence is overwhelming that standards throughout the education system, from infant classes right through to degree level, give cause for the most intense concern. Statistics are an erratic guide to any deterioration, since changes in criteria or

collection methods make comparisons notoriously unreliable. What can be said with confidence, however, is that the standard of knowledge of many thousands of schoolchildren, adults and even teachers is lamentable.

Melanie Phillips (1996)

Q8 Do you agree with Melanie Phillips? Have things changed since 1996, when she wrote this?

Q9 'Inner-city' schools, and boys in most schools, are often highlighted as a cause for concern. Why?

Phillips, Melanie (1996) *All Must Have Prizes* London: Little, Brown & Co.

Part 3 Population

I was ever of opinion, that the honest man who married and brought up a large family, did more service than he who continued single and only talked of population.

Oliver Goldsmith (playwright, novelist, poet and essayist, c.1728–74)

■ Population and economic growth

It had been thought that the more people there were, the more productivity there would be – and, therefore, the more economic growth. This is still the *optimistic* view. **Thomas Malthus** (political economist, 1766–1834) was a *pessimist*. In his 1798 *Essay on the Principle of Population as it Affects the Future Improvement of Society*, he contended that population growth would always outstrip economic growth.

According to him, population figures would rise geometrically, whilst food production would only increase arithmetically. Only poverty, disease, war – or late marriage and sexual self-restraint – would serve to keep population numbers in check.

It was a powerful message, and one that influenced middle-class attitudes towards the poor – and their treatment of them – for decades. It gave economic and theological authorization (since Malthus was a clergyman) to a *laissez faire* policy that put the children of the poor to work in the factories, mills and mines of the well-to-do. (For more details of *laissez faire* economics, see Unit 5.)

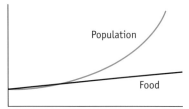

Q1 Why do you suppose Malthus' views gave support to an 'uncharitable' Victorian attitude towards the poor, and to *laissez-faireism* in particular?

■ Population sustainability – pessimistic and optimistic views

There are differing opinions on whether or not population growth can be sustained under various economic conditions. Broadly speaking, these opinions can be characterised as optimistic or pessimistic.

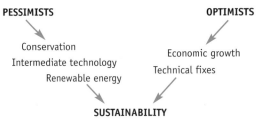

In 1972, The Club of Rome* published *Limits to Growth*. This was a pessimistic book full of graphs similar to the one in the left-hand column that issued dire warnings about how soon the world's natural resources might run out. In 1973, **Ernst Friedrich Schumacher** (economist, 1911–1977) published *Small is Beautiful*. He was also a pessimist, writing that large institutions, together with *laissez-faireism*, created social and environmental problems.

In 1995, **Wilfred Beckerman** published *Small is Stupid*. As an optimist, he recognized that there is a trade-off between economic growth and sustainability, but he believed that human ingenuity will always find a way to overcome a shortage of resources.

Malthus can be seen as a prophet who was proved wrong. There is arguably enough food in the world to feed a much bigger population than today's; the problem is that it is unequally distributed.

* The Club of Rome is a non-profit making non-government organization (NGO). Its members, from all over the world, are economists, scientists, business people, top civil servants, and current and former heads of state. They believe that each person can contribute to the improvement of the world's societies.

Q2 Would you call yourself an optimist or a pessimist in your views on population growth? Is this because you believe the case for the one is rationally better than it is for the other?

■ Population numbers

Two hundred years ago, when Thomas Malthus was writing, the total population of the world stood at 978 million – less than one billion. It now stands at something over six billion – more than three and a half billion of whom live in Asia. Not only are more babies being born, but – thanks to vaccines, antibiotics and the UN World Health Organisation – more of them live into adulthood. In Sri Lanka alone, towards the end of the 20th century, life expectancy rose by two years every twelve months. The following are the UN's own world population figures for the past 250 years.

World population

	1750	1800	1850	1900	1950	Millions 1999
Asia	502	635	809	947	1 402	3 634
Africa	106	107	111	133	224	767
Europe	163	203	276	408	547	729
Latin America & Caribbean	16	24	38	74	166	511
North America	2	2	26	82	172	307
Oceania	2	2	2	6	13	30
World	791	978	1 262	1 650	2 524	5 978

Q3 Work out the percentage rises in population in:
(a) Asia in the 19th century
(b) Asia in the 20th century
(c) Europe in the 19th century
(d) Europe in the 20th century.

Q4 Draw a line graph to represent the population growth over the period on all six continents.

There was more population growth between 1950 and 2000 than in the preceding four million years. However, UN calculations are that the growth may be slowing and that there may be only one more doubling of the world's total population. Its peak may be reached at 11 million by about 2050. **Bill McKibben** (writer and environmentalist) makes the case for one-child families in his book *Maybe One*, where he describes what he calls *good news–bad news*:

If it's relatively easy to explain why populations grew so fast after World War II, it is much harder to explain why that growth is now slowing. Experts confidently supply answers, many of them contradictory: "development is the best contraceptive", or education, or the empowerment of women, or hard times that force families to postpone children. For each example, you can find a counter example. Ninety-seven per cent of women in the Arab Sheikdom of Oman know about contraception, and yet they have 6.2 children apiece. Turks used contraception at the same rate as the Japanese, but their birth rate was twice as high. And so on. It's not AIDS that will slow population growth, save in a few African countries. It's not horrors like the civil war in Rwanda, which claimed half a million lives, a figure the planet restocks in

two days. All that matters is how often individual men and women decide that they want to reproduce…

Let's trust that the planet's population really will double only one more time. Even so, this is a good news–bad news joke. The good news is, we won't grow forever; we won't each of us have to stand on our own small patch of soil, surrounded by a sea of brethren. This has led some to say that we don't need to worry about population. Ben Wattenberg, writing in The New York Times *magazine last November, declared, "The population explosion is over".*

But the bad news is that there are six billion of us already, a number the world strains to support. One more near-doubling – four or five billion more people – will nearly double that strain. Will these be the five billion straws that snap the camel's back?

Bill McKibben (1999)

Q5 What do you suppose it is that persuades individual men and women that they do not want to reproduce?

Q6 In what ways is the world already straining to support six billion people? List as many of the strains and their effects as you can.

Population in the UK – how do the numbers add up?

Population by gender and age

	Under 16	16–24	25–34	35–44	45–54	55–64	65–74	75 & over	All ages (=100%) millions
				Percentages					
Males									
1901	33.6	19.9	15.7	12.2	8.8	5.8	3.1	1.2	18.5
1931	25.6	17.8	15.9	13.0	11.9	9.2	5.0	1.7	22.1
1961	24.8	13.9	13.1	13.9	13.9	11.2	6.3	3.1	25.5
1991	21.4	13.7	16.3	14.1	11.6	10.0	8.0	4.8	28.2
1998	21.3	11.4	16.2	14.7	13.3	9.9	7.9	5.3	29.1
Females									
1901	31.4	19.6	16.4	12.2	9.0	6.2	3.6	1.6	19.7
1931	23.0	17.0	16.0	14.0	12.5	9.3	5.7	2.4	24.0
1961	22.1	12.9	12.1	13.2	13.7	12.0	8.7	5.3	27.3
1991	19.3	12.5	15.1	13.4	11.1	10.0	9.5	9.0	29.6
1998	19.6	10.5	15.0	14.0	12.9	9.9	8.9	9.3	30.1

Source: Social Trends 30

Q7 What was the percentage decrease of males and females under 16, taken together, during the 20th century? Give suggestions as to why this decrease may have come about.

Q8 What was the percentage increase of males and females aged 65 and over, taken together, over this period? What are the likely explanations of this increase?

Q9 Are the figures for males and females different from each other in any significant respect? If so, is this a matter for concern?

Q10 "Americans currently bear children at a rate of just under two per woman, which sounds like we should simply be replacing ourselves. But happily, most of us do not die soon after becoming parents: we live on to see our kids reproduce, and perhaps their kids." (McKibben) What conclusions can we draw from this? For example, that one child per couple is enough?

McKibben, Bill (1999) *Maybe One* London: Anchor

Argument

What is an argument?

The word *argument* is most often used in one of three ways:

(a) a quarrel or dispute – e.g. "The neighbours were having a heated argument about who was responsible for mending the fence."

(b) a reason, or series of reasons, or items of evidence for or against a case – e.g. "My argument for abolishing the monarchy is based on the following facts …"

(c) a debate, or exchange of arguments, as in (b) – e.g. "The abortion argument is one as much about principles as about facts."

This section examines types (b) and (c). Of course, a debate (c) may or may not lead to a dispute (a). It will depend upon whether the two parties are friendly or hostile towards each other on other grounds, or on whether they allow *emotion* to overcome *reason*.

Much depends, in any argument, on whether there are *facts* on which it can be based.

> There is no good arguing with the inevitable. The only argument available with an east wind is to put on your overcoat.
>
> James Russell Lowell (1819–91)

Pythagoras' Theorem is an argument (in sense (b) of the word): it consists of a set of *premises* (it is a figure having three perfectly straight sides; it has three angles, adding up to 180°, of which one is a right angle; the side opposite the right angle is the hypotenuse …), and a *conclusion* (the square of the hypotenuse is equal to the sum of the squares of the other two sides).

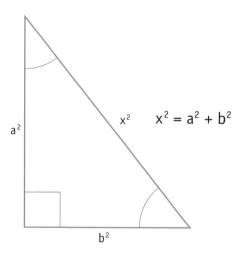

$$x^2 = a^2 + b^2$$

Q1 Pythagoras' Theorem is a type (b) argument. Why could it not lead to a type (c) argument?

Logic and rhetoric

Facts in geometry are of a rather particular kind, as discussed in Concept A, 'Facts'. In his work, *Elements* (c. 300 BCE), **Euclid** presented a set of arguments that remained unopposed for 2000 years. They were *deductive* arguments: the premises were certain and so the conclusions deduced from them were certain.

The Jewish-Christian philosopher **Baruch Spinoza** (1632–77) also thought that ethical principles could be deduced from certain premises. His *Ethics by the Geometrical Method* (1677) was an attempt to establish ethical truths by means of *logic*. Few would now think he succeeded.

Spinoza used logic to argue that God did not create the world, but that he *is* the world.

> *God is infinite, we say. Therefore, there can be nothing that is not God. Nature cannot be not-God.*

Descartes (1596–1650), a fellow rationalist, argued logically for the very existence of God:

> *God, we say, is perfect. It is more perfect to exist than not to exist. Therefore God must exist.*

Q2 What is your opinion of these two logical arguments about God? Give reasons for your answer.

Argument that cannot make use of logic turns to *rhetoric* instead. Rhetoric is the art of persuading others to your point of view. It was one of the seven liberal arts of the Medieval curriculum (see Concept B, 'The curriculum'). Nowadays, people tend to use the word *rhetoric* of any – generally political – argument with which they disagree (for example, "The Chancellor's speech was all empty rhetoric").

Here is a list of nine types of rhetorical argument:

(a) appeal to force – e.g. "If you don't complete the task, you will be sent to the headteacher."

(b) appeal to the purse – e.g. "Vote for us and we'll knock three pence off a litre of petrol."

(c) exploitation of a foible in one's opponent – e.g. "How can I believe what you say when you don't finish your sentences?"

(d) absence of proof to the contrary – e.g. "What evidence is there that you were not a communist?"

(e) appeal to prejudice – e.g. "My mother always advised me never to trust people with red hair."

(f) appeal to common sense – e.g. "All work and no play makes Jack a dull boy."

(g) appeal for pity – e.g. "How can he be blamed when he has been treated so badly by his father?"

(h) playing to the gallery (or appeal to popular opinion) – e.g. "The ordinary people of this country will never give up their sovereignty!"

(i) appeal to authority – e.g. "Churchill himself was an early advocate of a United Europe."

Q3 Give your own examples for arguments (a) to (i).

Empirical arguments

Empirical arguments are generally stronger, because these are based on *evidence* and *experience*. All of the nine arguments listed are still used on occasion. The appeal to authority, in particular, is often made by politicians, advertisers, scientists, barristers and priests.

Q4 An appeal to authority can be quite effective; equally, it might be ineffective. Find one appeal to authority – or think of one – that seems to you to fail in its purpose.

Other modern *empirical* forms of argument are based on:

- consequence – e.g. "If we were to let parents choose the gender of their baby, the country would be awash with boys."

- example – e.g. "The Swiss appear to do rather well outside the European Union, so withdrawal would not affect our prosperity."

- analogy – e.g. "Football is a kind of religion, with its own gods, its own rites, and its own bands of extremists."

Each of these three forms of argument is *evidence-based*: the evidence may be in the form of parallel cases or in the form of predicted effects based on observations of the here and now.

Consider this conversation between a teacher and a pupil:

"Walk round by the path, John, not across the grass."
"Why not, Miss? It's quicker that way."
"But what if everybody walked across the grass?"

The teacher is arguing by appealing to the *consequence* – or supposed consequence – that, in this case, that there would soon be another path across the grass, that mud would be brought into the corridor and so on. (These 'consequences' – the product of past experience, perhaps – are the reasons that the teacher would give if it weren't quicker to answer "It's a school rule!" – a sort of appeal to force.)

The teacher could have appealed to *example*, by saying: "You don't walk across the grass in front of the head's study, so why do it here?"

Speackers Corner at Hyde Park, London

Q5 Give examples of your own of arguments based on (a) consequence, and (b) example.

Argument by *analogy* can be both particularly effective and particularly risky.

Language courses in the 1960s and 1970s were advertised in something like the following way:

> **If you learned a foreign language when you were a child, you can do so again – by looking, and listening, and repeating.**
>
> Learn French in five weeks using tapes and slides. Immerse yourself in the sounds of the language as you did when you were young.

Teachers adopted the *direct method* in schools. The language laboratory arrived: students heard French through headsets and repeated the sounds they heard, over and over again. The language, it was hoped, would not be taught, but *caught* by analogy with the mother tongue.

The journalist Melanie Phillips took issue with this particular analogy:

> *There was growing confusion between the way children learn to speak their native tongue and the way to learn to speak a foreign language. Because very young children pick up the spoken language by being immersed in it, the belief grew that older children could pick up foreign languages in exactly the same way.*
> Melanie Phillips (1996)

Q6 In what respects was this analogy effective, and in what respects unsuitable, in your view?

Phillips, Melanie (1996) *All Must Have Prizes* London: Little, Brown & Company

Law and justice

Is there a universal law?

Just as natural scientists seek the hardness of evidence in their science that there is in physics and chemistry, and just as philosophers have sought to place knowledge on an objective base, so many thinkers throughout history have supposed that there is one universal law that underlies all particular laws.

Parliamentarian **Edmund Burke** (1729–97) put it like this:

There is but one law for all, namely, that law which governs all law, the law of our Creator, the law of humanity, justice, equity – the law of nature, and of nations.

If, as Burke stated, there is only one law, why have laws changed so much over time; and why are the laws different from one nation to another?

What is the law for?

The Roman orator **Cicero** (106–43 BCE) gave expression to an ideal:

The good of the people is the chief law.

Consider these two assertions:

Where no law is, there is no transgression.   Romans 4:15

Where laws end, tyranny begins.
                        Earl of Chatham (statesman, 1708–78)

Q1 (a) Explain in your own words what the two quotations mean?
       (b) Are these two assertions compatible?

Before there were nations there were communities, and each community had its own rules or laws. These laws protected the community against other communities (and so there had to be rules about who would fight, and for how long; who would supply the weapons and armour, and how). The laws also protected one group within the community against other groups. In other words they ensured communal *order*.

As a state came into being, so it adopted certain of these rules, and let others fall into disuse. The rules of the state were enshrined in law, and so became the law of the land. *Force* gave support to this law; the law was the consistent show of state force, or *power*.

Where did English law come from?

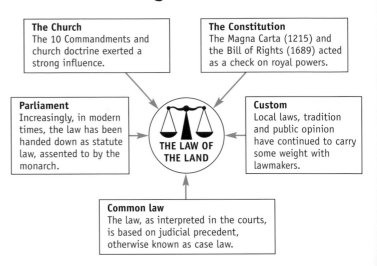

The Church
The 10 Commandments and church doctrine exerted a strong influence.

The Constitution
The Magna Carta (1215) and the Bill of Rights (1689) acted as a check on royal powers.

Parliament
Increasingly, in modern times, the law has been handed down as statute law, assented to by the monarch.

Custom
Local laws, tradition and public opinion have continued to carry some weight with lawmakers.

THE LAW OF THE LAND

Common law
The law, as interpreted in the courts, is based on judicial precedent, otherwise known as case law.

Q2 What laws or regulations can you think of that demonstrate the survival of Church influence?

Q3 One important article of Magna Carta was *habeas corpus*, formally enshrined in English law in 1679. Find out what it means and why it is important.

Q4 "Custom, that unwritten law/By which the people keep even kings in awe." (**Charles Davenant**, politician and economist, 1656–1714). What does this mean?

Custom vs law? Law vs justice?

Another influence on English law has been the pronouncements and writings of jurists and legal scholars down the ages – yet, of course, they themselves were giving expression to well-established customary, or common, law.

"Ignorance of the law is no excuse" has long been an article of legal faith. **John Selden** (jurist, 1584–1654) gave this reason:

Ignorance of the law excuses no man: not that all men know the law, but because `tis an excuse every man will plead, and no man can tell how to refute him.

Common law has usually been *bottom-up* (that is, influenced by the people); whilst statute law has often been *top-down* (in favour of the elite). In the past, the Church, the monarch and Parliament have acted in the interests of the aristocracy and the gentry. Thus the Attorney General **Francis Bacon** (1561–1626) could write, in an enlightened moment:

Laws are like cobwebs where the small flies are caught and the great break through.

Bacon was the prosecutor, in 1616, of one of his predecessors as attorney general, **Sir Edward Coke** (1552–1634). Coke was a champion of the common law and a more honourable man than his accuser. He had said:

> *How long soever it hath continued, if it be against reason, it is of no force in law.*

Reason is another word for what Edmund Burke meant by "the law of humanity", "the law of nature". But is *reason* a word or idea which can be described as having an *objective* force? In law, the accused is found either guilty or not guilty. The law is firm. But is it always fair?

The poet **John Dryden** (1631–1700) wrote:

> *Reason to rule but mercy to forgive:*
> *The first is law, the last prerogative.*

> **Q5** Put into your own words the main points of the last three quotations. How far do you agree with the ideas contained in them?
>
> **Q6** What do you take to be the difference between *law* and *justice*?

European law – bottom-up law

Statute law has always overridden common law; now, *European law* overrides laws made by the English Parliament. It was European law that imported new thinking into English law in the mid 1970s:

> *The legislation now represented by the Race and Sex Discrimination Acts currently in force broke new ground in seeking to work upon the minds of men and women and thus affect their attitude to the social consequences of difference between the sexes or distinction of skin colour. Its general thrust was educative, persuasive, and (where necessary) coercive.*
>
> **Bobby Vanstone** (1998)

On 2 October 2000, the Human Rights Act passed into English law, from Strasbourg.

Interior of the EU building, Strasbourg

HUMAN RIGHTS

- Right to Life (does not apply in the case of capital punishment or in war)
- Right to Liberty and Security (a reinforcement of *habeas corpus*)
- Right to a Fair Trial (to legal representation and presumption of innocence unless guilt is proved)
- Right to Respect for Private and Family Life (individual privacy can only be infringed if the law so requires)
- Right to Marry
- Freedom of Thought, Conscience and Religion
- Freedom of Expression (a state will still have the power to licence film and broadcast material)
- Freedom of Assembly and Association (including the right to join a trade union)
- Prohibition of Torture (and of degrading or inhumane punishment)
- Prohibition of Slavery and Forced Labour
- Prohibition of Discrimination (this applies to everyone without exception)

This is a new kind law: it is *bottom-up* law. It is as near as we have come to giving practical effect to what Cicero said (see the beginning of this section) more than 2000 years ago.

Judges and the interpretation of law

Judges have always had to interpret law: but their interpretation has generally been a *literal* one:

> *If there is no European law and no statute on a point of law, it is decided by the judge who hears the case in which the point arises. He or she is obliged to follow the decisions made by more senior judges in previous cases.*
>
> **Bobby Vanstone** (1998)

Judges have always had to argue from *authority*. Because one case will always be different from others, however, they have, in effect, argued by *analogy* (see Concept D, 'Argument'). Now the authorities and the analogies are shifting, and there is more room for creativity:

> *Judges, or at least the top appellate judges, have a creative role. They are influenced in their exercise of discretion by such factors as statutes, precedents, principles of the common law, their sense of justice, their sense of the community's sense of justice, the desire to settle the instant dispute, a wish to explain their decision consistently with the expectations of the legal profession so that it can be used as a precedent, the esteem of their peers, and so on.*
>
> **Josephine Hayes** in Vanstone 1998

> **Q7** Hayes refers to "… their sense of the community's sense of justice". Can we ever be sure what this is? How can it be ascertained and measured?

Vanstone, Bobby (1998) *Understanding Law* Harlow: Addison Wesley Longman

Unit 5 Economics

A definition

The word *economics* has its roots in two Greek words: *oikos*, house, and *nomos* which has a number of meanings but in this context refers to the idea of *control* or *management*.

Thus, the original meaning of the word is:

> *1 economics n. pl. management of the household.*

In the 17th century, the word *economics* extended to mean the management of a nation's resources:

> *2 economics n. pl. practical science of the production and distribution of the wealth of a country.*

This second meaning is what used to be called *political economy* and what is now called *macroeconomics* (from the Greek *macros*, large).

Macroeconomics and microeconomics

Macroeconomics is the study of economic decisions made by aggregates (or groups) of individuals, whether these be consumers or firms. This branch of economics is also interested in the role of government and the ways in which decisions about government spending, taxation and welfare payments affect employment, consumer confidence and private investment.

In contrast, *microeconomics* (from the Greek *mikros*, small) looks at economic behaviour at the level of the individual consumer or firm. Microeconomists will study, for example, the effects of taxation or mortgage payments on the budgets of a sample of individuals or households; or they may study the costs of production, marketing and distribution of goods in a cross-section of firms.

> **Q1** Consider for a moment any microeconomic decision you have made in the last 24 hours or week: did you earn, *spend*, *save*, *gamble*, *donate*, *invest* or knowingly *waste* money? What were your *motives* for so doing?

'Economic man'

Adam Smith (1723–90) is generally acknowledged to have been the founder of modern economics. He was, in fact, a philosopher, at a time when philosophers concerned themselves with the whole breadth of life and learning. In his first book *The Theory of Moral Sentiments* (1759), Smith spoke of 'economic man' as one driven by his *passions*, governed by *reason*, yet tempered by *sympathy*.

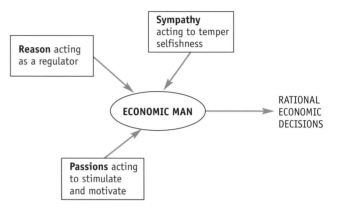

Economic man acted essentially out of self-interest, said Smith; a *rational* economic decision was one that maximized his own advantage (the *passion* and *reason* in the diagram). At the same time, Smith believed that as long as everybody acted like this, individual economic decisions would serve the general good. He said that *sympathy* with others would keep self-interest in check.

This was the famous phrase that Smith used to explain this:

> *Self-seeking men are often led by an invisible hand … without knowing it, without intending it (to) advance the interest of the society.*

The 'invisible hand' is a key concept underlying classical economic theory. Smith was effectively saying that everyone would benefit if individuals sought to make a profit for themselves. There was no need for government or anyone else to regulate individual self-interest – the 'invisible hand' would do the job, acting as 'the still, small voice of conscience'.

The 'invisible hand' was a phrase that he would use again in his *magnum opus* of 1776, *An Inquiry into the Nature and Causes of the Wealth of Nations*. There was a difference, however: in *Moral Sentiments*, Smith had thought it enough that individual sympathy or conscience should guide an individual's decisions, but in the *Wealth of Nations* the invisible hand on the tiller was *competition*:

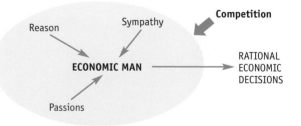

> **Q2** In what ways might competition act as an 'invisible hand'?
> **Q3** In what respects did competition influence any of the economic decisions that you considered in question 1?

Smith thought the consequences of the aggregate or sum of individual economic decisions would be beneficial. Perhaps he was an optimist. Pessimists and moralists who did not approve of self-interest feared the consequences of such decisions.

> *If the consequences [of self-interest] are thought of as beneficial, then the pattern identified in the explanation is traditionally described ... as an invisible hand; if they are thought of as harmful, it is sometimes described as an invisible backhand or an invisible foot.*
>
> Philip Pettit (philosopher, 1945–) in Honderich 1995

Laissez-faireism

In spite of the significance that Smith attached to human 'sympathy', his name was borrowed by the 19th century advocates of *laissez faire*. This was the idea that if people were free (hence liberalism, from the Latin *libero*, free) to get and spend as they wished, the result would be progress – and 'the greatest happiness of the greatest number' (to quote 19th-century philosopher **Jeremy Bentham**, 1748–1832) would follow. However, there have always been critics of free-market economics (see Unit 5, part 2), and one of the main criticisms has been the perception of economics as a science without a soul. **Thomas Carlyle** (historian and political philosopher, 1795–1881) was contemptuous both of economics and of economists:

> *Cash-payment is not the sole nexus [bond, connection] of man with man.*
>
> Past and Present 1843

> *Respectable Professors of the Dismal Science*
>
> The Present Time 1850

Q4 On the basis of the first of these quotations, explain why Carlyle thought economics a 'dismal' branch of knowledge.

Is economics a science?

In his criticism, Carlyle was thinking of economists such as **David Ricardo** (1772–1823) and **Thomas Malthus** (1766–1834, see Unit 4, part 3). Ricardo had said that growing numbers of workers would compete for work and food, and bosses would pay them the minimum necessary for subsistence. Malthus had said that profits would sometimes be spent, leading to prosperity, and sometimes saved, leading to depression. To many, these seemed like 'iron laws', but not to the economist **Alfred Marshall** (1842–1924):

> *There is general agreement of opinion among the leading English economists that economics is to be regarded as a science; and that therefore its laws are statements ... This view seems so reasonable that it would have been needless to insist on it had not the opposite one been taken by many writers in other countries, and especially France, who have included under the head of economic laws much which we class as principles of practical politics, or as utterances of individual publicists.*
>
> Alfred Marshall (1891)

In other words, economics might be a science if its practitioners gave an account of what happens – of what *is* – and did not preach about what *ought* to happen. Economic laws, said Marshall, are simply social science laws with a money-price attached to them.

What does a modern economist say?

> *A frequent complaint against economists is that, unlike the physical sciences, theirs does not afford the opportunity of testing theories in the laboratory. However, in this country and some others, notably in the United States, there have been many occasions when new governments have come to power determined to use the newly-given opportunity to try their theories in practice. From 1979 onwards ... this country was certainly exposed to a number of such experimental tests ... What they all have in common is that they are not carried out in the laboratory, but on the corpore virile [the living body].*
>
> *It is not to condemn a great discipline – as economics undoubtedly is – to say that what it currently furnishes to the politician is not as useful as one would wish it to be, or is sometimes thought to be by politicians and the general public. It is arguable that it is by its nature not capable of providing the sort of practical guidance physics renders to the engineer.*
>
> Eric Roll (1995)

Q5 In view of all that you have read so far – and, in particular, in view of what Marshall and Roll have to say – to what extent do you think economics is, or is not, a science?

Honderich, Ted (ed.) (1995) *The Oxford Companion to Philosophy* Oxford: OUP

Roll, Eric (1995) *Where Did We Go Wrong? From the Gold Standard to Europe* London: Faber & Faber

Part 1 Wealth and poverty

◼ Wealth

What does a nation's wealth consist of? What are the sources of that wealth, and how ought it to be earned or distributed?

Contemporary society still lives in the shadow of the long-held assumption that a nation's wealth is concentrated at the top and that that is perfectly proper. In 'A Prayer for the King's Majesty', loyal Anglicans ritually hoped that God would:

Grant him in health and wealth long to live.

Book of Common Prayer 1662

It seemed natural that the king and his family and friends should be wealthy: wealth was a badge of power and authority. A penniless king was as unthinkable as a dumb prophet or lascivious pope. For centuries, kings had rewarded the nobility for services rendered – so the *aristocracy* ('the rule of the best') was effectively a *plutocracy* ('the rule of the rich'). But by the time **Walter Bagehot** (economist, journalist, banker and shipowner, 1826–77) wrote *The English Constitution*, in 1867, a new breed of men enjoyed a new wealth that carried with it new power:

The order of nobility is of great use, not only in what it creates, but in what it prevents. It prevents the rule of wealth – the religion of gold. This is the obvious and natural idol of the Anglo-Saxon.

Walter Bagehot 'The House of Lords' in *The English Constitution*

Q1 Before the 19th century, the nobility had been the wealthy élite; now a new class of entrepreneurs – mine and factory owners, railway bosses – was amassing wealth. Why do you suppose Bagehot disapproved of "the rule of wealth"?

It had been supposed by previous generations of thinkers – **Thomas Mun** (1571–1641) and **Sir James Steuart** (1712–80) in Britain, **Jean-Baptiste Colbert** (1619–83) in France – that a nation's wealth depended on its treasury of precious metals, thanks to its owning mines or to its trade with mine-owning nations. Adam Smith called this theory *mercantilism*. He and the *physiocrats* (see the chart, top right) of France rejected it.

Q2 What seems to make
(a) an individual, and
(b) a nation wealthy nowadays?

> **MERCANTILISM**
> **Mun, Steuart and Colbert** believed that a nation's wealth lay in how much **gold** it possessed in its treasury.

> **PHYSIOCRACY**
> **François Quesnay** (1694–1774) and **Anne Robert Jacques Turgot** (1727–81) believed that 'nature ruled' and the only asset that yielded an economic surplus was **land**.

> **COMPETITION**
> **Adam Smith** (1723–90) believed that wealth could be measured by the annual production of **goods and services**.

> **MARXISM**
> **Karl Marx** (1818–83) believed that the real wealth of a state was its pool of **labour** exploited and undervalued by the bourgeoisie.

> **KEYNESIANISM**
> **John Maynard Keynes** (1883–1946) believed that a government should intervene to promote full employment by extending **credit** and encouraging an acceleration of money in the economy.

◼ The knowledge economy

Economists refer to knowledge as the new source of wealth, and talk about the *knowledge economy*.

An industrial transaction can be simplified down to an exchange of a ton of steel in return for a ton of coal or a bag of money. A knowledge transaction can be about the exchange of an idea for an idea. The result is very different: both parties now have two assets and the transaction is not about utilization but creation and growth ...

In a few short years, the notion of building and creating wealth will be radically different as knowledge becomes more the currency than the pound or the dollar ...

Getting ideas into action is about understanding that [an] organization's competitive advantage is increasingly governed by its people's ability to learn new things.

Mark Watson 'Status quo will have to change its tune'
The Guardian 9 September 2000

Q3 "Knowledge is the new wealth and ideas the new currency." What is your response to this sort of thinking? Is it possible to eat knowledge or wear ideas? Do you think wealth generated by ideas will benefit everybody?

It will still be necessary to produce food, and to manufacture clothes, furnishings and other household goods; plumbers and decorators, hairdressers and hospital porters will still be needed. Does this mean that a pool of employed (and unemployed) labour – of the relatively poor – will still be needed?

Poverty

In the last 20 to 25 years, there has been a marked growth in the percentage of people living below the poverty line in Britain. Consider these data (all relate to the UK):

A Distribution of wealth

	Percentages					
	1976	**1981**	**1986**	**1991**	**1995**	**1996**
Marketable wealth less value of dwellings. Percentage owned by:						
most wealthy 1%	29	26	25	29	28	27
most wealthy 5%	47	45	46	51	51	50
most wealthy 10%	57	56	58	64	64	63
most wealthy 25%	73	74	75	80	81	82
most wealthy 50%	88	87	89	93	93	94

B Income and wealth

Composition of weekly pay of employees: by gender and type of work, April 1998

	Average gross weekly earnings (£)
Males: manual	327
non-manual	505
Females: manual	210
non-manual	329
All employees	383

C Social security benefit expenditure

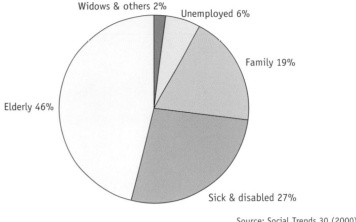

Source: Social Trends 30 (2000)

Q4 What were the trends in the distribution of wealth in the UK over the 20 years covered by Table A?

Q5 Who are the poor in Britain, according to B and C?

A report by the Joseph Rowntree Foundation included these findings:

● 9.5 million people cannot afford to keep their homes in a condition most regard as adequate – reasonably heated, free from damp or in a decent state of decoration.

● 3 million people cannot afford one or more essential household goods such as a fridge, a telephone or carpets for the living room in their homes.

● 4 million people are not fed properly and do not have enough money to afford fresh fruit or vegetables at least once a day or to provide adults with three meals a day.

● 6.5 million adults go without essential clothes, such as a warm waterproof coat, because of lack of money.

● 2 million children go without two or more basic necessities, such as adequate clothing or a healthy diet.

Source: Cherry Norton *The Independent* 11 September 2000

Q6 In 1983, 14 per cent of families were said to be living in poverty. This grew to 21 per cent in 1990 and is now above 24 per cent. Dr David Gordon of the University of Bristol, one of the authors of the report, said: "This rapid increase in poverty occurred during a period when the majority of British households were becoming more and more wealthy" (Cherry Norton). What in your view, could or should be done about this?

Part 2 The market

What is a market?

A market is a place where traders set up their stalls and lay out goods for sale. It is a place to which the general public comes to browse, to compare goods and prices, to haggle perhaps, and to buy. The traders who do best are the ones with one or more of the following:

- the lowest prices
- goods of the highest quality
- the loudest voice or the most charmingly persuasive manner.

Price, product and public relations: these make for the most effective sales pitch.

There are at least four parties to a market:

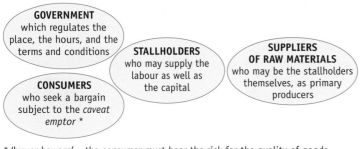

* 'buyer beware' – the consumer must bear the risk for the quality of goods bought, unless they are covered by the seller's warranty

Here are two comments on the workings of the market: the first by two free market economists, the second by a management guru:

> *Narrow preoccupation with the economic market has led to a narrow interpretation of self-interest as myopic selfishness, as exclusive concern with immediate material rewards. Economics has been berated for allegedly drawing far-reaching conclusions from a wholly unrealistic "economic man" who is little more than a calculation machine, responding only to monetary stimuli. That is a great mistake. Self-interest is not myopic selfishness. It is whatever it is that interests the participants, whatever they value, whatever goals they pursue.*
>
> Milton Friedman and Rose Friedman (1980)

> *Neither Adam Smith nor his successors, with a few extreme exceptions, believe that the whole of public activity should be left to the market. For one thing, a market system depends on a legal framework and a way of enforcing those laws. No one has seriously suggested that the police and the law courts should be run by private concerns for profit …*
>
> *Businesses live and die by the market. It is a wonderful discipline, giving out its automatic signals as to where shortages lie, or unnecessary surpluses. It is, with its built-in incentives and penalties, a spur to invention and improvement, but many do die in the process. Even big corporations seldom live longer than forty years, or deserve to. But schools, hospitals and welfare agencies cannot be allowed to die when they are inefficient, because there might not be any others nearby to replace them.*
>
> Charles Handy (1998)

Q1 Are the Friedmans attacking or defending Adam Smith's theory of 'economic man' (see Unit 5, introduction)? How different is their 'economic man'?

Q2 What does Handy approve of in the application of the market principle, and what does he disapprove of?

Case studies

Case study 1: The oil market

The market for one product is often very different from the market for other goods and services. For example, the market for cut diamonds is safe but exclusive, whereas the market for shoes is vast but subject to fashion. The diagram describes some of the players in the oil market.

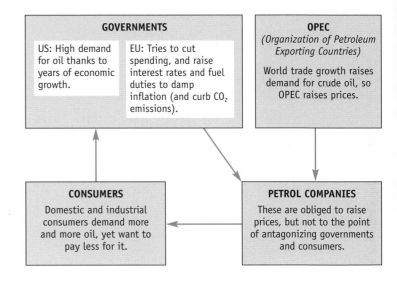

Q3 OPEC is a sellers' cartel, fixing the world price of crude oil according to changing economic indicators. What is meant when the oil market is described as a 'sellers' market'?

Case study 2: One day's trading

In practice, there are other players in the game than those referred to in Case study 1. The parts they play are both the *causes* and the *effects* of events that occur on the financial stage on a daily basis. Some of these events are predictable; most are unpredictable. Case study 2 records a series of interconnecting events that occurred on one particular day: Friday 22 September 2000. Like any other trading day, it was both typical and atypical. The key player was Intel, a company founded in 1968. Based in California, it is the world's biggest manufacturer of microchips, with an 85 per cent share of the market.

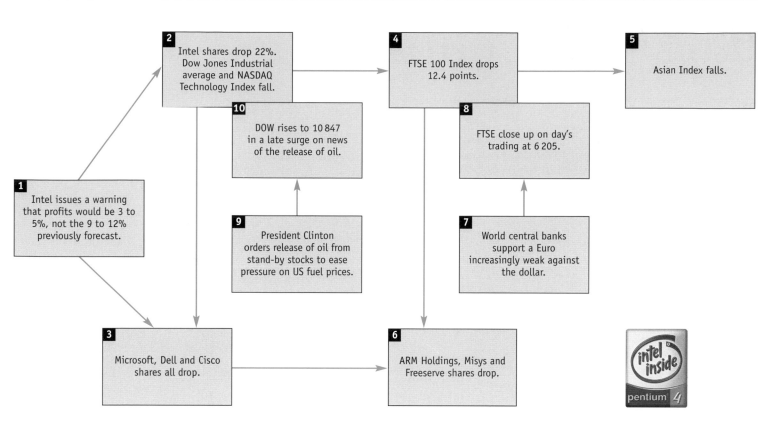

2 Intel shares drop 22%. Dow Jones Industrial average and NASDAQ Technology Index fall.

4 FTSE 100 Index drops 12.4 points.

5 Asian Index falls.

10 DOW rises to 10 847 in a late surge on news of the release of oil.

8 FTSE close up on day's trading at 6 205.

1 Intel issues a warning that profits would be 3 to 5%, not the 9 to 12% previously forecast.

9 President Clinton orders release of oil from stand-by stocks to ease pressure on US fuel prices.

7 World central banks support a Euro increasingly weak against the dollar.

3 Microsoft, Dell and Cisco shares all drop.

6 ARM Holdings, Misys and Freeserve shares drop.

Q4 Was European demand for microchips down because of the weak Euro, or because demand for computers and mobile phones was slowing? Which of the players involved would favour the former explanation for the day's events? Which would favour the latter?

Weaknesses in UK economic policy

It has been said of the period 1950 to 1990 that 'British living standards have fallen from among the highest in Western Europe to among the lowest' (Glynn and Booth 1996). Here are some reasons these authors give for Britain's failure as a stallholder in the world market:

- Governments have tended to boost the economy before an election (by cutting income tax, for example), but then reduce public spending afterwards. This has been called 'stop-go'.

- Too much scientific-technological expertise and too much R&D (research and development) expenditure went into defence. (Britain had the highest defence expenditure in relation to GNP of any NATO country.)

- Governments were slow to realize the trading opportunities opening up in Europe, preferring to deal with the sterling-area (Commonwealth) countries. Managers were similarly slow to expand into Europe, for reasons of language and culture, as well as currency.

- British manufacturers were uncompetitive: they did not invest in R&D, and so products were poorly designed, prices were set too high, and delivery dates and after-sales service could not be relied on.

- Company managers were poorly qualified in management, and so failed to assess the need for R&D, for economies of scale and for training of employees in new skills.

- Trade Unions engaged in demarcation disputes, and resisted moves to retrain and do away with restrictive practices.

Q5 Which of these six weaknesses persist in your view and which are being – or have been – overcome?

Q6 What can be done to make British industry more competitive?

Clark, Andrew (2000) 'Intel chills the silicon world' in *The Guardian* 23 September 2000

Friedman, Milton and Rose (1980) *Free to Choose* London: Secker & Warburg

Glynn, Sean and Booth, Alan (1996) *Modern Britain: An Economic and Social History* London: Routledge

Handy, Charles (1998) *The Hungry Spirit* London: Arrow Books

Part 3 Globalization

A global economy

If *privatization* was the economic theme of the 1980s, *globalization* was the theme of the 1990s and is likely to continue as a major theme of the early 21st century. What does globalization mean?

> *'Global' signifies the emergence of processes, and a system of social relations, that has little or no regard to nation states ... An increasing number of companies, operating outside their 'home' countries, see themselves as developing global strategies.*
>
> Leslie Skair 'Globalization' in Steve Taylor 1999

Globalization has been driven by the need to expand markets, reduce labour costs and realize economies of scale. It has been powered by new technology: by instantaneous communication and rapid access to information.

The trend has been in place for some time.

Case study 1: UK motor manufacture

From 1945 to the mid-1950s, car manufacture was dominated by US and UK firms.

There were six big car companies in the UK: Morris, Austin, Standard, Rootes (Hillman, Humber), Ford (a US entry in 1911) and Vauxhall (bought by US General Motors in 1925).

1952	Morris and Austin are combined in the British Motor Corporation (BMC). BMC holds 38 per cent of the car market until 1966.
1956	West Germany overtakes UK as second-biggest car manufacturer.
1967	Chrysler takes over Rootes Group (Hillman, Humber, Talbot).
1968	BMC is combined with Leyland Trucks (owners of Rover and Standard-Triumph) to make British Leyland (BL), the world's fifth largest car-maker, with 48 separate plants and a very wide product range. BL's first new models are the Marina and the Allegro, neither of them successful.
1975	The Labour Government nationalizes BL as the 'national champion'.
1977–82	The BL workforce is cut by 44 per cent.
1979	BL makes strategic links with Honda of Japan.
1985	BL is relaunched as Rover Group, receiving diminishing government subsidies.
1988	Rover is sold cheaply to British Aerospace (BAe).
1980s–1990s	Nissan, Toyota and Honda set up their EU production-bases in UK.
1991	Rover produces 0.4 million vehicles, just under 13 per cent of total UK production.
1994	Rover is sold to BMW of Germany.
1999–2000	BMW 'sells' Rover to Phoenix, which hopes to keep four per cent of the UK market.
2000	General Motors shuts down its Vauxhall plant in Luton.

Reasons for decline:

- multi-unionism; strikes
- unwieldy management structure
- out-dated working practices
- ill-advised factory location
- low levels of investment
- high labour costs
- high interest and exchange rates
- changes in government tax and HP terms
- failure to rationalize production.

The following prognosis was offered for motor manufacture in 1999:

> **Goodbye Fiat, Peugeot, Daewoo and ...**
>
> *It will be a bruising year for car companies, which are still the mainstay of manufacturing industry in most countries: a time of profitless prosperity. And as car companies go, so may go many others ... Expect more mergers to mop up excess capacity: the merger of Daimler and Chrysler has already triggered Renault's fusion with Nissan and Ford's purchase of Volvo ...*
>
> *Only Daimler Chrysler and Volkswagen are making decent profits. General Motors and Ford are barely making money on their huge European sales. Fiat is actually losing money. All this will get worse in 2000.*
>
> Iain Carson 'The World in 2000' in The Economist (1999)

Q1 How would you account for the success of car manufacture in the USA?

Q2 What lies behind the trend for big car companies to merge?

Does wealth equal power?

Times might be rough for big car companies, but they – and oil companies – were still the big forces in the corporate world in the mid-1990s. According to 1995 World Bank data, 400 transnational companies (TNCs) had annual sales in excess of US $10 billion.

The bar chart on page 57 compares the turnover of some of these companies with the gross domestic product (GDP) of a number of nation-states.

This table will look a little different now. Where is Microsoft, for example? And Nokia – Europe's biggest company in 2000?

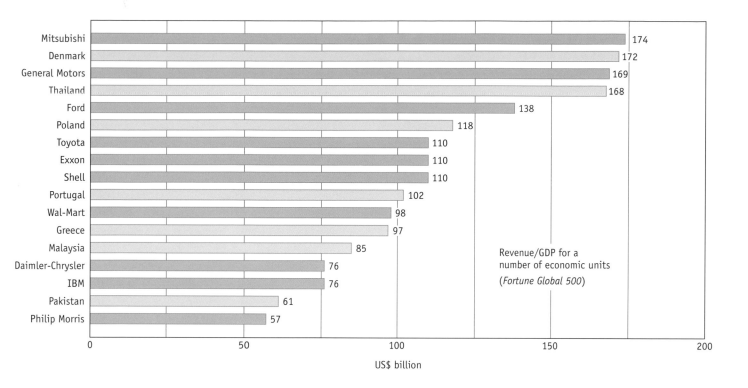

Revenue/GDP for a
number of economic units
(*Fortune Global 500*)

US$ billion

Q3 What are some of the negative effects of such a concentration of economic power in the hands of corporate giants?

Case study 2: Cargill

Cargill – a family-owned US corporation – has a greater sales turnover in coffee alone than the GNP of any of the African countries from which it buys its coffee beans. Cargill also accounts for over 60 per cent of the world trade in cereals. In most countries such a market share would automatically trigger a monopoly enquiry, but Cargill effectively belongs to no country. It is accountable only to itself. I have no reason to believe that Cargill exploits its position. The point is that whether it does or not entirely depends on the values and priorities of the family who own it ...

When corporations are bigger than nation states, you have to ask who governs them and for whom, and when those corporate states eschew democracy in favour of efficiency, you have to wonder how long they will last, because history suggests that when people get richer, they demand a voice. There are no rich dictatorships.

If a country decided, unilaterally, to disenfranchise and expel 40 000 of its citizens, voices would be raised around the world. When a corporation such as AT&T does it, the stock price goes up and with it the earnings of the Chief Executive.

Charles Handy *The Hungry Spirit*, Arrow Books (1998)

Case study 3: Nike

Nike paid Michael Jordan more in 1992 for endorsing its trainers ($20 million) than the company paid its entire 30 000-strong Indonesian workforce for making them.

Advertising today is not merely about selling products; it is about selling a brand, a dream, a message. So Nike's aim is not to sell trainers, but to "enhance people's lives through sports and fitness".

Nike runs an ad saying, "I believe high heels are a conspiracy against women". [It] signs up black stars such as Michael Jordan and Tiger Woods, and then adorns the walls of Nike Town with quotes from Woods saying, "There are still courses in the US where I am not allowed to play, because of the colour of my skin". It's anti-racism without the politics, 50 years of civil-rights history reduced to an anodyne advertising slogan.

Nike didn't seem too bothered about the campaign against it that took off so vehemently in the US in the mid-90s, until a group of black 13-year-olds from the Bronx, the company's target market and the one exploited by it to get a street-cool image, learned that the trainers they bought for $180 cost $5 to make, which led to a mass dumping of their old Nike trainers outside New York's Nike Town.

Katharine Viner 'Hand to brand combat', reviewing Naomi Klein *No Logo*,
in *The Guardian* 23 September 2000

Q4 How far can we be positive about the effects of globalization?

Q5 What has been done to counter the power of the big corporations, and the extent to which they may abuse their power? What else could be done?

Taylor, Steve (1999) *Sociology: Issues and Debates* Basingstoke: Macmillan

Ideology

A word has as many meanings as the uses that are made of it. The word *ideology* has not had a long history, but already it has been used in a number of ways.

The science of ideas

Perhaps ideology's earliest meaning was *the science of ideas*. **Antoine Destutt de Tracy** (1754–1836), an activist and prisoner in the French Revolution, wanted to sort out 'true' ideas from 'false' ones. He argued that the Revolution had been based on 'true' principles: it had been right and objectively necessary. The Terror* of 1793–4 had been 'false', in that it had served purely subjective interests. He wanted to show how the new science of ideas could distinguish between what was true and what was false. He called this new science ideology.

* *The phase of the French Revolution when the Jacobins, under Robespierre, were in power and systematically murdered their opponents.*

Ideology as power

Later in the 19th century, political philosophers **Karl Marx** (1818–83) and **Friedrich Engels** (1820–95) dismissed the idea that there could be a science of ideas. They argued that an ideology is a set of ideas that explains the world from the point of view of those who have wealth and power – the *bourgeoisie*, the bankers, the factory-owners. Ideology could not be a science, they said, because it could not be objective.

In 1846, they wrote:

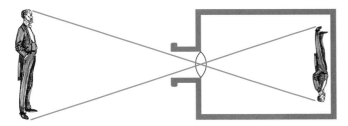

Consciousness can never be anything else than conscious existence, and the existence of men is their actual life-process. If in all ideology men and their circumstances appear upside-down as in a camera obscura, this phenomenon arises just as much from their historical life-process as the inversion of objects on the retina does from their physical life-processes.

Marx and **Engels** The German Ideology 1846

By "life-process", Marx meant *livelihood* – the way people earn their living and survive in the world. The ideology of the German *bourgeoisie* was as it was because of the political and economic power that they held. They were bound to view the world in a way that justified their power.

A person's *world-view*, according to Marx, will depend upon their class position, that is to say, whether this person is a member of the *bourgeoisie* or the *proletariat*, the exploiters or the exploited. The real power of the bourgeoisie lay in their ability to impose their ideology on the proletariat (through religion, education and the media), so that the proletariat accepted their powerless position. According to Marx and Engels, only a revolution would set the wage-slaves free from the ideology of their capitalist masters.

Terry Eagleton, the Marxist critic, puts it as follows:

> *There is, of course, no way of viewing reality except from a particular perspective, within the frame of specific interests or assumptions ... "Ideological" is not synonymous with "cultural": it denotes more precisely the points at which our cultural practices are interwoven with political power.*
>
> Ideology 1994

Everyone is part of a culture, but not everyone participates in the practices of that culture. Royal garden parties are a part of the culture, but only a select few receive invitations to them.

Q What do you think of the Marx/Engels theory that people's view of the world is conditioned by their material circumstances: for example, by whether they own a business or work on a production line? Is your own view of the world influenced by your family's socio-economic status?

The paradox is that Marx claimed that, after the revolution, there would be no more ideology, yet Marxism has itself become an ideology.

The end of ideology?

In the present day, someone who is committed to a particular ideology (an *ideologue*) tends to be seen as a fanatic or an extremist. *Laissez-faireism*, socialism, communism and fascism – all these ideologies are associated with conflict and struggle. Many modern writers have argued that this sort of struggle is out of date. For example, the American sociologist **Daniel Bell** (1919–) published his book *The End of Ideology* in 1960, when it seemed that all Americans could aspire to the same American dream. When communism fell in East and Central Europe in 1989, **Francis Fukuyama** (professor of public policy, 1952–) proclaimed "the end of history" (in *The End of History and The Last Man* 1992). If ideology was a struggle between different political ideas, liberal democracy emerged the clear winner. But if liberal democracy – where everyone is free and there are few controls, but nobody is allowed to fall below a minimum standard of living – has become the norm, is liberal democracy just another ideology?

Margaret Thatcher (Conservative Prime Minister, 1979–90) would probably have called herself a liberal democrat. But her policies – collectively called *Thatcherism* – tended to promote the good of the individual over the good of society. Indeed (see Unit 4, introduction), she said: "There is no such thing as society. There are individual men and women, and there are families."

Key points of Thatcherism:

- The "frontiers of the state" must be "rolled back".

- Market forces must be given free rein.

- The consumer must have freedom of choice.

- Government spending must be reduced to the minimum consistent with security.

- The cost of borrowing must be kept high to keep inflation low.

- Trade union powers are a burden on industry.

- The welfare state fosters a culture of dependency.

Q2 Is Thatcherism an ideology, would you say? Are the policies of the present-day Conservative Party an ideology?

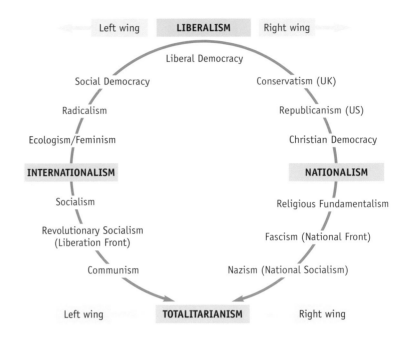

Left wing, right wing, or a middle way?

The possibility of distinguishing false ideological views of society from true ones seems to be fading into the distance ... How can we distance ourselves from the ideological assumptions of one position (say, conservatism) in order to comment on another particular ideology (say, socialism)?

Iain Mackenzie in Eccleshall 1994

Can there ever be objective knowledge? (This point is also discussed in Concept C, which asks whether it is possible to be objective in the social sciences.) Or does knowledge always serve the interests of a particular social group? If it does, then what is knowledge for one person is ideology for another, and the idea of knowledge being 'true' and 'false' doesn't make any sense. Or can there be a 'third way', a 'middle way', that is non-ideological?

Of the range of political beliefs, the extreme left wing and extreme right wing tend to be seen as ideological, with liberal democracy as a sort of middle way.

Left wing ———— Liberal democracy ———— Right wing

But perhaps the political spectrum is not so much a line as a circle, since the ends of the line come close together as *totalitarianism*.

Q3 What do you understand by (a) totalitarianism, and (b) liberalism?

Broadly speaking, moderate right-wing politics emphasizes the rights of the *individual*, and moderate left-wing politics the needs of *society*. Perhaps there will always be 'right' and 'left' ideologies.

The North/South divide

It is generally accepted that the struggle between the Eastern (communist) and Western (liberal democratic) ideologies is over and that they are reconciled in a 'third' or 'middle' way. However, there is still, arguably, a post-colonial struggle between North and South – between the rich countries and the poor countries of the world. Can the North justify its economic superiority on the grounds of a supposed ideological superiority?

Q4 If it is no longer appropriate to talk about 'true' and 'false' ideologies, is it at least possible to talk of 'better' and 'worse' ideologies?

Q5 What role does ideology play, if any, in the struggle between North and South? Is it merely a question of economics or are there more fundamental questions of ideology at stake?

Eagleton, Terry (ed.) (1994) *Ideology* London: Longman

Mackenzie, Iain in Robert Eccleshall *et al.* (1994) *Political Ideologies* (2nd edn) London: Routledge

Marx, Karl and Freidrich Engels (1974) *The German Ideology* (ed. C.J. Arthur) London: Lawrence & Wishart

Nationalism and internationalism

The word *nation* has Latin roots:

Natio, –onis n.
1 A being born, birth, origin
2 A breed, stock, kind, species, race, tribe
3 A race of people, nation

How is a nation defined?

In the diagram in Concept E, nationalism is associated with right-wing politics, and internationalism with the politics of the left. Political conservatives have generally identified themselves with the nation, nationality, nationhood and national sovereignty.

A nation is a body of people bound together by a common cultural heritage. These words will not, however, serve as a definition, for they might equally be employed to describe a tribe or a clan. To constitute a nation, the group needs to be quite numerous and to have achieved a certain level of political maturity. Normally, the unifying cultural factors include language, religion, historical heritage and tradition – but these objective factors do not always need to be present: the German nation does not share a single religion, the Swiss nation embraces several linguistic groups, and so on. Much more important are the subjective factors, involving an awareness among members that they belong to the nation and wish to be governed by themselves, and nobody else.

Richard Muir (1997)

Q1 According to this definition, does (a) Scotland, and (b) Wales qualify as a nation?

Q2 Is England a nation? Or Great Britain (the name given to the union of England and Wales with Scotland in 1707)? Or the United Kingdom (following the Union of Ireland with Great Britain in 1800)?

Nationalism

It is precisely the subjective view of what a nation is that gives rise to nationalism.

Charles Stewart Parnell (1846–91) was an Irish nationalist and leader of the late-19th-century Irish movement for Home Rule.

No man has the right to fix the boundary of the march of a nation; no man has a right to say to his country – thus far shalt thou go and no further.

Charles Stewart Parnell, speech at Cork, 22 January 1885

Nationalism is an ideology which thrives when a nation comes under threat, real or imagined. It features on a continuum, between *xenophobia* and *patriotism*, where xenophobia is a morbid dislike of foreigners, and *jingoism* is a bellicose patriotism.

Xenophobia	Nationalism	Jingoism	Patriotism

'Good' and 'bad' nationalism

Nationalists not only articulate a universal message, but also narratives tied to the specific and unique circumstances of the nation whose cause they espouse. These identify its legitimate boundaries and membership, and set out its claims. They trace its history, the key dates in its development, its enemies, allies, patriots, martyrs and traitors. Its culture, character and traditions, what values it stands for, are articulated, as well as its future goals … The intelligentsias of nationalism have tended to comprise few great philosophers, but more than their fair share of poets, musicians, antiquarians and linguists, who have explored and created the cultural artefacts that allegedly give meaning to the life of the nation.

Richard Jay in Eccleshall et al.1994

Under the impact of a racially defined conception of statehood, a new European nationalism began to develop: one nourished by the conviction that the unification of both Italy and Germany was the outcome of an intoxicating mixture of "blood and iron" … Power and morality were fused and the interests of the nation displaced any attachment to the rule of international law and the universal rights of man … Consistent with his unwavering belief in racial hierarchy, egalitarianism was anathema to Hitler, whether within or among peoples. What mattered was the moulding of a common unity among Germans as nationalists … Hitler was a racial nationalist, obsessed by a fanatical belief in the redemptive power of blood.

Rick Wilford in Eccleshall et al. 1994

Q3 What appears to you to be 'good' about nationalism, and for what reasons might it go 'bad'?

Q4 Do you think there is an English nationalism, good or bad?

Internationalism

It was the failure of nations to live at peace, and the fact that nationalism was so often a cause of war, that gave rise to internationalism. In the 19th century, this took the form of *imperialism*:

The day of small nations has long passed away. The day of Empires has come.

Joseph Chamberlain (statesman, 1836–1914)

After the First World War, it was the League of Nations that flew the flag for internationalism. This was followed, after the Second World War, by the United Nations Organization.

There are something like 4 500 international bodies – most of them formed since the Second World War. Many began life as groups pledged to defend their sovereignty against military aggression and to promote peace. More recently, they have evolved as associations for the promotion of regional economic and social development. Development banks are likely to have more significance, in the long run, than military pacts.

The United Nations

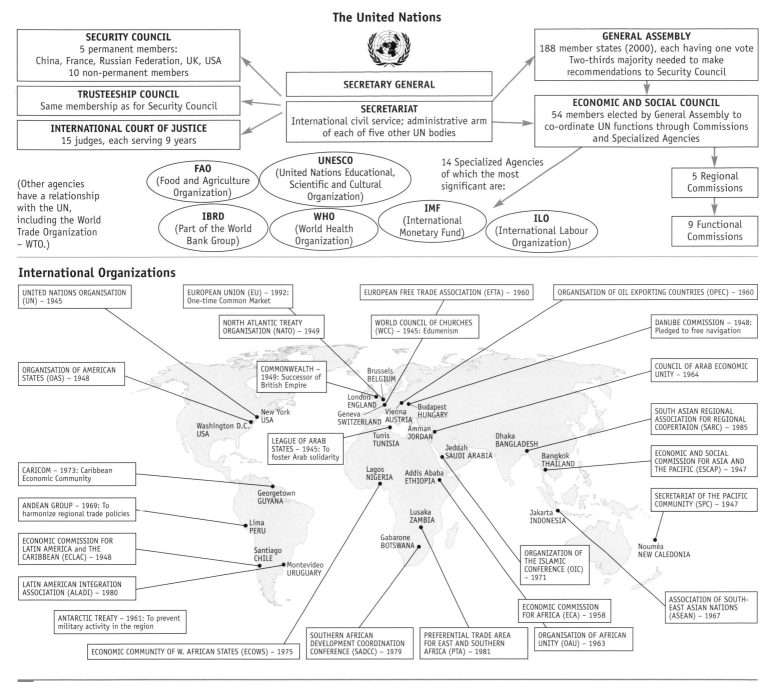

SECURITY COUNCIL
5 permanent members:
China, France, Russian Federation, UK, USA
10 non-permanent members

TRUSTEESHIP COUNCIL
Same membership as for Security Council

INTERNATIONAL COURT OF JUSTICE
15 judges, each serving 9 years

SECRETARY GENERAL

SECRETARIAT
International civil service; administrative arm
of each of five other UN bodies

GENERAL ASSEMBLY
188 member states (2000), each having one vote
Two-thirds majority needed to make
recommendations to Security Council

ECONOMIC AND SOCIAL COUNCIL
54 members elected by General Assembly to
co-ordinate UN functions through Commissions
and Specialized Agencies

5 Regional
Commissions

9 Functional
Commissions

(Other agencies
have a relationship
with the UN,
including the World
Trade Organization
– WTO.)

FAO
(Food and Agriculture
Organization)

UNESCO
(United Nations Educational,
Scientific and Cultural
Organization)

14 Specialized Agencies
of which the most
significant are:

IBRD
(Part of the World
Bank Group)

WHO
(World Health
Organization)

IMF
(International
Monetary Fund)

ILO
(International Labour
Organization)

International Organizations

UNITED NATIONS ORGANISATION (UN) – 1945

EUROPEAN UNION (EU) – 1992: One-time Common Market

EUROPEAN FREE TRADE ASSOCIATION (EFTA) – 1960

ORGANISATION OF OIL EXPORTING COUNTRIES (OPEC) – 1960

NORTH ATLANTIC TREATY ORGANISATION (NATO) – 1949

WORLD COUNCIL OF CHURCHES (WCC) – 1945: Edumenism

DANUBE COMMISSION – 1948: Pledged to free navigation

ORGANISATION OF AMERICAN STATES (OAS) – 1948

COMMONWEALTH – 1949: Successor of British Empire

COUNCIL OF ARAB ECONOMIC UNITY – 1964

SOUTH ASIAN REGIONAL ASSOCIATION FOR REGIONAL COOPERTAION (SARC) – 1985

CARICOM – 1973: Caribbean Economic Community

LEAGUE OF ARAB STATES – 1945: To foster Arab solidarity

ECONOMIC AND SOCIAL COMMISSION FOR ASIA AND THE PACIFIC (ESCAP) – 1947

ANDEAN GROUP – 1969: To harmonize regional trade policies

SECRETARIAT OF THE PACIFIC COMMUNITY (SPC) – 1947

ECONOMIC COMMISSION FOR LATIN AMERICA and THE CARIBBEAN (ECLAC) – 1948

ORGANIZATION OF THE ISLAMIC CONFERENCE (OIC) – 1971

LATIN AMERICAN INTEGRATION ASSOCIATION (ALADI) – 1980

ASSOCIATION OF SOUTH-EAST ASIAN NATIONS (ASEAN) – 1967

ANTARCTIC TREATY – 1961: To prevent military activity in the region

ECONOMIC COMMISSION FOR AFRICA (ECA) – 1958

ECONOMIC COMMUNITY OF W. AFRICAN STATES (ECOWS) – 1975

SOUTHERN AFRICAN DEVELOPMENT COORDINATION CONFERENCE (SADCC) – 1979

PREFERENTIAL TRADE AREA FOR EAST AND SOUTHERN AFRICA (PTA) – 1981

ORGANISATION OF AFRICAN UNITY (OAU) – 1963

Brussels BELGIUM
London ENGLAND
Geneva SWITZERLAND
Vienna AUSTRIA
Budapest HUNGARY
New York USA
Washington D.C. USA
Amman JORDAN
Tunis TUNISIA
Jeddah SAUDI ARABIA
Dhaka BANGLADESH
Bangkok THAILAND
Lagos NIGERIA
Addis Ababa ETHIOPIA
Georgetown GUYANA
Lima PERU
Lusaka ZAMBIA
Jakarta INDONESIA
Santiago CHILE
Montevideo URUGUARY
Gabarone BOTSWANA
Nouméa NEW CALEDONIA

Globalization

Unit 5, part 3 looked at globalization as an economic development: that is, the trend for companies to expand on a massive, international scale, often through mergers and take overs. Globalization is a political phenomonen, too, as groups of nations form economic and political alliances, as in the integration of European states into the European Union, for example.

> *There has been speculation about the consequences of globalization for nationalism and for human identifications with locality and place, but most remains uncertain. Globalization and regional integration must surely be weakening more traditional loyalties. If nation-states endure – as they probably will for quite some time to come – it will be because people are not yet ready to make the transition from a nation-based form of mental-bonding to some other form of psychopolitical association.*
>
> Richard Muir (1997)

Q5 The European Union is an example of "regional integration". To what extent do you think it is "weakening traditional loyalties" within its member states? What evidence is there of this happening in Britain?

Q6 Is there a difference between *internationalism* and *globalization*?

Q7 To what extent are you yourself an internationalist?

Eccleshall, Robert *et al.* (1994) *Political Ideologies* (2nd edn)
London: Routledge

Muir, Richard (1997) *Political Geography: A New Introduction,*
Basingstoke: Macmillan

Unit 6 Politics

Origins of the word

Policy, politburo, police, political and (indirectly) polite, all spring from a single Greek root: polis, meaning – at first – city. In the context of Ancient Greece, the city was also the state, and all free men were citizens of that state.

Greek philosopher, **Aristotle** (384–322 BCE) said "Man is a social animal" (see Unit 4, introduction). His actual words (anthropon physei politikon zoon) can equally be translated as "man is by nature a civil animal", or "a political being". It is through such translations that the Greek word polis has come into the English language. The various nuances of meaning the word has had are shown in the diagram:

(Greek) **Politikos** ← (Greek) **POLIS**
civil, political   city, state

(Latin) **Politicus**   (Latin) **Polire, Politus**
relating to the state   to polish, polished, polite

(English) Politics, political,   (English) Polish, polished   (English) Police
politician, policy, etc.   (civilised, urbane*)
                                 polite (as in 'polite
* From Latin **Urbs** = city   society')

Opinion about politics

If to be political was to be social, civilized, urbane and polite, why are politicians at the bottom of most people's list of favourite people? Why does politics have such a bad name? Why did **Samuel Johnson** (compiler of the first great English Dictionary, 1709–84) scorn politics?

> BOSWELL: So, Sir, you laugh at schemes of political improvement?
>
> JOHNSON: Why, Sir, most schemes of political improvement are very laughable things.
>
> James Boswell Life of Johnson 1791

And why did the yet-to-be-elected US President Ronald Reagan tell a conference in Los Angeles:

> Politics is supposed to be the second oldest profession. I have come to realize that it bears a very close resemblance to the first.
> 2 March 1977

Q1 'Politics is war without bloodshed' (**Mao Zedong**, leader of Chinese Communist Party, 1893–1976). Is this why many are cynical about politics? Do people think of politics as meaning party politics (where rival groups do verbal battle with each other)?

Q2 The distinction is often made between government and politics, and between a statesman and a politician. What do these words mean to you? In the following quotations what does the word politics mean?

> Politics is the art of the possible.
> Otto von Bismarck (Prime minister of Prussia and Chancellor of German Empire, 1815–98)

> Politics is not the art of the possible. It consists in choosing between the disastrous and the unpalatable.
> John Kenneth Galbraith (US economist, 1908–)

> In politics, there is no use looking beyond the next fortnight.
> Arthur James Balfour (Conservative prime minister, 1848–1930)

> A week is a long time in politics.
> Harold Wilson, 1964 (Labour prime minister, 1916–95)

Q3 "A week is a long time in politics." What do you think Wilson meant by this?

What makes a politician?

Author and poet, **Robert Louis Stevenson** (1850–94) wrote, in 1882: "Politics is perhaps the only profession for which no preparation is thought necessary." Did **John Major** (Conservative prime minister 1990–7) agree with him?

> Politics attracted me from an early age. I longed to be involved, and loathed the thought that I would have no part in making the decisions that would shape my life and times. The thought of a run-of-the-mill job did not appeal; I wanted excitement and the stimulus of the unexpected – although, I was to learn, one can overdose on that. I did believe in public service and public obligation, and if I'd had a double first, I would have been attracted to a career in the Civil Service. But I had no wish to be a second-rank civil servant, and my background and lack of paper qualifications would more or less have dictated that fate, irrespective of any talent I might have shown. Being insufficiently educated to advise ministers, I decided early on to be a minister myself, and to harness others' learning to my native good sense.
> John Major (1999)

Q4 Give reasons for and against politicians being specially trained for the job.

Is politics a science?

Political science exists as an academic discipline, but so too does political philosophy. Can 'hard' evidence be produced for political theories, or is it a 'soft' evidence subject?

Bismarck spoke of politics as an art when he referred to it as the "art of the possible" in 1867, but four years earlier, he had said:

> Die Politik ist keine exacte Wissenschaft.
> Politics is not an exact science.
> 1863

Note: Wissenschaft can as well be translated by the word knowledge as by science.

Earl Latham (political scientist), in his article on political science in *Encyclopaedia Britannica*, says:

If the term science is to be applied to any body of systematically organized knowledge based on facts ascertained by empirical methods and described by as much measurement as the material allows, then political science is a science, just as are the other social disciplines. If, on the other hand, the term science is to be limited to those disciplines in which the scholar can control the materials to be studied and can perform experiments that others can reproduce under the same conditions and in which predictability is possible, then the label is less appropriate, although not entirely misapplied.

Eric Roll (see Unit 5, introduction) claimed that economics tests its theories in a scientific way. Although its theories are not tested in a laboratory (unlike the theories of physical and natural science), they are tested on the body politic. It is the same with political theory. It would be surprising if, after hundreds of years of politicking and political history, political scientists could not make some generalizations of a 'true' and 'objective' kind.

Such generalizations are represented in the following diagram (the beginnings of this diagram can be found in Concept E, Ideology).

Q5 Do you agree with the diagram? Would you change the position of any of the ideologies or representative policies? Can you add to the diagram?

Q6 Bernard Crick, author of *The American Science of Politics*, is quoted in the *Encyclopaedia Britannica* as having said that:

The hope of creating an artificial science of politics on natural principles, although not originally and uniquely American, has been largely generated and sustained by two aspects of the American culture – an agreement on liberal doctrine that has made politics less a matter of serious doctrinal splits than of mere disagreement among partisans of the same creed, and a general national preoccupation with technology.

Here Crick suggests that there are no great ideological divisions in contemporary American politics. What are the defining policies of each of the main political parties in the UK? Are they still based on distinctive ideologies?

Q7 "History is past politics, and politics is present history." (E.A. Freeman *Methods of Historical Study* 1886) Discuss.

Ideologies and policies

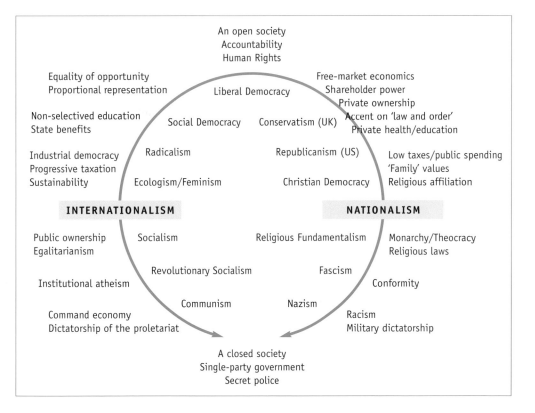

Latham, Earl (1976) 'Political Science' in *Encyclopaedia Britannica* (15th edn), Chicago/London: Encyclopaedia Britannica Inc.

Major, John (1999) *John Major: The Autobiography* London: HarperCollinsPublishers

Part 1 Government

Is government necessary?

Just as the subject of politics gives rise to debate, so too does the idea of government.

> *Government, even in its best state, is but a necessary evil; in its worst state, an intolerable one. Government, like dress, is the badge of lost innocence.*
>
> **Thomas Paine** (English political writer, 1737–1809) *Common Sense* 1776

> *I heartily accept the motto, "That government is best which governs least". Carried out, it finally amounts to this, which I also believe, "That government's best which governs not at all".*
>
> **David Thoreau** (US author and essayist, 1817–62) *Civil Disobedience* 1849

Yet Thoreau came to believe that slavery must be abolished. And it could only be abolished by a government, such as that of **Abraham Lincoln** (US president, 1809–65, who announced the freedom of slaves in 1863). Arguably, it is impossible to live without some form of government.

Thoreau (in the quotation above) could be described as a Romantic. **John Ruskin** (art and social critic, 1819–1900) was perhaps more of a realist when he wrote:

> *Government and co-operation are in all things the laws of life; anarchy and competition the laws of death.*
>
> *Unto this Last* 1862

This view agrees with one set down by **Thomas Hobbes** (political philosopher, 1588–1679) that no government at all would mean:

> *'No arts; no letters; no society; and which is worst of all, continual fear and danger of violent death'*
>
> *The Leviathan* 1641

Q1 To what extent do you agree or disagree with the Paine, Ruskin and Hobbes statements quoted above?

Systems of government

The real question about government is what system should be adopted. At one time the simple choice seemed to be between *monarchy* and *republicanism*:

> *The best reason why Monarchy is a strong government is that it is an intelligible government. The mass of mankind understand it, and they hardly anywhere in the world understand any other.*
>
> **Walter Bagehot** (writer and economist, 1826–77) *The English Constitution*

> *The Republican form of Government is the highest form of government; but because of this it requires the highest type of human nature – a type nowhere at present existing.*
>
> **Herbert Spencer** (Darwinist, founder of Social Darwinism, 1820–1903) *Essays*

Formally speaking, Britain still has a monarchical system of government. Within this system there are separate bodies responsible for different government functions. The organization of these bodies has its roots in centuries of political thought. One influential figure was the philosopher **John Locke** (1632–1704). He argued against putting too much power in any one pair of hands and so distinguished between the *executive* (decision-making) and the *legislative* (law-making) functions of government. The French political philosopher, **Montesquieu** (1689–1755), proposed that the three functions of government (executive, legislative and judicial) should be placed in three separate bodies. This proposal – the doctrine of separation of powers – was influential in the drafting of the American constitution, and most others.

The British system of government

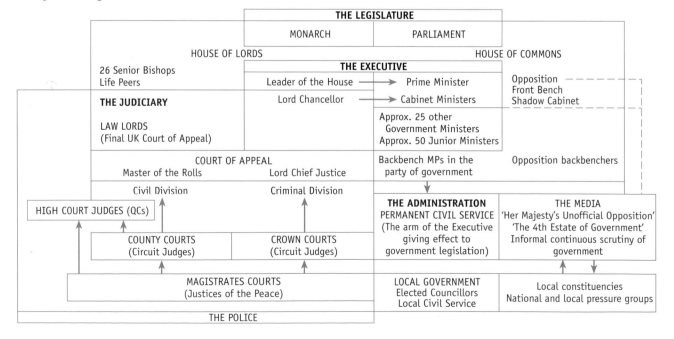

Q2 Are these three functions of government separate in the British system of government?

Q3 What checks are there in this system on the power of the executive?

Q4 Why did Herbert Spencer (quoted earlier) think that the republican form of government was virtually impossible to achieve?

What is government for and how does it work?

Broadly speaking, right-wing thinkers have tended to view government as necessary to secure the state against its external enemies, and to maintain law and order at home. Thus, the Foreign Office and the Home Office are key ministries. To run armed services and a police service, a government needs revenue, and so a Treasury (or finance ministry) is necessary, too. Left-wing thinkers have been inclined to want to spend the Treasury's money on various social goods. **John Ruskin** thought along these lines:

The first duty of a State is to see that every child born therein shall be well housed, clothed, fed and educated, till it attain years of discretion.

John Ruskin *Time and Tide* 1867

If the government and all its 'spending ministries' now have this authority, it is (presumably) because the people have given it to them. They could not supply an education service, a health service and social insurance by themselves.

Below is an examination of how the government acts on the people's behalf.

Q5 What are the advantages and disadvantages of what seems to be a very long-winded process?

Q6 What part does the general public play in the legislative process?

Q7 Does the House of Lords have a useful role or not? Is a second chamber needed at all?

Passing a bill

Proposals for government bills come from:

THE CABINET
(the executive and policy-making body of a country, consisting of all government ministers, or just the senior ministers)

LEGISLATION COMMITTEE
Via: ● Party Conference
● Ministers
● Pressure Groups
● Commissions of Enquiry

QUEEN'S SPEECH
at State Opening of Parliament at start of a new session

↓

FIRST READING
Speaker introduces sponsoring minister;
Clerk reads the title of the bill

↓

Printing and distribution to MPs (approximately two weeks)

↓

SECOND READING
Sponsoring minister makes main speech, followed by opposition speech and debate on principles of the bill. If it is a government bill (from the Cabinet), the vote will be subject to a three-line whip.

↓

WHIP
A business schedule sent to party members each week. Each item is underlined indicating its importance: one line means no division is expected, two lines means that the item is fairly important, and three lines means that the item is very important and every member must attend and vote according to the party line.

↓

VOTE → OR → **STANDING COMMITTEE**
for line-by-line scrutiny and amendments

↓

COMMITTEE OF WHOLE HOUSE
for most significant bills

↓

REPORT STAGE
At the Report stage the Speaker selects the amendments for debate. The government may cut this short by moving the guillotine motion (meaning it can be separated into components with each component being completely dealt with each day).

↓

THIRD READING → **THREE READINGS IN THE HOUSE OF LORDS**
A bill can be delayed by one session. Finance bills go straight through.

↓

ROYAL ASSENT
announcement in both Houses

The State Opening of Parliament

Part 2 The fourth estate

The estates

The three *estates* (group of people in a political community) in the Estates General (*Etats Généraux*) in pre-Revolutionary France were the nobility, the clergy and the peasantry. In the British system, their counterparts were Lords, Bishops and Commons – and then there was the press gallery, known as the *fourth estate* and seen as a powerful force.

> *The gallery in which the reporters sit has become a 'fourth estate'*
> *of the realm.*
>
> Lord Macaulay (historian, essayist, poet, politician, 1800–59)

> *Burke said there were Three Estates in Parliament; but, in the*
> *Reporters' Gallery yonder, there sat a* Fourth Estate *more*
> *important far than they all.*
>
> Thomas Carlyle (essayist and historian, 1795–1881) *Heroes and Hero-worship*

Press barons

In the first half of the 19th century, stamp duty was levied on all newspapers. The radical, unstamped newspapers were suppressed in the 1830s, but certain titles struggled on illicitly, and *The Times* held the field among papers that paid their dues. Stamp duty was abolished in 1855, not in the interests of free speech, so much as in the interests of free trade. Ironically, the radical press collapsed in favour of dailies run by the bourgeoisie for the bourgeoisie. Only big money could launch new titles and only big money could run what became highly organized industries. Thus it was that the big titles fell into the hands of big-money men: Lord Northcliffe (*Daily Mail*), Lord Rothermere (*Daily Mirror*), Lord Beaverbrook (*Daily Express* and *Evening Standard*), Lord Camrose (*Daily Telegraph*) and Lord Kemsley (*Scotsman, The Sunday Times, The Times*).

> *The press barons are usually accused of using their papers as*
> *instruments of political power. But they were hardly unique in*
> *this. What made the press magnates different is that they sought*
> *to use their papers, not as levers of power within the political*
> *parties, but as instruments of power against the political parties.*
> *The basis of the Establishment's objection to men like Rothermere*
> *and Beaverbrook was not that they were politically ambitious, but*
> *that they were politically independent ...*
> *An independent 'fourth estate', prematurely announced in the*
> *mid-nineteenth century, came much closer to reality during the*
> *inter-war period, under the aegis of the press barons.*
>
> James Curran and Jean Seaton (1997)

Much has been said about the influence of newspaper proprietors (not so much *barons* nowadays as *tycoons*) on the policies and story lines of their editors. James Curran and Jean Seaton in their book *Power without Responsibility* give this example of a spot of bother at *The Sunday Times*.

Rupert Murdoch was threatened by the Malaysian government in 1994 with reprisals against his business empire, at a critical moment in the development of his Asian satellite TV business, following prominent reports in *The Sunday Times* that senior officials

and ministers had received backhanders in the building of the Pergau dam, funded with British aid. Murdoch first remonstrated with the *Sunday Times* editor, Andrew Neil: "You're boring people. You are doing too much on Malaysia ... They're all corrupt in that part of the world." He then transferred Neil to a job in his US TV business reportedly assuring Malaysia's Prime Minister Mahathir that a "rogue editor" had been "sorted out".

Q1 What question does the extract on Rupert Murdoch and the Malaysian government raise about the possibility that newspapers might act as a fourth estate?

The power of the press in Britain

To what use has the press put its independent power? Here are a few examples:

1924 On the 25 October, the *Daily Mail's* headline was: "Civil war plot by socialists' masters". It was reported that Zinoviev, President of the Third Communist International in Moscow had written to the British Communist Party, inciting it to engage in subversive activities. The letter was bogus, but four days later, the first Labour government fell.

1930 Beaverbrook and Rothermere backed the United Empire Party candidate in a Paddington by-election. The candidate won in what had been a 'safe' Tory seat. The imperialist wing of the Conservative party was more vocal after this.

1945 The press had made much of the 1942 Beveridge Report on the welfare state: thus there was already popular support for the Labour Party and its pledge to implement the report. It duly won the post-war election resoundingly.

1974 What had been the Labour-supporting *Daily Herald* – now *The Sun* – switched its allegiance to the Conservatives. Until 1997 it could be relied on to back Thatcherism and in particular – with other tabloids – all legislation which 'bashed' the trade unions.

1992 *The Sun* claimed to have won the election for the Conservatives (under John Major) with its attack on Neil Kinnock's Labour party under the headline "Will the last person to leave the country please switch off the lights". The *Daily Mail* might also have had a hand in the victory thanks to its claim that Kinnock and Labour would add £1 250 to everyone's mortgages.

1996 Tabloid newspapers ran stories about "loony left" councils. They were variously alleged to have spent almost half a million pounds on "24 super-loos for gypsies"; ceased using black bin liners because they were "racist"; banned the singing of 'Baa baa black sheep' in nursery schools; and placed gays at the head of council house waiting lists.

1997 *The Sun* turned its back on the Conservative Party and stated its support for New Labour leader, Tony Blair.

2000 The *Daily Mail* ran a campaign to "dump the pump" to spite the Chancellor for his "highway robbery" in the matter of fuel duties. It set up a "hotline" so that readers could tell their "petrol price horror stories".

Q2 Look at a selection of current daily and Sunday newspapers, and make a judgement as to their political leanings.

Q3 Why do you suppose so many titles support Conservative party policy?

Q4 Can you think of other campaigns that newspapers have run in recent months?

Perhaps the most concerted, and most influential, campaign waged by the press in recent years has been in defence of British 'sovereignty' against European 'federalism', and of the Pound against the Euro. The *Daily Mail*, for example, critical of the Blair government for seeking to 'scrap the pound', ran a story claiming, "Now they want to scrap the British passport!" (28 October 2000). It was a story based on a rumour based on hearsay.

Roy Greenslade, himself a newspaperman, takes editors to task for calling for a 'grown-up' debate on the Euro, prior to a referendum, when they have, by their skewed reporting, undermined all possibility of genuinely open debate. Here are two brief extracts from his article.

The Euro's not for spinning

I had to rub my eyes. A *Daily Mail* leading article 10 days ago made an impassioned plea for a "debate" on the single currency. Soon after, the *London Evening Standard* – same owner, same hymn sheet, same tune, different organist – looked forward to a "prolonged debate". Both calls followed in the wake of *The Sun* demanding "a full, honest public debate" around the question Tony Blair intends to ask in the forthcoming, but unscheduled, referendum.

Can they be serious? *The Daily Mail* and *The Sun*, having run hysterical, xenophobic, myth-making campaigns against the Euro for years, now want an informed debate! This must surely rank as one of the most perfect definitions of chutzpah …

The editors of *The Sun*, *The Daily Mail* and *The Daily Telegraph* are not for turning. Whether their hostility to the EU is born of genuine ideological concerns or more commercial worries about losing their audience in an integrated Europe, they will not change their minds. Having made the concept of 'government spin' into the enduring leitmotif of Blair's administration, they will scupper any moves to spin the Euro.

The Guardian 10 July 2000

◼ Broadcasting and politics

Broadcasters are rather less free to run campaigns, either for or against government policy, than newspaper owners or editors. Nevertheless, there has been suspicion among many Conservatives over the years that the BBC is staffed by Labour supporters bent on influencing public opinion and wasting public money. This suspicion was given expression in an article in *The Sunday Telegraph*.

Labour sympathizer takes over at BBC

By **Joe Murphy**
Political Editor

Robin Oakley, the BBC's political editor, is to retire early to make way for a Left-leaning newspaper columnist.

The surprise appointment of Andrew Marr, the former editor of *The Independent*, alarmed some Conservatives who claimed that the BBC's traditional impartiality was being put at risk.

Oakley, 58, who is regarded as privately having Conservative views, will stand down this summer, a year before his 60th birthday when he was due to retire …

Marr, 40, who writes in the Labour-supporting *Daily Express* and *Observer*, is a former Labour Party member. However, as a lobby journalist at Westminster during the 1980s and 1990s he had a reputation for impartiality. Senior Tories close to William Hague praised him as "a very straight journalist" last night and said there would be no official protest to the BBC over his appointment.

The Sunday Telegraph 14 June 2000

The BBC is independent of government, as its charter requires. Some have argued it was too independent for the liking of **Margaret Thatcher** (Prime Minister 1979–90):

> Mrs Thatcher never saw much television, except when she was on it. However, her husband, who watched a lot, was widely reported to have given her daily résumés of its iniquities …
>
> In contrast, print journalism caused the Conservative government few problems in the 1980s. In her first term of office, the Prime Minister gave knighthoods to the editors of the Sun, Sunday Express and Daily Mail. In return, these and other newspapers softened their criticisms of the government and concentrated their fire on its enemies – a novel interpretation of the duties of the Fourth Estate.

Curran and Seaton (1997)

Q5 In today's media there is a lot of talk about 'spin'. What is it and who does it? Is it new? Is there anything wrong with it?

Q6 How far is the BBC in a position to act as a fourth estate?

Curran, James and Seaton, Jean (eds) (1997) *Power without Responsibility* (5th edn) London: Routledge

Part 3 The people

◼ Democracy

The word *democracy* comes from the Greek words *demos* (community) and *krates* (sovereign power) – power in the hands of the people.

The Greek philosopher, **Plato** (c. 427–347 BCE), had a very low opinion of democracy:

> *Because of the liberty which reigns there, they have a complete assortment of constitutions, and he who has a mind to establish a state ... must go to a democracy as he would to a bazaar at which they sell them, and pick out the one that suits him ... And there being no necessity for you to govern in this state, even if you have the capacity, or to be governed, unless you like, or to go to war when the rest go to war, or to be at peace when others are at peace, unless you are so disposed...*
>
> Plato *The Republic*, Book 8 (translated. B. Jowett)

For Plato, democracy meant anarchy, and out of anarchy would come a despot. Democracy also meant anarchy to **Edmund Burke** (British Whig politician, 1729–97): "A perfect democracy," he said, "is the most shameless thing in the world." The French Revolution had begun as a "perfect democracy", and out of it there had come anarchy – and a despot, **Napoleon Bonaparte** (1769–1821).

◼ Different interpretations of democracy

The phrase "of the people, by the people, for the people", is associated with US President **Abraham Lincoln**, and his Gettysburg Address (1863). However, the anti-slavery campaigner **Theodore Parker** (1810–1860) used the phrase first:

> *A democracy, that is, a government of all the people, by all the people, for all the people; of course, a government after the principles of eternal justice, the unchanging law of God; for shortness' sake, I will call it the idea of freedom.*
>
> Speech at Anti-Slavery Convention, 29 May 1850

Perhaps when he used these words, Lincoln did well to drop the word "all".

> **Q1** Plato and Burke appear to have been critical of *direct* democracy; Parker and Lincoln spoke up for *representative* democracy. What is the difference? Is direct democracy anywhere to be found?

At the turn of the last century it seemed that the Americans believed more strongly in democracy than most educated Britons:

> *Democracy means simply the bludgeoning of the people by the people for the people.*
>
> Oscar Wilde 'Soul of Man under Socialism' 1891

> *Democracy substitutes election by the incompetent many for appointment by the corrupt few.*
>
> G.eorge Bernard Shaw 'Maxims for Revolutionists' in *Man and Superman* 1903

The cynicism of **Oscar Wilde** (Irish writer, 1854–1900) might be put down to snobbery, but why should a socialist such as George Bernard Shaw have sneered at democracy? These were educated men; they feared what government by the uneducated mass would mean.

The Labour party held the torch for democracy – but the first Labour administration lasted only eight months (in 1924), and the second collapsed after just over two years (1929–31). (In 1931, the parties united in a government of national unity, to fight the depression and the Second World War.) In 1945, after 16 years of 'national' government, **Clement Attlee** (Prime Minister 1945–51) presided over something like popular democracy and **Winston Churchill** (Prime Minister 1951–55) did not think to undo it – but neither man had any illusions about the workings of democracy:

> *No-one pretends that democracy is perfect or all-wise. Indeed, it has been said that democracy is the worst form of government except all those other forms that have been tried from time to time.*
>
> Winston Churchill, speech 11 November 1947

> *Democracy means government by discussion, but it is only effective if you can stop people talking.*
>
> Clement Attlee, speech 14 June 1957

◼ Democracy versus individualism

One aspect of democracy that Plato had disliked was the fact that "the offices are too minutely subdivided and too many hold them" (*Statesman*). In his book *The English: A Portrait of a People*, Jeremy Paxman gives an example of this subdivision when he writes about the individualism of the English:

> *One consequence of this English obsession with privacy and individualism has been to create a people who are not easily led. They distrust exhortation, and the further away they are from metropolitan life, the stronger their cussedness. In the Fens, for example, they simply don't give a damn. The Bishop of Norwich was told by his predecessor, "Welcome to Norfolk. If you want to lead someone in this part of the world, find out where they're going. And walk in front of them."*
>
> Jeremy Paxman (1999)

> **Q2** Is Britain (or England) a democracy? Can we British citizens be democrats and individualists?

Paxman makes the point that in the past the vote was associated with home ownership:

Historically, participation in the political life of the country depended upon owning your own home. Before 1832, you could only vote if you had property valued for land tax at more than forty shillings a year; and every time the franchise was extended in the nineteenth century, the right to participate in democracy was dependent upon being a male householder ... It was a mark of Margaret Thatcher's deep understanding of some of the instincts of the English ... that she recognized the power of the urge to own property, forcing municipal authorities to give their tenants the right to buy.

Jeremy Paxman (1999)

67.6 per cent (1998) of Britons are home owners, yet barely one-third shut their front doors behind them to vote in local elections – those closest to home.

Q3 Why do you suppose the turn out for local (and European) elections is so low?

Living in a democracy

Voting is only one way of being a democrat. There are others as illustrated in the two case studies below:

Case study 1: The Snowdrop Campaign

It was the first lesson of the morning at Dunblane Primary School, on 13 March 1996. Thomas Hamilton walked into the gymnasium and shot dead 16 children and their teacher.

Anne Pearston and a friend of one of the bereaved parents got up a petition for controls on handguns. The snowdrop was adopted as the emblem of the appeal, since this was the only flower then in bloom. The campaign lobbied MPs at the Scottish Grand Committee in Inverness, and gave evidence to the Cullen Enquiry set up by the Westminster government.

The Snowdrop Campaign caught the public imagination – especially when, on 19 March, two youths were arrested for the theft of firearms from a private house in Buckinghamshire. Keeping guns in secure places was no longer enough. An outright ban was now demanded.

The House of Commons Select Committee on Home Affairs report of August 1996 concluded that a complete ban was not necessary. *The Sun* printed telephone numbers of all Tory members of this committee, inviting its readers to ring them in protest. A BBC *Panorama* programme interviewed bereaved parents of Dunblane.

The Cullen Report, published in September 1996 fell short of recommending a ban but, by this time, the Labour Party had committed itself to legislation. Handguns were banned by Act of Parliament, 21 November 1997.

Case study 2: Export of live animals

Animal welfare groups, such as Compassion in World Farming (CIWF), had given publicity to the conditions in which live calves, in particular, were exported, and how they were treated at their destination. Following this publicity, protesters wrote to the ferry companies concerned, with threats to boycott passenger services. Adverse publicity was such that P&O and Stena pulled out of the trade.

Exporters now had to charter ships and aircraft from small ports and airfields. Brightlingsea, Essex, was such a port. To reach it, lorries had to pass through the town on a narrow, house-lined street. From January 1995, residents and others harassed lorries on this route. Of the protesters associated with the campaign (Brightlingsea Against Live Exports), 80 per cent had never protested against anything before. The BALE protest attracted huge national publicity – the doleful faces of the calves made the point eloquently.

Such local protests (Shoreham, Sussex, was another centre of protest) gave a boost to the CIWF to lobby for changes to the law at a European level.

The protests generated by the campaign to ban live exports appear to illustrate that the activity of protesting has become increasingly acceptable socially as a mechanism which enables 'ordinary' members of the public to communicate and register their concern to governmental bodies.

David Simpson Pressure Groups 1999

Q4 Identify the democratic actions taken in the two case studies.

Q5 Why do you think "the activity of protesting has become increasingly acceptable" in Britain, in recent years?

Democracy rules OK

Voting in central, local and European elections

Writing to one's MP the press signing a petition

Joining a political party pressure group or lobbying an MP

Demonstrating with placards, speeches, marches, happenings

Paxman, Jeremy (1999) *The English: A Portrait of a People* London: Penguin Books

Simpson, David (1999) *Pressure Groups* London: Hodder & Stoughton

Culture

Origins of the word

Some words have their roots in one soil, their shoots in another, and their fruits in a third. *Culture* is such a word. It has grown from its Latin roots along the following lines:

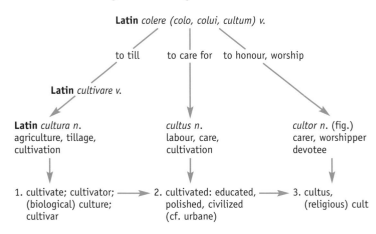

Latin *colere (colo, colui, cultum) v.*

to till   to care for   to honour, worship

Latin *cultivare v.*

Latin *cultura n.*
agriculture, tillage,
cultivation

cultus n.
labour, care,
cultivation

cultor n. (fig.)
carer, worshipper
devotee

1. cultivate; cultivator;
   (biological) culture;
   cultivar

2. cultivated: educated,
   polished, civilized
   (cf. urbane)

3. cultus,
   (religious) cult

Tillage, husbandry, food-growing is the primary sense of the word. At one time, cultivating crops was thought of as a *religious* activity and in people's minds it was never far from growing crops to growing children – training them up and educating them to be fully-grown, cultivated adults. The stick was used to discipline both plants and pupils.

Q1 Why should farming the land, growing crops – husbandry – have anything to do with religion? What were *fertility cults* for, and what did their priests do?

Q2 Philosopher and writer, **Roger Scruton** (1944–) wrote: "Culture, I suggest, has a religious root and a religious meaning. This does not mean that you have to be religious in order to be cultivated. But it does mean that the point of being cultivated cannot, in the end, be explained without reference to the nature and value of religion.

"That suggestion is controversial; to many it will seem absurd."

Does it seem absurd to you?

Definitions of culture

The philosopher **Jean Jacques Rousseau** (1712–78) developed the idea of the 'noble savage'– the perfectly natural human, uncorrupted by civilization. In his treatise on education, *Émile*, he wrote:

Everything is good when it leaves the Creator's hands; everything degenerates in the hands of man.

Jean Jaques Rousseau (1762)

To be 'civilized' – urbane, polished, refined – was no commendation as far as Rousseau was concerned. He defined culture as everything that nature wasn't – as the antithesis of nature.

GOD   MAN
NATURE versus CULTURE

Sociologist Ronald Fletcher defines culture in the following way:

The 'social heritage' of a community: the total body of material artefacts (tools, weapons, houses, places of work, worship, government, recreation, works of art, etc.) of collective mental and spiritual 'artefacts' (systems of symbols, ideas, beliefs, aesthetic perceptions, values, etc.) and of distinctive forms of behaviour (institutions, groupings, rituals, modes of organisation, etc.) created by a people (sometimes deliberately, sometimes through unforeseen interconnections and consequences) in their ongoing activities within their particular life-conditions, and (though undergoing kinds and degrees of change) transmitted from generation to generation.

Ronald Fletcher (1999)

In this definition, culture is everything that human have made.

Classifying culture

So various is culture, viewed as everything human, that it became usual to speak of *primitive* culture and *civilized* culture, or *peasant* and *urban* culture – of *cultures*, or *subcultures*, in the plural. Anthropologists classified 'primitive' cultures much as sociologists classified 'civilized' societies. The West has tended to describe itself as a 'civilized' culture. Everyone else, by this definition, has been seen as 'uncivilized' and in need of 'civilization' (despite Rousseau's claims to the contrary).

Q3 What implications has the West's assumed cultural superiority had in the past? Are there any implications today?

Two cultures? Science and the humanities

In Britain in the 19th century, scholarly debate made a distinction between science and the humanities. Public schools taught Latin, Greek and Religion; Mathematics was an 'extra'; science was for dissenting academies. **Thomas Henry Huxley** (scientist and humanist, 1825–95) argued forcefully in *Science and Culture* (and elsewhere) that one must have scientific understanding to be fully educated or 'cultured'. **Matthew Arnold** (poet and critic, 1822–88) argued, just as forcefully, that culture meant great literature (and particularly poetry), and the work of the 'human spirit' – and it is Arnold's definitions of culture that are most often quoted:

Culture, being a pursuit of our total perfection by means of getting to know, on all the matters which most concern us, the best which has been thought and said in the world.

Matthew Arnold *Culture and Anarchy* 1869

Culture, the acquainting ourselves with the best that has been known and said in the world, and thus with the history of the human spirit ...

Culture is the passion for sweetness and light, and (what is more) the passion for making them prevail.

Matthew Arnold *Literature and Dogma*, 1873

The Huxley/Arnold debate was re-ignited in the 20th century by the scientist-novelist **C.P. Snow** (1905–80) and literary critic **F.R. Leavis** (1895–1978). Snow gave the Rede lectures in 1959, entitled 'The Two Cultures and the Scientific Revolution'. There were two 'high' cultures now, he said: "the literary and the scientific". Leavis disagreed with Snow in his Richmond Lecture in 1963 – stating his view that only the study of literature can give us "critical awareness". The debate on what is valuable or meaningful in cultural terms seems to approach the most fundamental questions of what a society considers to be important.

Q4 Are there two cultures, or only one? Roger Scruton agrees with Arnold and Leavis:

High Culture is not a source of scientific or technical knowledge (knowledge that or knowledge how), but a source of practical wisdom (knowledge what). Its meaning lies in the ethical vision that it perpetuates, and in the order that results in our emotions. On such a view, there can no more be a scientific culture than there can be a scientific religion; culture like religion, addresses the question which science leaves unanswered: the question what to feel. The knowledge that bestows on us is a knowledge not of facts nor of means but of ends: the most precious knowledge we have.

Many people will find the view that I am advancing preposterous.

Does it seem preposterous to you?

A hierarchy of culture?

In countries such as Britain, a distinction is frequently made between 'low' culture (or popular culture) and 'high' culture.

Q5 Brainstorm what you think of when you hear the term 'high' culture.

Q6 Do the same for 'popular' culture.

It seemed to be taken as read amongst the academic establishment in England, who had sole privilege of defining cultural worth, that 'high' culture was of greater value. In the 1950s and 1960s this assumption was challenged by two English writers, **Richard Hoggart** (1918–) and **Raymond Williams** (1921–88), who turned their attention to cultures that had previously been marginalized and viewed as less important, such as working-class culture. Their work laid the foundations for an entirely new

approach to thinking about and studying culture – what has come to be called *cultural studies*.

It has ceased to be ridiculous to make the sorts of comparisons that **Chris Smith**, former Culture Secretary, makes between 'pop art' and 'high art'. In his book *Creative Britain* (1998), he argued that what he called a "cultured democracy" should:

embrace the best of everything, no matter what labels others may put on it.

The question here is whether it makes sense to compare Bob Dylan with John Keats, Catherine Cookson with William Golding, Damien Hirst with J.M.W. Turner? Is it just a question of time, or taste, or fashion? Is it all relative: is one 'culture' as good as another?

Q7 In his *Notes towards a Definition of Culture* (1948), T.S. Eliot wrote:

Culture may be described simply as that which makes life worth living.

(a) Is this too broad a definition to be useful? From what you have read above, how would you define culture?
(b) What examples of modern 'popular' culture do you reckon will survive another generation or more?

Fletcher, Ronald (1999) in *The New Fontana Dictionary of Modern Thought* (eds) Alan Bullock and Stephen Trombley (3rd edn) London: HarperCollinsPublishers

Scruton, Roger (1998) *An Intelligent Person's Guide to Modern Culture* London: Duckworth

Europe

Some English and British views on Europe

British people ('Us') have tended to think of Europeans as 'Them'. We are here and Europe is over there. We know that Europe is not one state but many, but it has often served our purposes to think of it as one entity. Queen Elizabeth I addressed her troops at Tilbury in 1588, as the Armada approached, with these famous words:

I know I have the body of a weak and feeble woman, but I have the heart and stomach of a king, and a king of England too; and think foul scorn that Parma or Spain, or any prince of Europe, should dare to invade the borders of my realm.

The first Prime Minister, **Sir Robert Walpole** (1676–1745), said to Queen Caroline, in 1739:

Madam, there are fifty thousand men slain this year in Europe, and not one Englishman.

He could not have put it more plainly that Englishmen were not considered to be Europeans. In the year of Trafalgar, 1805, Prime Minister William Pitt (1759–1806) boasted to Londoners:

England has saved herself by her exertions and Europe by her example.

On the day that Germany declared war on France, 3 August 1914, Foreign Secretary Edward Grey (1862–1933) said:

The lamps are going out all over Europe; we shall not see them lit again in our lifetime.

Once again, it appears, 'we' did not consider ourselves to be a part of Europe. In 1991, Prime Minister **John Major** (1943–), no anti-European:

soon realized that getting your own way in Europe was a specialized affair. It had its own natural rhythms. It was better to play by club rules. Britain needed to raise its voice from within the charmed circle.

John Major (1999)

Q1 Brainstorm in a group the associations, stories and impressions that come to mind when you think of Europe. Are your impressions, in fact, of different countries of Europe?

European cultures

Europe is not only many different countries, of course: it is many different cultures. Given its geography, it was bound to be, as Alastair Bruton explains:

Europe's geography could hardly have been better designed to encourage the growth and clash of cultures. The bays and archipelagos of the Mediterranean, the fertile river valleys inland, the Atlantic estuaries and offshore islands offered countless secure refuges within whose shelter different peoples could develop their own customs and traditions. And yet as soon as these people ventured further afield, Europe's topography ... all but forced them into contact with each other.

Alastair Bruton (1996)

Of the British who went abroad for holidays in 1998, 72 per cent stayed in EU-member countries. Many took their own culture with them, but at some stage, they confronted another culture, in terms of:

- language
- food and drink
- buildings and their upkeep
- dress sense
- ways of driving and parking cars
- gestures and interpersonal relations
- leisure activities
- religious customs
- social etiquette.

Holidays abroad by destination, 1998

	%
Spain	27.5
France	20.2
Greece	5.3
Italy	4.0
Portugal	3.6
Irish Republic	3.5
Netherlands	2.7
Belgium	2.3
Germany	1.8
Austria	1.3
Total	72.2

Source: Social Trends 30

Q2 To what do you attribute the popularity of Spain and France as holiday destinations?

Q3 In groups, choose one European country and give a brief account of its culture in terms of the points listed above, and any others that strike you as important.

A new Europe

Contacts of every kind among Europe's peoples are multiplying all the time. And out of the resulting culture clash – out of the day-to-day exchange of ideas as businessmen, encouraged by the Single Market, set up subsidiaries in other countries or families take holidays abroad; out of the innumerable educational and cultural exchange programmes; out of the football matches and athletics meetings; out of the developing co-operation among national, regional and municipal politicians; out of the regular meetings of the Council of Ministers, the debates in the European parliament and the Council of Europe, the legal sparring in the Court of Human Rights and the European Court, and the routine contact of civil servants gathered from across the Continent – out of all these things, a new Europe is being made.

Alastair Bruton (1996)

Q4 Do you want Britain to play a bigger part in this "new Europe"? Give reasons for your answer.

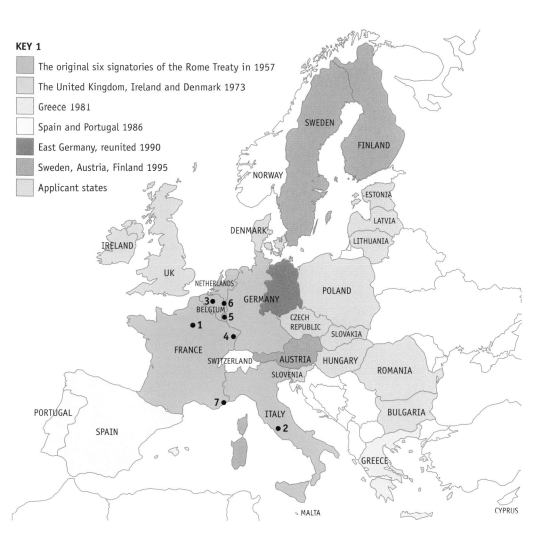

KEY 1

- The original six signatories of the Rome Treaty in 1957
- The United Kingdom, Ireland and Denmark 1973
- Greece 1981
- Spain and Portugal 1986
- East Germany, reunited 1990
- Sweden, Austria, Finland 1995
- Applicant states

KEY 2

1 PARIS
The Treaty of Paris 1950 created the European Coal and Steel Community (ECSC)

2 ROME
The Treaty of Rome 1957 created the European Economic Community (EEC)

3 BRUSSELS
Home of:
- The European Council (Heads of Government)
- Council of Ministers (Meetings of Ministers of Finance, Justice, etc.)
- European Commission (full-time nominated officials with particular briefs)

4 STRASBOURG
European Parliament (MEPs directly elected) (also in Brussels)

5 LUXEMBOURG CITY
European Court of Justice

6 MAASTRICHT
The Treaty of Maastricht 1991 created the EU Economic and Monetary Union (EMU) and EU citizenship

7 NICE
The Treaty of Nice 2000 prepared for enlargement and reduced veto powers of members

Regionalism

The Maastricht Treaty, in creating European citizenship, laid the foundations of a common currency, a common foreign and security policy, and many other common policies in the fields of justice, education (mutual recognition of qualifications), public health and labour mobility – a common *political culture*.

Maastricht also established a *Committee of the Regions*, however. This Committee is a consultative body representing local and regional authorities. It is designed to keep a check on EU decisions, to make sure the various regions are not disadvantaged or overlooked. Alongside integration at one level, therefore, goes a promotion of regional identities.

Despite official bodies such as the Committee of the Regions, some fear that there is not enough protection of regional identities and cultures, and that too much power has been given to Brussels.

Bruton takes the view that:

- control from Brussels would be a tyranny
- the nation-state is commanding less and less loyalty
- it is the regions that will save democracy.

Regionalism's most obvious appeal is that it is everything that the European Union is not. It is about culture and identity, about what it means to be Catalan or Bavarian, Flemish, Basque or Scots, and its origins lie deep in that astonishingly resilient and selective memory of our homeland's past glories which is common to us all.

Alastair Bruton (1996)

Q5 How would you describe your own regional or cultural identity?

Q6 What does it mean now to be 'British'?

Bruton, Alastair (1996) *A Revolution in Progress* London: Little, Brown & Company

Major, John (1999) *John Major: The Autobiography* London: HarperCollinsPublishers

The idea of the past

If you were asked the question, "What is history?", you might reply something like, "The study of the past". But ideas about what "the past" is have changed with time; in fact, they depend on how people view time itself.

The Ancient Greeks thought of time as *cyclical* – as repeating itself. Each cycle lasted one *aeon*, or one thousand years. A variation of this was the belief that there was some development: that time was better thought of as a spiral, combining repetition with progression:

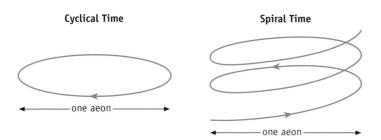

Cyclical Time   **Spiral Time**

— one aeon —   — one aeon —

Jews and Christians think of time as *linear*, with a clear starting point – "In the beginning, God created the heaven and the earth" (Genesis 1:1) – and with a clear end point – the Day of Judgement.

Dialectical time, associated with **Gregory Wilhelm Friedrich Hegel** (philosopher, 1770–1831), was a refinement of linear time. Hegel thought of history as a process of resolution (*synthesis*) of the conflict between the spirit of one time (*thesis*) and the contrary spirit of the next (*antithesis*).

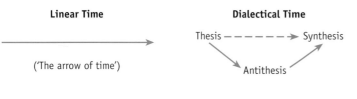

Linear Time   **Dialectical Time**

Thesis - - - - - ► Synthesis

('The arrow of time')   Antithesis

Q1 How would you say contemporary Western society views the past? How might this be different from the way people viewed the past in Hegel's time?

Hegel lived at a time when writers were beginning to look back at the great 'sweep of history', to see whether anything might be learned from it. They were not greatly encouraged by what they saw:

History is indeed little more than the register of the crimes, follies and misfortunes of mankind.
  Edward Gibbon *The Decline and Fall of the Roman Empire* 1776–88

What experience and history teach is this – that nations and governments have never learnt anything from history, or acted upon any lessons they might have drawn from it.
  G.W.F. **Hegel** *Letters on the Philosophy of World History* 1830

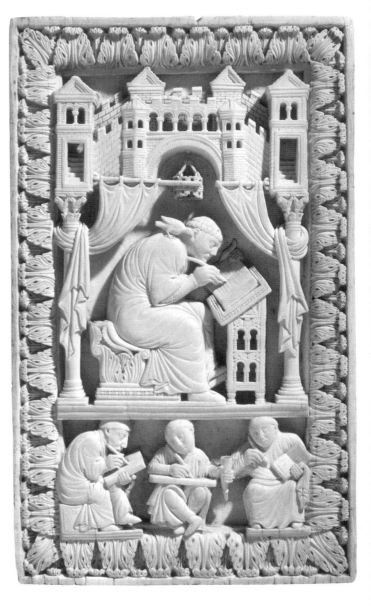

Gregory I, the Great: Pope (c.540–604). Doctor of the Church, Saint and historian. Religious figures concerned themselves with history

Q2 Do you think we can learn anything at all from history? Can you think of examples where individuals or nations do seem to have learned a lesson from history?

Q3 Is learning from the past the main purpose of the study of history? If not, what is the point of studying history?

Is history a science?

When people talk of 'science', they usually imply a process of the following sort:

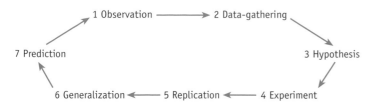

This process holds good for certain physical sciences, but not all. Astronomers, for example, do not conduct experiments – they have to wait for replication of their observations.

Social scientists don't conduct experiments either, but by observing particular groups, they seek to make generalizations about society at large. Most historians, however, avoid making generalizations altogether.

Here is what **James Anthony Froude**, a 19th-century historian, said of history as science:

> *A science of history, if it is more than a misleading name, implies that the relation between cause and effect holds in human things as completely as in all others … When natural causes are liable to be set aside and neutralised by what is called volition, the word Science is out of place... History is but the record of individual action.*
>
> James Anthony Froude *Short Studies on Great Subjects* 1867–83

In other words, history cannot be a science, according to Froude, because people have free will (*volition*). If people did not have free choice (and could be examined scientifically), historians would not be able to praise or blame them.

> **Q4** Do you agree with Froude that history cannot be a science and that historians are, therefore, free to praise and blame people in the past?

Is history biography?

Perhaps the word 'science' is out of place, but even so, most historians do aim to be 'scientific' in their approach. It is true that historians are concerned not with things, but with people, as social scientists are. It is also true that historians are concerned with *particular* people, and *particular* events – with what is essentially *unique*. **H.A.L. Fisher** (historian and education minister, 1865–1940) put it like this:

> *Men wiser and more learned than I have discerned in history a plot, a rhythm, a predetermined pattern … I can see only one emergency following upon another as wave follows upon wave … there can be only one safe rule for the historian: that he should recognize in the development of human destinies the play of the contingent and the unforeseen.*
>
> H.A.L. **Fisher** *A History of Europe* 1935

Others, like Fisher – despairing of plots, and rhythms and patterns – concluded that history is nothing but biographies. Froude, for

example, views history as simply "the record of individual action", describing mankind as an "aggregate (collection) of individuals":

> *History is the essence of innumerable biographies.*
>
> **Thomas Carlyle** *Critical and Miscellaneous Essays* 1838

> *There is properly no history; only biography.*
>
> Ralph W. Emerson *Essays* 1841

Philip Guedalla (historian and writer, 1889–1944) took a different view: for him, history and biography were not one and the same thing:

> *Biography is a very definite region bounded in the north by history, on the south by fiction, on the east by obituary, and on the west by tedium.*
>
> *The Observer* 3 March 1929

> **Q5** Do you agree that history is merely a chronicling of lives? Does this mean that historians are little more than true-to-life novelists?

Summary – historiography

Academic history seems to live somewhere between social *science*, and the *art* of historical fiction. It does not construct *laws*, but is attentive to *facts*. Historians go about their work systematically; they collect all the relevant data possible and try to be *objective*. In these ways history might be called 'scientific'.

E.H. Carr (historian, 1892–1982) writes:

> *This is what may be called the common-sense view of history: history consists of a corpus of ascertained facts. The facts are available to the historian in documents, inscriptions and so on, like fish on the fishmonger's slab. The historian collects them, takes them home, and cooks and serves them in whatever style appeals to him …*
> *The facts are really not at all like fish on the fishmonger's slab. They are like fish swimming about in a vast and sometimes inaccessible ocean; and what the historian catches will depend, partly on chance, but mainly on what part of the ocean he chooses to fish in and what tackle he chooses to use – these two factors being, of course, determined by the kind of fish he wants to catch. By and large, the historian will get the kind of facts he wants. History means interpretation …*
>
> E.H. Carr (1961)

> **Q6** Carr refers to "documents, inscriptions and so on": what sort of documents does he mean? Where else can a historian "fish" for facts?
>
> **Q7** "History gets thicker as it approaches recent times" (**A.J.P. Taylor**, historian, 1906–90). What do you think Taylor means by "thicker"? Can historians be truly objective about their own times?

Carr, E.H. (1961) *What is History?* London: Penguin Books

Part 1 Progress

Defining progress

The history of England is emphatically the history of progress.
Lord Macaulay (historian, 1800–59)1843

Q1 From your knowledge of British history, what kind of progress do you think Lord Macaulay had in mind?

Progress is a concept that lies at the heart of many discussions of history: it may be the progress from barbarism to civilization, from poverty to wealth, or from ignorance to enlightenment. The concept contains an unspoken suggestion that progress is a good thing: that progress means *improvement*. So what is progress?

When Elizabeth I went on a royal 'progress', she toured her kingdom, staying at the houses of her wealthiest subjects. She did not expect that each act of hospitality would outdo the last. A *progress* was simply a *journey*.

Q2 Look up the word *progress* in a good dictionary, to see how it is used.

Q3 Now look it up in a thesaurus, to see what words are associated with it.

Progress didn't mean 'things getting better' until the 19th century. The idea took root, especially in Britain, between the 'Terror' in France after the Revolution of 1789 and the horror – much of it again in France – of the First World War (1914–18). But the seeds of the idea were sown long before this.

Q4 Why do you suppose that when Darwin's contemporaries first read his book *On the Origin of Species*, they took evolution to imply improvement? Why should they not have done?

MESSIANISM

The Jews, and later the Christian Church, believed that God had a purpose. Adam's sin (the Fall) thwarted this temporarily, but God would send his anointed (Messiah) to fulfil his purpose and establish the kingdom of heaven.

RATIONALISM

The belief in reason as the foundation of knowledge was promoted by René Descartes (1596–1650); Isaac Newton (1642–1727) was one of the first presidents of the Royal Society, established in 1662. Reason and science made for a new self-confidence.

CIVIL RIGHTS

The execution of Charles I in 1649 put an end to the doctrine of the Divine Right of Kings and secured the power of Parliament above the Crown, confirmed in the Bill of Rights (1689). John Locke (1632–1704) Thomas Paine (1737–1809), Baron Montesquieu (1689–1755), Voltaire (1694–1778) and Jean Jacques Rousseau (1712–78) all added their voices to the call for freedom.

EVOLUTION

Charles Darwin (1809–82) published his theory of evolution by natural selection, but did not e ncourage a belief in human improvement. Other evolutionists, such as philosopher Herbert Spencer (1820–1903), spoke of "the ultimate development of the ideal man" as "logically certain".

ENLIGHTENMENT

Marie Jean Condorcet (1743–94) believed in the "perfectibility" of humankind. For Immanuel Kant (1724–1804), progress was the work of Providence. George Wilhelm Friedrich Hegel (1770–1831), Auguste Comte (1798–1857) and Karl Marx (1818–83) believed, in different ways, that history had logic and direction.

INDUSTRIALIZATION

Scientific and technical advances led to the marvels of gas lighting, electricity, vaccination and motive power. Great exhibitions in London (1851) and Paris (1889) celebrated 'modern' technological achievements.

DEMOCRACY

Optimism and confidence in politics came with developments such as universal education (the Education Act of 1870), the Victorian ideal of self-help, voting reform (Reform Acts 1832, 1867 and 1884), and the strengthening of the ethical basis of law.

1914–18

Pessimism towards progress

Progress is not an accident, but a necessity … It is a part of nature.

Herbert Spencer *Social Statics* 1851

Comte and Spencer came to be thought of as *progressivists*, so strongly did they believe in the inevitability of progress. The self-made men and empire-builders of the Victorian period were all too happy to present themselves as evangelists of progress. Not all of their contemporaries agreed with them, chiefly for social-economic reasons:

So long as all the increased wealth which modern progress brings goes but to build up great fortunes, to increase luxury and make sharper the contrast between the House of Have and the House of Want, progress is not real and cannot be permanent.

Henry George (social philosopher, 1839–97) *Progress and Poverty* 1879

The accumulation of wealth, with its daily services at the Stock Exchange and the Bourse, with international exhibitions for its religious festivals, and political economy for its gospel, is progress, if it be progress at all, towards the wrong place.

James Anthony Froude (1818–94) 'On Progress'

Q5 In what respect are these two writers saying the same thing? In what respect are they saying something different?

Here is how **Morris Ginsberg**, Professor of Sociology in the University of London, brought his book *The Idea of Progress* to an end, in 1953:

The optimism of the early theories of progress which assumed that intellectual development was the chief or sole determinant of social progress is dead and beyond hope of resurrection. It is only too obvious that knowledge can be used for evil purposes … Yet it is a futile thing to rail against science and technology. If they can be used as instruments of oppression and destruction, they can also be used to promote freedom and well being; if they facilitate the concentration of power, they can also show us how to prevent its abuse. The moral neutrality or indifference of the sciences leaves the path open to progress or regress. The choice is ours. It remains that if knowledge is not a sufficient, it is a necessary condition of progress. It can give no assurance of ultimate success, but it can point to the possibilities open to men and thus help to provide the will with the opportunity to choose among them. Knowledge offers no apocalyptic visions, but it can do something to help man to make his own history before the end is reached.

Q6 (a) Think of some ways in which knowledge has been "used for evil purposes".
(b) What does Ginsberg appear to mean by the "moral neutrality or indifference" of the sciences?

Q7 Ginsberg was writing soon after the Second World War, half a century ago. The question is: is it possible to believe sincerely in progress today? Consider whether it is appropriate to believe in progress in:
- the arts
- medicine
- scientific understanding
- education
- social justice
- international relations.

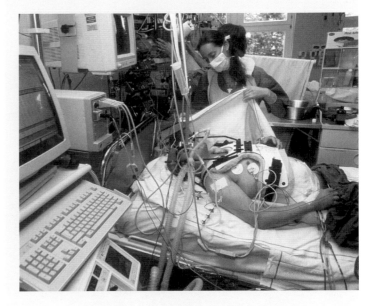

Ginsberg, Morris (1953) *The Idea of Progress: A Revaluation* London: Methuen

Part 2 Science past

Important events in science and technology from 1500–2000 are listed here. Where relevant, these take the form of a significant publication. The arrows suggest influences between certain events.

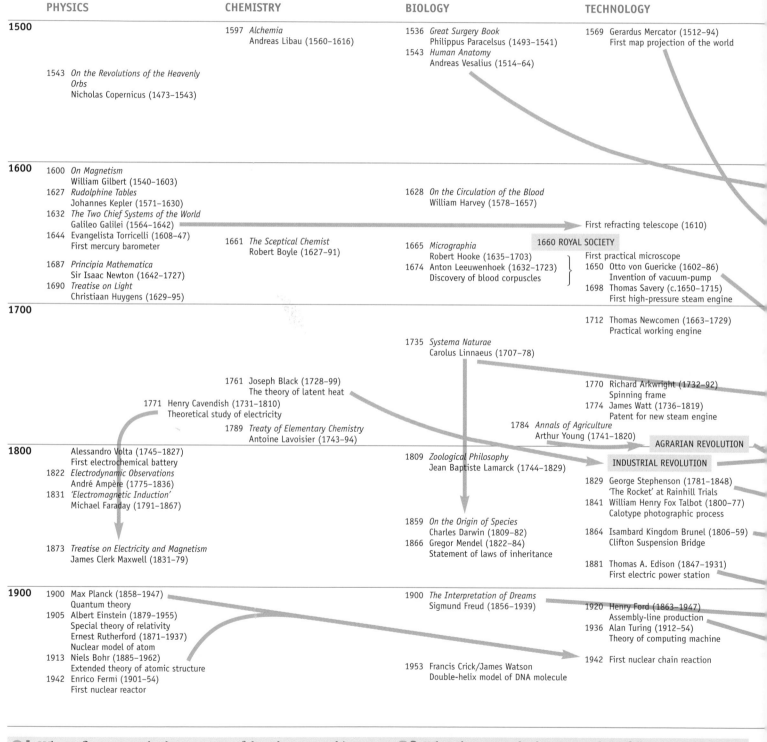

PHYSICS	CHEMISTRY	BIOLOGY	TECHNOLOGY

1500

1597 *Alchemia*
Andreas Libau (1560–1616)

1543 *On the Revolutions of the Heavenly Orbs*
Nicholas Copernicus (1473–1543)

1536 *Great Surgery Book*
Philippus Paracelsus (1493–1541)
1543 *Human Anatomy*
Andreas Vesalius (1514–64)

1569 Gerardus Mercator (1512–94)
First map projection of the world

1600

1600 *On Magnetism*
William Gilbert (1540–1603)
1627 *Rudolphine Tables*
Johannes Kepler (1571–1630)
1632 *The Two Chief Systems of the World*
Galileo Galilei (1564–1642)
1644 Evangelista Torricelli (1608–47)
First mercury barometer
1687 *Principia Mathematica*
Sir Isaac Newton (1642–1727)
1690 *Treatise on Light*
Christiaan Huygens (1629–95)

1661 *The Sceptical Chemist*
Robert Boyle (1627–91)

1628 *On the Circulation of the Blood*
William Harvey (1578–1657)

1665 *Micrographia*
Robert Hooke (1635–1703)
1674 Anton Leeuwenhoek (1632–1723)
Discovery of blood corpuscles

First refracting telescope (1610)

1660 ROYAL SOCIETY

First practical microscope
1650 Otto von Guericke (1602–86)
Invention of vacuum-pump
1698 Thomas Savery (c.1650–1715)
First high-pressure steam engine

1700

1712 Thomas Newcomen (1663–1729)
Practical working engine

1735 *Systema Naturae*
Carolus Linnaeus (1707–78)

1761 Joseph Black (1728–99)
The theory of latent heat
1771 Henry Cavendish (1731–1810)
Theoretical study of electricity
1789 *Treaty of Elementary Chemistry*
Antoine Lavoisier (1743–94)

1770 Richard Arkwright (1732–92)
Spinning frame
1774 James Watt (1736–1819)
Patent for new steam engine

1784 *Annals of Agriculture*
Arthur Young (1741–1820)

AGRARIAN REVOLUTION

1800

Alessandro Volta (1745–1827)
First electrochemical battery
1822 *Electrodynamic Observations*
André Ampère (1775–1836)
1831 *'Electromagnetic Induction'*
Michael Faraday (1791–1867)

1809 *Zoological Philosophy*
Jean Baptiste Lamarck (1744–1829)

INDUSTRIAL REVOLUTION

1829 George Stephenson (1781–1848)
'The Rocket' at Rainhill Trials
1841 William Henry Fox Talbot (1800–77)
Calotype photographic process

1873 *Treatise on Electricity and Magnetism*
James Clerk Maxwell (1831–79)

1859 *On the Origin of Species*
Charles Darwin (1809–82)
1866 Gregor Mendel (1822–84)
Statement of laws of inheritance

1864 Isambard Kingdom Brunel (1806–59)
Clifton Suspension Bridge

1881 Thomas A. Edison (1847–1931)
First electric power station

1900

1900 Max Planck (1858–1947)
Quantum theory
1905 Albert Einstein (1879–1955)
Special theory of relativity
Ernest Rutherford (1871–1937)
Nuclear model of atom
1913 Niels Bohr (1885–1962)
Extended theory of atomic structure
1942 Enrico Fermi (1901–54)
First nuclear reactor

1900 *The Interpretation of Dreams*
Sigmund Freud (1856–1939)

1953 Francis Crick/James Watson
Double-helix model of DNA molecule

1920 Henry Ford (1863–1947)
Assembly-line production
1936 Alan Turing (1912–54)
Theory of computing machine

1942 First nuclear chain reaction

Q1 What influences might the invention of the telescope and/or the microscope have had on 17th century painting?

Q2 With what 'revolution' in science do we associate the name of Sir Isaac Newton?

Q3 What changes in thinking came about following publication of *The Origin of Species*, in 1859?

Art past

In the diagram below, the major painting of important artists are cited. In some cases, a painting that seems to have been inspired by a development in science and technology is referred to.

The distinction made between 'Realism' and 'Metaphor' is open to discussion.

REALISM	METAPHOR	ABSTRACTION	
			1500
	1503 *Mona Lisa* Leonardo Da Vinci (1452–1519)	1513 *The Knight, Death and the Devil* Albrecht Durer (1471–1614)	ITALIAN RENAISSANCE
1537 *Henry VIII & Jane Seymour* Hans Holbein (1497–1543)	1510 *The School of Athens* Raphael (1483–1520)		
	1512 The Sistine Chapel Ceiling Michelangelo (1475–1564)		
	1570 *The Fall of Man* Titian (c.1490–1576)		
	1586 *The Burial of Count Orgaz* El Greco (1541–1614)		
			1600
1624 *The Laughing Cavalier* Frans Hals (c.1580–1666)			DUTCH RENAISSANCE
1632 *The Anatomy Lesson of Dr Tulp* Rembrandt (1606–1669)	1635 *The Rape of Sabines* Peter Paul Rubens (1577–1640)		
1633 *The Operation* Adriaen Brouwer (1605–38)	1636 *The Inspiration of the Poet* Nicolas Poussin (1594–1665)		
1637 *King Charles* (Triptych) Anthony Van Dyck (1599–1641)			
1658 *The Rokeby Venus* Velázquez (1599–1660)			
1669 *The Geographer* Jan Vermeer (1632–75)			
			1700
BAROQUE	1717 *Embarkation for Cytherea* Jean Antoine Watteau (1684–1721)		
1740 *Grace Before Meat* Jean-Baptiste Chardin (1699–1779)	1726 *The Adoration of the Magi* Giovanni Tiepolo (1696–1770)		
1756 *Dr Samuel Johnson* Sir Joshua Reynolds (1723–92)			
1768 *Experiment with an Air–pump* Joseph Wright of Derby (1734–97)	1751 *Gin Lane* William Hogarth (1697–1764)		
1769 *A Lion Devouring a Horse* George Stubbs (1724–1806)			
1785 *Mrs Siddons* Thomas Gainsborough (1727–88)	1799 *The Rape of the Sabines* Jacques Louis David (1748–1825)		
1805 *Greta Bridge* John Sell Cotman (1782–1842)	1826 *Illustrations to the Book of Job* William Blake (1757–1827)		**1800**
1810 *3 May 1808* Francisco de Goya (1746–1828)	1831 *Liberty Guiding the People* Eugène Delacroix (1798–1863)		ROMANTICISM
1819 *The Raft of the Medusa* Théodore Géricault (1791–1824)			
1821 *The Hay Wain* John Constable (1776–1837)			
1844 *Rain, Steam and Speed* J.M.W. Turner (1775–1851)	1856 *The Scapegoat* Holman Hunt (1827–1910)		IMPRESSIONISM
1850 *Burial at Ornans* Gustave Courbet (1819–77)			
1873 *Gare St. Lazare* Claude Monet (1840–1926)	1865 *Battersea Bridge* James Abbott McNeill Whistler (1834–1903)		
1876 *Moulin de la Galette* Pierre Renoir (1841–1919)		1885 *L'Estaque* Paul Cezanne (1839–1906)	
	1889 *Self Portrait* Vincent Van Gogh (1853–90)		
		1907 *Les Demoiselles d'Avignon* Pablo Picasso (1881–1973)	**1900**
		1920 *The Mechanic* Fernand Léger (1881–1955)	
	1931 *The Persistence of Memory* Salvador Dali (1904–89)	1943 *Broadway Boogie Woogie* Piet Mondrian (1872–1944)	
1961 *Green Coca-Cola Bottles* Andy Warhol (c.1926–87)		1946 *The Blue Unconscious* Jackson Pollock (1912–56)	

Q4 What are the defining characteristics of Italian Renaissance painting?

Q5 What effects might the Industrial Revolution have had on 19th century art?

Q6 What seem to have been some of the effects on painting of (a) the invention of photography (b) Freudian psychology?

Part 3 Positions of power

■ The Establishment

Before the Second World War, Britain was ruled by what came to be called 'the Establishment'. This was a term popularized in a *Spectator* article in 1955, and was much used by a new wave of satirists. The Establishment was essentially upper class; it represented tradition and was seen as resistant to change, especially by those who believed that power should be earned, not inherited (meritocrats). **Sir Alexander Douglas-Home** was, perhaps, the last Establishment prime minister (1963–64); and **Lord Hailsham** was the last Establishment Lord Chancellor (1970–74; 1979–87).

Though elements of the Establishment persist, most have been subject to reform or faced with increased competition. At the same time, there has been a general decline in deference towards all authority. Power is more widely spread – and more diffuse – than ever before.

 Monarchy (Royal family and retainers)

 Parliament and the **Civil Service** (especially the Foreign Office)

 The City (merchant banks, Lloyd's)

 The BBC

 The armed forces (especially the army)

 Oxford and **Cambridge Universities**

 Top public schools

 The Church of England (archbishops and senior bishops in the House of Lords)

 The Law (Law Lords, judges and barristers)

 The Times

■ Institutions that have lost some of their power

 The Established Church
Numbers of regular churchgoers have dropped steadily. The Archbishop of Canterbury still has some authority, but bishops are no longer regarded as powerful figures. The possibility of disestablishment (separation of the Church of England from the state) is regularly raised.

 The universities
Oxford and Cambridge are still at the top of the educational tree, but there are many departments in other universities that are as good as, or better than, their Oxbridge counterparts. The influence of universities in general has been diluted.

 Parliament
MPs have lost some of their influence in government, to the Prime Minister and cabinet. The media are often briefed by ministers and their press secretaries before MPs. Televising of Parliament has increased some people's disenchantment with politicians.

 The armed forces
These are an extension of the Ministry of Defence, and are part of bigger NATO/OSCE machines.

 The trade unions
In terms of numbers of members, the Trades Union Congress (TUC) is still Britain's largest pressure group. The TUC still has a 50 per cent vote at the Labour Party Conference, but membership of unions affiliated to the TUC dropped from 12.2 million in 1979 to 6.8 million in 1997.

 Public schools
The old public schools retain prestige, but 'the old school tie' is not now the passport to success that it used to be.

 Local government
Conservative governments' capping of revenue and expenditure levels reduced the influence of councils. Councils now have fewer powers, as services are contracted out. Voter turnout at local elections is low.

 The BBC
The 'Beeb' has lost its broadcasting monopoly and is now in ratings competition with commercial channels, as well as terrestrial, satellite and cable channels. The licence fee, from which only the BBC benefits, is under permanent review.

Q1 What were the forces that combined to undermine 'the Establishment'?

Q2 Is the monarchy as significant in the new establishment as in the old?

Institutions that have won more power

The press
It may no longer be true, as the advertisement claimed, that "top people read *The Times*", but the press in general reflects, and moulds, public opinion more powerfully than ever before. *The Daily Mail*, for instance, considers itself the voice of 'middle England', while the *Sun* was quick to claim credit for Tony Blair's 1997 general election victory.

Europe
European law now supersedes law in England and Wales in many dimensions. All new Westminster legislation has to take into account the 1986 Single European Act and the 1992 Maastricht extension of European powers.

Regulators
All the utilities (suppliers of essential services) are regulated by bodies such as Ofgas, Ofwat and Oftel, whose role is to champion the interests of the consumer and to ensure fair competition.

Pressure groups
Well-established groups such as the National Trust, the NSPCC, Oxfam, and the pro- and anti-smoking lobbies, can apply pressure to those in power. The environmental lobby has a particularly strong voice. New groups, such as the Countryside Alliance, can make an impact by mobilizing support.

Television
TV is powerful because it reaches inside almost every home. Many people's view of the world is formed by television viewing, and political parties take a keen interest in the coverage they are given.

Advertisers
Advertisers and the public relations industry are big players in the power game. Saatchi & Saatchi helped sell the Conservative Party to millions of voters. Advertisers sustain newspapers and independent TV companies.

Big retailers
Big retailers put small retailers out of business, dominate the urban environment with their superstores, and change people's shopping habits.

Q3 Think of as many ways in which pressure groups have influenced policy as you can.

Q4 Think of examples of the impact of television programmes on national life.

Institutions that have neither lost nor gained power

The Law
Judges have been found to be fallible, and the Lords are no longer the final court of Appeal, but the Home Secretary has surrendered to judges the power to modify prison sentences.

Doctors
The British Medical Association (BMA) and individual medical experts enjoy influence, particularly in times of health scares, but the NHS is under constant pressure from lack of resources and high demand on services.

Scientists
The public respects scientists, but is dismayed when they cannot provide clear-cut solutions to problems such as BSE. Conflicting views from experts, for example, over genetically modified food, undermine trust in scientists.

The banks
Since 1997, the Bank of England has been independent of the Treasury with regard to setting interest rates, but the large high street banks are subject to increasing competition from ex-building societies.

The House of Lords
Whilst the hereditary peers have been shorn of power, a (soon) to-be modernized and democratized Lords should enjoy more leverage and respect.

The police
Chief Constables and the Metropolitan Police Commissioner are always listened to, but charges of 'institutional racism' and abuse of power have dented public confidence.

Business executives
There is admiration of entrepreneurs such as Richard Branson and Bill Gates, but there is also concern about 'fat cat' executives receiving huge payouts, and multinationals exploiting the poor in developing countries.

Q5 To what extent have the following groups gained or lost power: (a) journalists (b) sportspeople (c) farmers (d) miners? What are the reasons for their change in status?

Q6 How do you think power will shift in the coming decades? Which groups of people and institutions do you think will gain more power, and which will lose it?

Q7 When Kenneth Clarke was Secretary of State for Education in the early 1990s, he said the study of history in school should omit the most recent 20 years, because we were too close to them to be objective. Do you agree with him? If so, is the analysis on these two pages historically invalid?

Opinion

Connotations of the word

The word *opinion* can be used in negative or positive ways. The following quotations exemplify the difference.

Negative

opinion n. belief or judgement, not based on proof or evidence; view held as probable, provisionally, e.g. personal ~; private ~; public ~; a matter of ~.

There are as many opinions as there are men; each a law to himself.
Terence (Roman dramatist, c. 190–159 BCE) *The Eunuch*

The coquetry of public opinion, which has her caprices, and must have her way.
Edmund Burke (parliamentarian, 1729–97)

To be independent of public opinion is the first formal condition of achieving anything great or rational whether in life or in science.
Georg Wilhelm Friedrich Hegel (philosopher, 1770–1831)
Philosophy of Right 1821

Opinion is ultimately determined by the feelings, and not by the intellect.
Herbert Spencer, (Victorian free-thinker, 1820–1903) *Social Statics* 1850

Positive

opinion n. formal statement by an expert as to the fact of the matter or the proper course of action, e.g. second ~; professional ~; scientific ~; legal ~.

Where there is much desire to learn, there of necessity will be much arguing, much writing, many opinions; for opinion in good men is but knowledge in the making.
John Milton (poet, 1608–74) *Areopagitica* 1644

New opinions are always suspected, and usually opposed, with any other reason but because they are not already common.
John Locke (philosopher, 1632–1704) *Essay on the Human Understanding* 1690

Every reform was once a private opinion.
Ralph Waldo Emerson (philosopher, essayist and poet, 1803–82) *Essays* 1841, 44

Bigotry may be roughly defined as the anger of men who have no opinions.
G.K. Chesterton (novelist and poet, 1874–1936)

Q1 What does Burke mean by the 'coquetry' of public opinion, having 'caprices'?

Q2 Is what Spencer says fact or opinion?

Q3 Do you agree with Milton that opinion is "knowledge in the making"? Give reasons for you answer.

The negative definition of opinion would have it that *fact* and *opinion* are opposites. The positive definition of opinion, on the other hand, sees a connection between them, placing them on a single continuum of knowledge.

KNOWLEDGE

law/fact   theory/belief   judgement/opinion   impression/hunch

Objectivity ——————————————————→ **Subjectivity**

NOTE: perhaps 'bigotry' (see Chesterton quote) or 'prejudice' is the real negation, belonging still further to the right on this continuum.

The Right to belief

In practice, whether people take a positive or negative view of someone's opinion will depend upon *who* that person is. Opinion of an acknowledged expert will always count for more than the opinion of a 'nobody'.

The right of the individual to hold their own opinion – whatever the rest of society think of it – is a controversial issue. English philosopher **John Stuart Mill** (1806–73) is still thought to have made the most significant contribution to this debate.

If all mankind minus one were of one opinion, mankind would be no more justified in silencing that one person than he, if he had the power, would be justified in silencing mankind. Were an opinion a personal possession of no value except to the owner, if to be obstructed in the enjoyment of it were simply a private injury, it would make some difference whether the injury was inflicted only on a few persons or on many. But the peculiar evil of silencing the expression of an opinion is that it is robbing the human race, posterity as well as the existing generation – those who dissent from the opinion, still more than those who hold it. If the opinion is right, they are deprived of the opportunity of exchanging error for truth; if wrong, they lose what is almost as great a benefit, the clearer perception and livelier impression of truth produced by its collision with error.

John Stuart Mill *On Liberty* 1859

Q4 Mill rules out the silencing of an opinion in any circumstances. Are there circumstances in which democratic societies do constrain public expression of opinion?

Q5 If an opinion is not a 'personal possession', what does Mill suggest that it is?

Q6 How far do you agree with Mill's assertion of the value of individual opinion?

Opinion in hindsight

Opinion carries doubt with it in that the 'orthodox', or 'received' opinion of one time may change in the next; and in that 'experts' disagree with each other. Mill speaks of the collision of truth with error – though in a social, as opposed to physical science, context, it is not easy to distinguish which is which, or even whether these categories are actually helpful. It is a question which faces the individual (as **Sir Thomas Browne** says), and society (**Hobbes**):

I could never divide myself from any man upon the difference of an opinion, or be angry with his judgement for not agreeing with me in that, from which perhaps within a few days, I should dissent myself.

Sir Thomas Browne (writer and physician, 1605–82) *Religio Medici* 1643

They that approve a private opinion, call it opinion; but they that mislike it, heresy: and yet heresy signifies no more than private opinion.

Thomas Hobbes (philosopher, 1588–1679) *Leviathan* 1651

The practice of eugenics (the science of 'improving' the population by controlled breeding) is associated with the worst excesses of the Nazi regime. However, in the 1930s many respected members of European society proposed theories of 'selective breeding'.

Sidney and Beatrice Webb, George Bernard Shaw, Harold Laski, John Maynard Keynes, Marie Stopes, the New Statesman, *even, lamentably, the* Manchester Guardian. *Nearly every one of the left's most cherished iconic figures espoused views which today's progressives would find repulsive.*

Jonathan Freedland *The Guardian* 30 August 1997

Bertrand Russell (philosopher and mathematician, 1872–1970) even proposed that the government allocate 'procreation tickets', and fine those who mated with holders of the wrong colour tickets.

Q7 Can you think of other examples of 'public opinion' that have radically changed from one generation to the next?

Q8 Have you yourself undergone a change of opinion of a significant kind?

Opinionated writing

Lytton Strachey (1880–1932) inherited an exalted public opinion of Queen Victoria. A free-thinker and member of the Bloomsbury set, Strachey set about writing short biographies of Victorian figures that critically examined their lives. He was, thus, a founder of the 'debunking' school of historians. Here are three extracts from his biography *Queen Victoria*:

The vast changes which, out of the England of 1837, had produced the England of 1897, seemed scarcely to have touched the Queen. The immense industrial development of the period, the significance of which had been so thoroughly understood by Albert, meant little indeed to Victoria. The amazing scientific movement, which Albert had appreciated no less, left Victoria perfectly cold. Her conception of the universe, and of man's place in it, and of the stupendous problems of nature and philosophy remained, throughout her life, entirely unchanged ...

From the social movements of her time Victoria was equally remote. Towards the smallest no less than towards the greatest changes she remained inflexible. During her youth and middle-age smoking had been forbidden in polite society, and so long as she lived she would not withdraw her anathema against it. Kings might protest; bishops and ambassadors, invited to Windsor, might be reduced, in the privacy of their bedrooms, to lie full-length upon the floor and smoke up the chimney – the interdict continued. It might have been supposed that a female sovereign would have lent her countenance to one of the most vital of all the reforms to which her epoch gave birth – the emancipation of women – but, on the contrary, the mere mention of such a proposal sent the blood rushing to her head ...

For more than half a century no divorced lady had approached the precincts of the Court. Victoria, indeed, in her enthusiasm for wifely fidelity, had laid down a still stricter ordinance: she frowned severely upon any widow who married again. Considering that she herself was the offspring of a widow's second marriage, this prohibition might be regarded as an eccentricity; but, no doubt, it was an eccentricity on the right side.

Lytton Strachey *Queen Victoria* 1921

Q9 What are the opinions of Queen Victoria that Strachey is examining in these extracts?

Q10 To what extent is Strachey examining them in a factual way, and to what extent is his presentation influenced by his own opinions?

Substance abuse and health

Facts and opinions

Nowhere is opinion more divided than in matters of personal and public health, and in particular the right of the individual to eat unhealthy food, smoke, drink and take recreational drugs. Such issues also provide good examples of how complex and difficult it is to make an informed judgement on a subject where opinions differ widely. Policy-makers, for example, such as politicians, base their publically-held opinions on facts, often in the form of statistical information – though it is worth remembering that the views that people already hold influence the way such facts are selected and presented. Study the source information that follows, and use it to develop an informed opinion on the subject of personal freedom and public responsibility in relation to health.

Food

Body mass: by gender and age, 1997

England									%
	Underweight		Desirable		Overweight		Obese		Total
	M	F	M	F	M	F	M	F	
16–24	17	17	56	56	22	19	5	9	100
25–34	4	8	46	51	43	27	13	15	100
35–44	2	7	32	44	48	32	18	18	100
45–54	1	4	25	38	52	37	22	23	100
55–64	1	4	25	29	47	37	27	30	100
65–74	1	4	25	27	56	44	18	25	100
75 and over	4	8	34	30	50	41	12	22	100
All aged 16 and over	4	7	34	40	45	33	17	20	100

Source: Social Trends 30, 2000

Mortality from coronary heart disease in the United Kingdom is among the highest in the world, accounting for more deaths and more premature deaths than any other single cause ... About half the risk is attributable to smoking, high blood pressure, and raised serum cholesterol concentrations, with the last two being profoundly affected by diet.

The average serum cholesterol concentration in British adults is currently 5.8 mmol/l, and about two thirds of the population have concentrations above the desirable level of 5.2 mmol/l.

There have been some recent changes in the British diet, such as increased sales of skimmed milk, low-fat spreads, and wholemeal bread, yet intakes of fat as a percentage of total energy have apparently not decreased ...

The possibility of curbing or opposing the massive amount of advertising for unhealthy food and drink must be considered. Regular television screening within the home goes a long way to overturning the hard work of all those presently participating in health education.

S. Bingham in The Health of the Nation 1991

Q1 Which groups appear to be particularly vulnerable to weight problems?

Q2 In 1980, 6% of men were obese, and 8% of women; in 1986–87, 8% of men were obese, and 12% of women. What is driving up the figures for obesity?

Drugs

Percentage of 16–24-year-olds who have used drugs in past year, 1998

England & Wales			%
	Males	Females	All
Cannabis	32	22	27
Amphetamines	12	8	10
Ecstasy	6	4	5
Magic mushrooms	5	2	4
LSD	5	2	3
Cocaine	4	3	3
Any drug	36	24	29

A distinctive feature of injecting-drug use is the extent to which it changes over time. The Home Office figures (2 000 addicts in 1970, 6 000 in 1980, and 17 000 in 1990) suggest relentless progression in the face of which any health strategy might be futile.

John Strang in The Health of the Nation 1991

In 1997, the Independent on Sunday called for the decriminalization of cannabis:

Cannabis is the focus of more than 85 per cent of all drug seizures, and its users account for more than 80 per cent of people charged with drug offences (40 000 in 1991) ... Cannabis has been used as a medicine in China, India, the Middle East, southern Africa and South America for centuries ... In the 19th century it was respectable enough to be used by Queen Victoria's doctor to alleviate her labour pains.

Dr Philip Robson Independent on Sunday 28 September 1997

On the other hand, neuropharmacologist, Susan Greenfield, would not want it legalized:

She decries the attempt to legalize cannabis except for medicinal purposes, and points out that the drug is pretty potent: it takes 0.3mg to induce the same kind of effects as 7 000mg of alcohol.

Anjana Ahuja The Times 15 June 2000

Q3 What have been of the effects be of reclassifying cannabis? What might some of the effects be of (a) decriminalizing (b) legalizing it?

Smoking

Current smokers: by gender and socio-economic groups

Great Britain								%
	1972		1982		1996–97		1998–99	
	M	F	M	F	M	F	M	F
Professional	33	33	20	21	12	11	15	14
Employers and managers	44	38	29	29	20	18	21	20
Intermediate and junior non-manual	45	38	30	30	24	28	28	24
Skilled manual	57	47	42	39	32	30	33	30
Semiskilled manual	57	42	47	36	41	36	38	33
Unskilled manual	64	42	49	41	41	36	45	33
All aged 16 and over	52	42	38	33	29	28	28	26

Current estimates suggest that about 115 000 deaths, and roughly 106 000 admissions to hospital in Britain every year are attributable to smoking. Passive smoking increases the risk of lung cancer by 10–30 per cent and causes respiratory complaints in children.

Smoking costs the NHS at least £500 million annually, but the costs of ill health to society are considerably more, with an estimated 50 million working days being lost through sickness absence.

Most (54 per cent) regular adult smokers would like to stop smoking for good (Dept. of Health, unpublished data) ...

The reasons why children and young people take up smoking are complex and a relation has been shown between advertising and under-age smoking. Peer pressure, parental and sibling smoking, desire to look grown up, and availability are all factors. By the age of 10, more than 28 per cent of children have tried their first cigarette.

Jacky Chambers in The Health of the Nation 1991

Q4 Among which group has there been the biggest proportionate fall in the numbers of smokers between 1972 and 1999?

Q5 What could/should be done to discourage the adoption of the smoking habit among children and young people?

Alcohol

Percentages of adults consuming over selected weekly limits of alcohol: by gender and age

Great Britain			%
	1988	1994–95	1998–99
Males			
16–24	31	29	36
25–44	34	30	27
45–64	24	27	30
65 and over	13	17	16
All aged 16 and over	26	27	27
Females			
16–24	15	19	25
25–44	14	15	16
45–64	9	12	16
65 and over	4	7	6
All aged 16 and over	10	13	15

NOTE: the recommended weekly limit for males is 21 units; for females it is 14 units

The harms related to alcohol consumption are many and act at both population and individual levels. They include physical ill health; psychological ill health; public disorder, violence, and crime; family disputes; child neglect and abuse; road traffic accidents; accidents at work and in the home; fire; drowning; and employment problems ... Estimates of the deaths attributable to alcohol consumption in England and Wales vary from 5 000 to 40 000.

The most important indicator of health for alcohol consumption is liver cirrhosis. Correlations between alcohol consumption and liver cirrhosis lie between 0.8 and 0.9.

Differential changes in tax for different alcoholic beverages in Britain have provided clear evidence of the importance of tax in determining alcohol consumption. Over the past 20 years the prices for spirits and wines have dropped more than 50 per cent relative to income whereas the prices of beers have dropped by only 16 per cent. Over this period the proportion of total alcohol consumed as beer has fallen from 74 per cent to 55 per cent and the proportion of alcohol consumed as wines and spirits increased from 24 per cent to 40 per cent.

John Garrow in The Health of the Nation 1991

Q6 What can be said about the trends in alcohol consumption over the period 1988–99?

Q7 On the basis of Garrow's figures, what would a wise Chancellor do in relation to tax on alcohol?

Q8 Why should a government be concerned with people's smoking and drinking habits?

Smith, Richard (ed.) (1991) *The Health of the Nation: The BMJ View* London: British Medical Journal

8 Philosophy

Thinkers in Ancient Greece were called philosophers, or *lovers of knowledge and wisdom*. At that time philosophy was not a separate subject or discipline – or department of knowledge – as it is today; instead it took in all aspects of knowledge and the quest for knowledge. It was an enquiry into the nature of things. It was *science*.

Few of the men who are now regarded as philosophers were *professional* philosophers: **John Locke** (1632–1704) was a physician; **George Berkeley** (1685–1753) and **Søren Kierkegaard** (1813–55) were clergymen; **David Hume** (1711–76) was a librarian and historian; **Baruch Spinoza** (1632–77) was a lens grinder; **John Stuart Mill** (1806–73) was a civil servant.

The search for truth

Philosophers have almost all been concerned with truth: that is, they have looked for ways of describing the world, have asked questions about it and have given answers in the form of statements (or *propositions*) about it. The hope has been that these propositions are a close fit with things as they really are. It has been a high hope – but it persists:

I start with the assumption that there is some class of true propositions which it is the special business of philosophy to discover, and that their discovery is of some importance.

A.J. Ayer (1990)

The purpose of philosophy is ... to discover true propositions or to acquire correct solutions to as many problems as possible.

George N Schlesinger (1983)

Pursuit of the truth requires more than imagination: it requires the generation and decisive elimination of alternative possibilities until, ideally, only one remains ...

Thomas Nagel (1986)

From earliest times, philosophers have looked for the truth about different aspects of the world and human life in it. The following

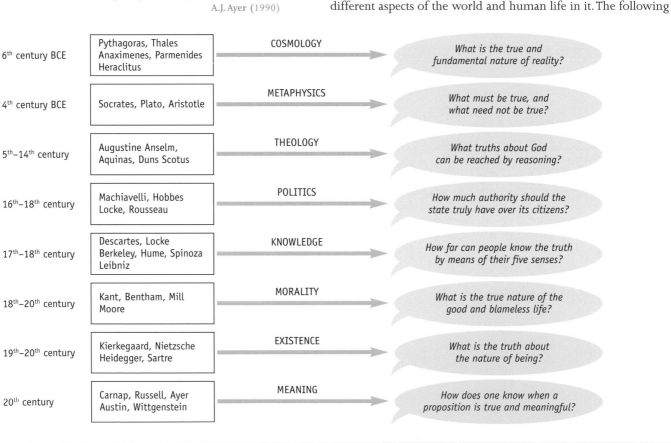

6th century BCE	Pythagoras, Thales Anaximenes, Parmenides Heraclitus	COSMOLOGY	What is the true and fundamental nature of reality?
4th century BCE	Socrates, Plato, Aristotle	METAPHYSICS	What must be true, and what need not be true?
5th–14th century	Augustine Anselm, Aquinas, Duns Scotus	THEOLOGY	What truths about God can be reached by reasoning?
16th–18th century	Machiavelli, Hobbes Locke, Rousseau	POLITICS	How much authority should the state truly have over its citizens?
17th–18th century	Descartes, Locke Berkeley, Hume, Spinoza Leibniz	KNOWLEDGE	How far can people know the truth by means of their five senses?
18th–20th century	Kant, Bentham, Mill Moore	MORALITY	What is the true nature of the good and blameless life?
19th–20th century	Kierkegaard, Nietzsche Heidegger, Sartre	EXISTENCE	What is the truth about the nature of being?
20th century	Carnap, Russell, Ayer Austin, Wittgenstein	MEANING	How does one know when a proposition is true and meaningful?

Q1
(a) "It is true that the consent of citizens is what gives the state its authority."
(b) "It is true that all matter is made up of fundamental particles."
(c) "It is true that the soul is to be distinguished from the mind."

Is "true" being used in the same way or in different ways in these three statements? What other words or phrases could you use in place of "It is true ..." in each of these statements (e.g. "It can be proved that ...", "It is commonly agreed that ...").

are loose groupings of philosophers who asked truth-seeking questions in particular contexts:

As knowledge has grown, so one 'subject' after another uprooted itself from philosophy and established itself as a separate discipline (as shown in Concept B, 'The curriculum'). **Bertrand Russell** (philosopher, 1872–1970) explains:

Philosophy, like all other studies, aims primarily at knowledge ... as soon as definite knowledge concerning any subject becomes possible, this subject ceases to be called philosophy, and becomes a separate science. The whole study of the heavens, which now belongs to astronomy, was once included in philosophy; Newton's great work was called "the mathematical principles of natural philosophy". Similarly, the study of the human mind, which was a part of philosophy, has now been separated from philosophy and has become the science of psychology ... those questions which are already capable of definite answers are placed in the sciences, while those only to which, at present, no definite answer can be given, remain to form the residue which is called philosophy.

Bertrand Russell (1912)

Q2 What sorts of questions, according to Russell, remain for philosophers to answer? Can you think of a few examples of such questions?

The philosopher's toolkit

What special tools do philosophers have at their disposal for making propositions that are true? Socrates hoped that by engaging in *dialogue*, people would find the truth that underlies their assumptions. Descartes and Spinoza applied a sort of mathematical *reasoning* to problems. Frege, Russell, Quine, Dummett and others have tried *logic*. Logic is all about whether statements are consistent with each other.

Q3 Consider the statement: "He sang wonderfully but the applause was brief."

What would you need to know in order to test the truth of this statement? Could it ever be shown to be absolutely true?

A logician will divide the statement into its constituent sentences and construct a *truth table* (where T is True, and F is False):

A [He sang wonderfully] *but* B [the applause was brief].			
	A	**B**	**A but B**
(i)	T	T	T
(ii)	T	F	F
(iii)	F	T	F
(iv)	F	F	F

If sentences A and B are both true, as in (i), the statement as a whole is true, but if either A or B is false, as in (ii), (iii), and (iv), the whole sentence is false. But can the sentence "the applause was brief" be *absolutely* true or *absolutely* false? Some in the audience might have thought the applause was brief and some might not.

This is a simple example – and it may do a disservice to logic – but the philosopher and mathematician **Wilfrid Hodges** readily admits that logic has its limitations:

Life seems full of half-truths, grey areas, borderline cases, but logic stands with sword uplifted to divide the world clearly into the true and the false ... We are forced to admit that where borderline cases may arise, logic is not an exact science.

Wilfrid Hodges (1997)

The Roman type is Hodges' own: he knew he was saying something rather important. Most things in life are neither A nor B, neither true nor false, neither right nor wrong. There are beautiful buildings; there are ugly buildings; and there are borderline cases. Most cases are borderline cases.

What is left for philosophy?

Philosophers Richard Rorty and Mary Midgley pour scorn on the claim that philosophy has a special "knowledge about knowledge" (see Concept B). Ian Mackenzie doubts the possibility of distinguishing between *true* and *false* ideologies (see Concept E). And post-modernist thinkers are suspicious of anything that looks like an overarching truth (a *grand narrative*) about the world.

Bertrand Russell spoke of the way in which sciences have broken away from philosophy and become independent. The philosopher A.C. Grayling counts this among philosophy's great strengths:

Consider what [philosophy] has directly or indirectly given birth to in modern times: in the 17th century the natural sciences, in the 18th century psychology, in the 19th century sociology and empirical linguistics, in the 20th century computing, and cognitive science ... If [philosophers] bring to bear the ideals of their vocation – clarity, principle, insight, and illumination – they do a service to mankind. And sometimes, as the progress of human knowledge shows, they even find answers.

A.C. Grayling "The last word on philosophy" *The Guardian* 14 August 2001

Philosophy might have given birth to many children, but it may now be beyond childbearing age. Philosophers-turned-scientists might have found answers in the past, but philosophy doesn't have any monopoly on clarity, principle, insight or illumination. If that is so, does that mean everyone is now a philosopher?

Q4 Consider this statement: "It is better to live with a life expectancy of, say, 15 years, than to have been aborted and not to live at all."

This is the sort of proposition that philosophers – which arguably means everyone – might discuss.
(a) Are there *facts* that you would need to know before you could agree or disagree with the proposition?
(b) Are there *values* implicit in the proposition?
(c) Can these values, and therefore the proposition itself, be said to be objectively *true*?

Ayer, A.J. (1990) *The Meaning of Life and Other Essays* London: Weidenfeld and Nicolson

Hodges, Wilfrid (1997) *Logic* London: Penguin Books

Nagel, Thomas (1986) *The View from Nowhere* Oxford: OUP

Russell, Bertrand (1912) *The Problems of Philosophy* Oxford: OUP

Schlesinger, George N. (1983) *Metaphysics* Oxford: Basil Blackwell

Part 1 The sanctity of life

▌ Medical ethics

One area where philosophers make a valuable contribution is in the ongoing debates about *bioethics*, the ethics of medical and biological research. Medical science is beset with philosophical questions: What does it mean to be 'alive'? Does 'death' mean brain death, or the irrecoverable loss of consciousness? When does a living entity become, or cease to be, a 'person'?

As science opens up new possibilities for healing and preserving life, it also throws up new challenges concerning, for example, the ethics of cloning, manipulation of genes and use of human embryos for research.

▌ A duty to save life?

In his book *Rethinking Life and Death* (1995), Peter Singer raises ethical questions about the value that society places on human life. He quotes a Christian bioethicist on this subject:

Traditional medical ethics ... never asks whether the patient's life is worthwhile, for the notion of a worthless life is as alien to the Hippocratic tradition as it is to English criminal law, both of which subscribe to the principle of the sanctity of human life which holds that, because all lives are intrinsically valuable, it is always wrong intentionally to kill an innocent human being ...

John Keown in *Singer* 1995

Some doctors still take the Hippocratic Oath, which states the obligations and proper conduct of physicians. In doing so, they make the following promise: "I will give no deadly drug to any, though it be asked of me, nor will I counsel such, and especially I will not aid a woman to procure abortion." In reality, doctors daily prescribe "deadly drugs" – often to kill pain, and sometimes with the consequence that they hasten the patient's death. Since 1967, when abortion was legalized in most of the UK, doctors have also regularly "procured" abortions.

Under the European Convention of Human Rights, Article 2, "Protection of Life": "Everyone's right to life shall be protected by law." Does "everyone" mean *everyone*? This extract begins to outline some of the complexities of Article 2.

It is unclear how far Article 2 places states under any obligation to seek to ensure the continuance of life where the individual involved, or those acting on his or her behalf, wish it to end. The Commission has found that passively allowing a person to die need not attract criminal liability in order to satisfy Article 2. This might apply to allowing a handicapped baby or a patient in a persistent vegetative state to die.

Fenwick (1998)

Q1 The law and codes of conduct send out conflicting signals about what is ethically acceptable. What is the effect of this inconsistency on: (a) doctors (b) relatives of someone in a persistent vegetative state?

Birth

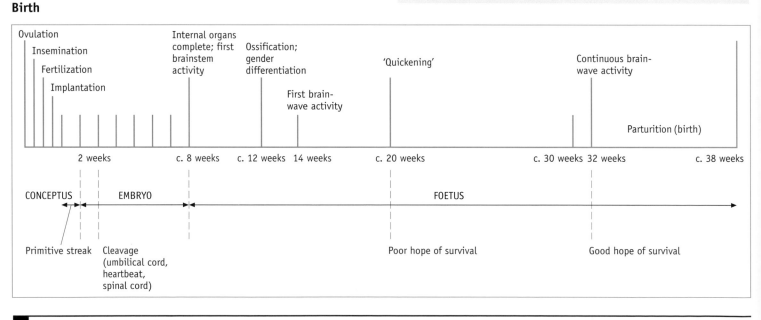

▌ The value of life

The Latin word *sanctus* means: sacred, inviolable, holy. Those who believe in the sanctity of human life set an *absolute* value on all (human) life and can, therefore, approve neither of abortion nor of voluntary euthanasia. They believe that, in nature, life has a beginning and an end, and that it is always wrong to try to prevent the beginning or to hasten the end. Singer tells the story of Laura Campo, a young woman who was told, in the eighth month of her

pregnancy, that the foetus was anencephalic – that is, most of its brain was missing. It was too late for an abortion, so Campo opted to give birth to the baby, so as to make its organs available for transplant:

Baby Theresa was born on 21 March 1992. But the doctor in charge said that since Theresa had some brainstem function, she

was not brain dead and he could not remove her organs. Together with Justin Pearson, the baby's father, Campo went to court to try to get a declaration that organs could be removed, but Judge Estella Moriaty refused, saying that "death is a fact, not an opinion", and that she could not authorize anyone to take Baby Theresa's life to save another child, "no matter how short or unsatisfactory the life of Baby Theresa might be".

Singer (1995)

Q2 How far do you agree, or disagree, with Judge Moriaty's decision? How would you defend her decision from a philosophical and ethical point of view?

Q3 In your view, is a belief in the sanctity of life consistent with:
(a) eating meat (b) supporting capital punishment
(c) declaring war?

Sanctity of life vs quality of life

Whilst death may be a fact, to quote Judge Moriaty, it is also a process – as is birth. Both events take time, and this creates problems for those who believe in the sanctity of life, in that it gives medical technology more opportunity to intervene actively in the process. Technology enables medical professionals to bring to term a foetus that in the past nature might have aborted, and to

keep 'alive' a patient who is 'braindead'. Faced with ethical uncertainty, doctors increasingly turn to the law for guidance, as in the case of Baby C, who was born eight weeks prematurely and then caught a virulent form of meningitis.

A profoundly brain-damaged three-month old girl should be taken off the ventilator keeping her alive and be allowed to die in peace, England's senior family judge said yesterday.

Sir Stephen Brown, president of the High Court's family division, said Baby C's future was hopeless. "It is a terrible thing to have to say … it is almost a living death."

The prognosis was that she would never develop beyond the level of a six-week-old baby, would be blind and deaf. She had a life expectancy of up to two years. However, she would suffer distress and pain from the treatment, and also if she were left without treatment.

The judge said the parents, who were in court, had faced the situation bravely and recognized what was in the best interests of their child.

Clare Dyer *The Guardian* 4 April 1996

Q4 To what extent does this case, and Sir Stephen's verdict, give support to Singer's view that the "sanctity of life" ethic is out of date? How would you defend Sir Stephen's verdict, from a philosophical and ethical standpoint?

Death

Local cell and tissue decay	Loss of brain function (brain-wave activity)	Cessation of breathing	Fall of body temperature to ambient level (algor mortis)	Body discoloration (livor mortis)

Persistent Vegetative State (PVS)

| Irretrievable loss of consciousness | Cessation of heartbeat and peripheral pulse | Stoppage of blood circulation | Stiffening of skeletal muscle (rigor mortis) | Putrefaction/ dehydration |

| Late 20th-century understanding of 'living death' | Harvard Brain Death Committee definition of death (1968) | Clinical death as historically determined |

At the beginning of this section, the question was asked: "When does a living entity become, or cease to be, a 'person'?" Jonathan Glover's answer is challenging: "The prospect for drawing a satisfactory line round 'being a person' is poor … being a person is a matter of degree."

It is Singer's view that the "sanctity of life" ethic should be abandoned in favour of a "quality of life" ethic. He offers a provisional rewriting of the rules:

Five old commandments

1 *Treat all human life as of equal worth.*

2 *Never intentionally take human life.*

3 *Never take your own life, and always try to prevent others taking theirs.*

4 *Be fruitful and multiply.*

5 *Treat all human life as always more precious than any non-human life.*

Five new commandments

1 *Recognize that the worth of human life varies.*

2 *Take responsibility for the consequences of your decisions.*

3 *Respect a person's desire to live or die.*

4 *Bring children into the world only if they are wanted.*

5 *Do not discriminate on the basis of species.*

Q5 Give your own definition of a 'person'.

Q6 Discuss any or all of Singer's new commandments.

Fenwick, Helen (1998) *Civil Liberties* (2nd edn) London: Cavendish Publishing

Glover, Jonathan (1977) *Causing Death and Saving Lives* London: Penguin Books

Singer, Peter (1995) *Rethinking Life and Death* Oxford: OUP

Part 2 Rights and duties

Philosophers have always sought to arrive at their positions using reason, logic and detailed linguistic analysis. In practice, philosophers have resorted to *common sense*, but the opinions that they form are more *coherent* than most.

The role of the state

Ever since Plato, philosophers have tried to work out a coherent view as to the proper relationship between the state and its citizens.

For **Thomas Hobbes** (1588–1679), the state was a *referee*, holding warring citizens apart; it represented legitimate force. For **John Locke** (1632–1704) and **Jean Jacques Rousseau** (1712–78), the state and its citizens were parties to a *social contract*: both conceded rights, and acknowledged duties, in the interests of peace and justice.

Political philosopher **John Rawls** (1921–) has revived the social contract theory of justice:

> *Justice is the first virtue of social institutions, as truth is of systems of thought.*
> *The concept of justice I take to be defined by the role of its principles in assigning rights and duties, and in defining the appropriate division of social advantages.*
> *A society is properly arranged when its institutions maximize the net balance of satisfaction.*
> *Just as it is rational for one man to maximize the fulfilment of his system of desires, it is right for a society to maximize the net balance of satisfaction taken over all of its members.*
> *This view of social co-operation is the consequence of extending to society the principle of choice for one man.*
>
> John Rawls (1972)

Q1 Explain what you think Rawls means by "the net balance of satisfaction"? What are the "social institutions" involved in achieving this balance?

Basic rights and natural duties

Rawls defined the "basic liberties", or rights, of citizens and gave examples of what he called "natural duties".

Rights

- Political liberty (the rights to vote and be eligible for political office) together with freedom of speech and assembly
- Liberty of conscience and freedom of thought
- Freedom of the person along with the right to hold (personal) property
- Freedom from arbitrary arrest and seizure as defined by the concept of the rule of law.

Duties

- The duty to help one another when in need or jeopardy, provided that one can do so without excessive risk or loss to oneself

- The duty not to harm or injure one another
- The duty not to inflict unnecessary suffering.

The right to hold opinions – freedom of thought – has long been recognized as one of the fundamental rights in a democratic society. **John Stuart Mill** (1806–73) describes the silencing of one man's opinion as robbing both the person holding the opinion and those doing the silencing (see also Concept G). But the freedom to *hold* an opinion is one thing; the freedom to *express* that opinion is another; and the freedom to *act* upon it is different again.

> *No one pretends that actions should be as free as opinions. The liberty of the individual must be thus far limited; he must not make himself a nuisance to other people.*
>
> John Stuart Mill On Liberty 1859

Q2 Rawls is quite specific in respect of rights (to vote, to own property, etc.), but both he and Mill emphasize the negative duty of not doing harm to others. Make a list of positive duties that fall to citizens in a democratic society.

Conflicts of interests

In a mature democracy, the social contract is not just between one group of citizens and another; rather there are many contracts, between many groups, to cover multiple cases where there may be a conflict of interests. The following studies examine two cases where there is such a conflict.

Case Study 1: Fox-hunting

Supporters of fox-hunting claim that:

- foxes are pests, and hunting with hounds is the most humane way of culling them
- hunting is a part of the rural economy and of long tradition
- banning hunting would infringe their rights as citizens.

Opponents of hunting claim that:

- animals have rights just as humans do
- hunting is a cruel, outmoded sport, unworthy of a civilized society.

The philosopher and farmer Roger Scruton argues that animals are not moral beings (a cat is not doing wrong when it kills a mouse), therefore, they have neither moral duties nor moral rights. Human beings have both. Scruton defends fox-hunting on the grounds that it perpetuates the "harmony of the natural world":

We must discharge our responsibilities wisely and humanely, showing sympathy for all species which do not unduly threaten us. We must extend our sympathy not to individuals only, but to species and to the needs of species in a world of harsh competition for survival. When it comes to pests we should try to live with them on respectful terms, and to kill them humanely, rather than to engage in those wars of extermination, which threaten everything. And we should cultivate piety – the virtue placed so vividly before us by Wordsworth. We have no God-given right to do as we like with the natural world, but a God-given duty to preserve it.

General Studies, No.2, January 2001, Philip Allan Updates
(originally from: *Animal Rights and Wrongs*, 2000, Metro)

It has been alleged that overturning the rights of hunters to hunt may infringe the European Convention on Human Rights. There is no doubt at all that it contravenes John Stuart Mill's maxim that "The sole end for which mankind are warranted individually or collectively, in interfering with the liberty of action of any of their number, is self-protection".

Q3 Identify the groups who have (a) a direct, and (b) an indirect interest in this issue. Does the interest, or right, of one group outweigh the interest or right of others?

Q4 Vegetarians cannot prevent the slaughter of animals for food, because they are in a minority in our society. Would they have a right to ban meat eating if they were in the majority?

Q5 How, if we accept Mill's maxim, can (a) hunt sabotage, and (b) a ban on hunting be justified?

Case Study 2: Justice seen to be done

In 1993, two 10-year old boys, Robert Thompson and Jon Venables, abducted James Bulger, nearly 3, in a Liverpool shopping centre, while his mother's back was turned. They led him along two miles of streets to a little-used railway line, where they stoned and beat him to death. The public was scandalized. Had the boys not been given the utmost protection, angry crowds would almost certainly have meted out the same treatment to them. The pair were ordered to be detained "at Her Majesty's Pleasure" for a minimum of eight years. The Lord Chief Justice raised this to 10 years. In 1994, the then Home Secretary Michael Howard raised the term again, to 15 years. Following a ruling of the European Court, sentencing was made the entire responsibility of judges, in March 2000. Lord Chief Justice Woolf reviewed the case of Thompson and Venables, among others, and recommended that they be released to begin the new lives, with new identities, for which they had been carefully prepared while in custody.

Here are two views expressed in the *Daily Mail* of 27 October 2000.

The enormity of the offence is reason enough for the profound public unease over the ruling yesterday by the Lord Chief Justice, Lord Woolf. Robert Thompson and Jon Venables will probably be freed early next year, having served less than eight years in detention.

And yet there are arguments on the side of mercy. At 10 years old, the killers' moral characters were not fully formed. By all accounts, they have come to recognize the gravity of their crime and nobody would wish to see a penal system that doesn't allow for redemption.

But when all that has been said, eight years is lamentably low on the scale of punishments demanded by their crime. Justice has not been seen to be done …

The hurt inflicted on the Bulger family is already apparent. Now they are devastated by yet another ruling from a judicial system which has badly let them down. Their sentence will never end.

Daily Mail Comment

[The release of Thompson and Venables] will not please those people who like to nurse their anger. For them, forgiveness is wet and redemption fraudulent.

But if anger is not leashed by justice, it will beget self-righteousness and moral myopia. That is what justice is for, to find the even hand and dissolve wrath in reason …

The feelings of James's parents, however, reside at a level far deeper than anger. They have experienced the unfathomable pain of having their son snatched from them and destroyed.

Their bereavement is eternal, their torment unmitigated by time. They are bound to think that the killers should likewise suffer interminably, and who dare blame them? …

The sooner they are able to forget these individuals, or recognize that they are no longer the people they were, the better they will be able to recover.

Brian Masters

Q6 Whose interests are at stake here, and what weight should be attached to their interests?

Q7 "Justice must be seen to be done." What is meant by this? Is there potentially a conflict between justice being seen to be done and justice actually being done?

Rawls, John (1972) *A Theory of Justice*, Oxford: Oxford University Press

Part 3 Direct action

The general public's sense of justice is a shifting thing. It did not outrage the public's sense of justice until the 1960s that those who attempted suicide and failed should be brought to court. It did not outrage the public's sense of justice until the 1990s that a man who raped his wife was not arrested. The law was changed in both cases to reflect the changing sense of what is acceptable and what is not. Sometimes a change in the law modifies public opinion, as the law concerning capital punishment has gradually done; most often, perhaps, it is public opinion that changes the law.

Changes in public opinion

What brings about a change in public opinion? One possibility is direct action – perhaps civil disobedience – taken by individuals or groups. Consider the following two cases:

In the 1980s, the CND activist Bruce Kent was arrested at the US nuclear base at Sculthorpe, with a pair of wire-cutters. He was about to cut the perimeter wire. He was charged with intent to commit criminal damage.

His defence was that the threat to use nuclear weapons was contrary to international law, and that his intent was to obstruct the commission of a crime. The judge ruled that this defence was irrelevant. The jury, accordingly, found Kent guilty as charged.

In 2000, Lord Melchett, of Greenpeace, was arrested, with others, following their destruction of a field of genetically modified (GM) maize. He was charged with actual criminal damage.

His defence was that their actions were necessary to prevent a still greater harm: the release of "contaminated" seed into the environment. The judge allowed this defence, and the jury found Lord Melchett not guilty. He was acquitted.

Q1 Why is it, do you think, that two such similar cases had quite different outcomes? Did public opinion have any part to play?

Direct action has a long, and some would say honourable, tradition in the United Kingdom; a notable example is that of the Suffragettes in the first two decades of the 20th century, whose campaign for voting rights for women included concerted direct action. More recent examples include the following:

1981	Riots in Brixton, Southall and Liverpool Toxteth
1984/5	Battles between miners and police, notably at Orgreave
1990	Protests against the poll tax
1993	Obstruction of motorway building at Twyford Down
1994	Protests against the M11 at Wanstead and the M65 at Blackburn
1995	Demonstrations against the export of live animals
1999	Protests against the World Trade Organization in Seattle and London
2000	Blockade of petrol refineries by farmers and hauliers

Q2 What other direct action can you think of that has taken place at particular times or that is ongoing?

Q3 How successful is direct action in changing public opinion and the law? Was it the Suffragettes' campaign that won women the vote or did other factors play a part? What about the more recent instances?

Direct action: a non-absolute right?

Article 11 of the European Convention on Human Rights provides for Freedom of Association and Assembly. It is this article that is invoked by those who join in public protest. Just as there have to be limits on the Freedom of Expression (Article 10), so there have to be some limits on the Freedom of Assembly, as Helen Fenwick (legal writer) explains:

Clearly the State has a duty to protect citizens from the attentions of the mob. The need to give weight to these interests explains the general acceptance of freedom of assembly as a non-absolute right even though it may be that violent protest is most likely to bring about change …

The individual right to assemble to make public protest is bolstered by the interests justifying freedom of speech – furthering the search for truth and the participation of the citizen in the democracy …

It is clear that these justifications are not equally present in relation to all forms of what may loosely be termed protest. The argument from democracy most clearly supports peaceful assemblies or marches which use speech in some form to persuade others, including the authorities, to a particular point of view. If the group seeks not to persuade others but to bring about the object in question by direct action, the democratic process may be said to have been circumvented rather than underpinned …

However, some forceful action may not be intended in itself to bring about the object in question directly, but may be used as a desperate expedient to draw attention to a cause where peaceful means have failed.

Helen Fenwick (1998)

Q4 Why is freedom of assembly a "non-absolute right"?

Q5 When is protest democratic and when may it be anti-democratic? Where does direct action fit into the notion of civic rights and duties?

Breaking the law

The issue of direct action becomes most controversial at the point where direct action involves criminal action. Those breaking the law often claim justification on the grounds that the law is wrong and their action is based on a higher moral authority. Others claim that the law must be upheld at all costs: the alternative being anarchy. Ann Mallalieu, Labour life-peer, and President of the Countryside Alliance, was highly critical of the destruction of GM maize by Greenpeace:

I do not believe that it is right, whatever the provocation, to break the law ... It was not the poll tax riots which changed government policy but the non-cooperation of taxpayers in such numbers that enforcement became impossible for the authorities.

The Independent on Sunday 1 October 2000

However, those who refused to pay their poll tax were breaking the law no less than those who caused damage in the riots. So are there circumstances when breaking the law can be justified? The following four cases, reported in the newspapers, examine this question.

A

Legalization or criminalization?

Being almost a septuagenarian, my partner rolled our celebratory joints shortly after Ann Widdecombe's* clarion call for zero tolerance on drugs. This old Labour codger is deeply indebted to the charismatic representative of the self-styled party of law and order for making this quite idiotic pronouncement. The prospect of this very respectable retired public servant (and former magistrate) being fined and criminalized for smoking cannabis in privacy, having been belatedly introduced to this very pleasurable pursuit for the first time earlier this year, is mind-boggling.

*Then Conservative Shadow Home Secretary   Name and address supplied
The Guardian 7 October 2000

B

Greenpeace boards disused rig

Police in Aberdeen will today meet Shell executives to draw up plans to tackle 10 Greenpeace demonstrators who have occupied a disused North Sea oil platform, writes John Arlidge.

The environmentalists, who scaled the Brent Spar platform 120 miles Northeast of Shetland on Sunday, said yesterday that they would remain on board until the oil company abandoned plans to dispose of the decaying structure by 'sinking' it offshore.

They argue that the tanker loading-bay is contaminated with more than 100 tons of toxic and radioactive material, including cadmium and arsenic. Sinking it, instead of towing it inshore for destruction on land, would cause 'irreparable damage to the marine environment'.

The Guardian 2 May 1995

Q6 What (if anything) makes the protest of the pot-smoker different from the refusal to pay poll tax?

Q7 In what sense (if any) were the Greenpeace demonstrators breaking the law?

C

The Government has to stand up to the bullying of the fuel protesters

This is a defining moment for the Government when it must show that it will not permit policy to be made on the streets. If Mr Brown does the right thing and refuses to cut fuel duty, we will be treated to the disruptive activity of a minority of road hauliers, farmers and other special-interest groups. This time we can be sure that ministers will be better prepared than they were in September. They have made no secret of the lengths to which they will go – including training a thousand troops to take over tanker-driving duties – to protect us from an arrogant minority ...

The Government surely hopes to weaken the resolve of the protesters; it is right to do so. The militants need to know that the first duty of any government is to uphold the rule of law.

The Independent 2 November 2000

D

Roads Protesters 'reclaim' high street

Five hundred anti-roads protesters took over a main route in London yesterday as part of a new campaign to reclaim the streets for pedestrians and cyclists.

Camden High Street in north London was blocked and a half-mile stretch turned into a giant open-air party.

Jugglers, mime artists and fire-eaters entertained the crowds while bunting, flags and banners were strewn between lamp-posts and shops.

Three specially provided cars were ceremonially destroyed by the protesters to show their determination to overthrow what they see as the tyranny of the motor vehicle.

Picnic tables were set up and food doled out to passers-by. A 200-yard stretch was carpeted and a rainbow zebra crossing unfurled across the road.

Within minutes of the street being occupied, thousands more who had been happily shopping in the market nearby spilled on to the road, joining the party. The event was the result of two weeks of planning by Reclaim the Streets.

Danny Penman The Independent 15 May 1995

Q8 The Independent refers to the fuel protesters as an "arrogant minority". How far might this description fit any protest group – Reclaim the Streets, for example?

Q9 Did the Reclaim the Streets protesters exceed the limits of freedom of expression?

Fenwick, Helen (1998) *Civil Liberties* (2nd edn) London: Cavendish Publishing Ltd

Values

A definition

Tracing the use of a word to its Latin root gives an opportunity to reflect on its contemporary usage. The word *value*, and several words similar to it, comes from the Latin verb *valere*, which has at least three layers of meaning, literal and figurative:

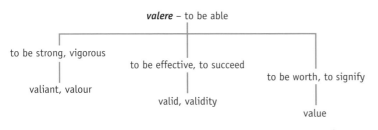

valere – to be able

to be strong, vigorous — valiant, valour

to be effective, to succeed — valid, validity

to be worth, to signify — value

What we value, we attach importance to; we measure its worth. Naturally enough, we have always tended to measure this worth in money-units. Hence, Oscar Wilde's definition of cynicism:

> Cecil Graham: What is a cynic?
>
> Lord Darlington: A man who knows the price of everything and the value of nothing.
>
> Lady Windermere's Fan 1892

And hence our talk of the face *value* of a bill of exchange; the surrender *value* of a bond; shareholder *value*; *value* for money; cash-*value*; and *value*-added tax.

A ten-pound note has no *intrinsic* value; the face, the signature and the watermark on it give it *extrinsic* value to the exchange value of ten pounds. A statement (such as a promise) has no intrinsic value, either – a judgement must be made as to how far the speaker can be trusted:

> Any general statement is like a cheque drawn on a bank. Its value depends on what there is to meet it.
>
> **Ezra Pound** (poet and cultural critic, 1885–1972) *The ABC of Reading* 1934

Society and values

Sometimes the word *value* has negative connotations. A contrast is made between a *fact-statement* and a *value-judgement*. The sociologist, **Max Weber** (1864–1920), claimed that if sociology was to be a science, it must be free from value-judgements. For inferences to be valid, they must be value-free, or value-neutral.

> **Q1** Is this possible? Can conclusions be drawn about poverty, inequality of access to education, suicide rates and so on, without making value-judgements?

When value is discussed in a positive sense, it is often in the plural – *values*. When **William Ralph Inge** (1860–1954) stated in 1917

that "the aim of education is the knowledge not of facts, but of values" (see Concept A), he was not decrying facts, he was elevating values.

During her time as Prime Minister, Margaret Thatcher often invoked the notion of values, in the form of Christian values, family values, even Victorian values:

> I was asked whether I was trying to restore Victorian values. I said straight out I was. And I am.
>
> Margaret Thatcher (1983)

She liked to think of herself, and to be thought of as, a 'conviction politician', whose values were manifest in all that she said and did:

> Me? A cold-war warrior? Well, yes – if that's how they wish to interpret my defence of values and freedoms fundamental to our way of life.
>
> Margaret Thatcher (1976)

> **Q2** What do you think these values were that Mrs Thatcher was resolved to defend?
>
> **Q3** Mrs Thatcher often drew (grudging) admiration from opponents. Why do you think this was?

Hierarchy of values

Just as needs can be classified according to whether they are basic (physical) or sophisticated (intellectual), as in Maslow's Hierarchy of Needs (see Unit 3, part 3), so values can be classified as 'lower order' and 'higher-order'. Values might be described as the mirror image of needs.

A hierarchy of values

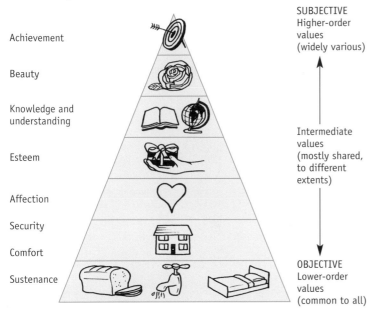

Achievement — SUBJECTIVE Higher-order values (widely various)

Beauty

Knowledge and understanding

Esteem — Intermediate values (mostly shared, to different extents)

Affection

Security

Comfort

Sustenance — OBJECTIVE Lower-order values (common to all)

> **Q4** What is beautiful to you, and what constitutes an achievement? If you were to ask friends or relatives this question, what would their answers be?
>
> **Q5** "There are no objective values" (Mackie, 1977). Do you agree?

Life: the ultimate value?

It is becoming increasingly difficult to claim that all life is intrinsically valuable (see Unit 8, part 1). Life is, perhaps, the ultimate value – yet sometimes a choice has to be made between death and a certain sort of life. This involves making a value-judgement, or giving an *opinion*, as Lord Justice Ward did in the case of the conjoined twins Jodie and Mary. Jodie's heart and lungs kept Mary alive, but the strain of supporting both of them would kill Jodie in a matter of weeks or months. As Roman Catholics, the parents believed that the lives of both were equally sacred. They could not, therefore, consent to an operation that would save one baby at the other's expense.

Here is an extract from Lord Justice Ward's judgement, in which he ruled in favour of the operation to save Jodie:

Balancing scales of life and death

The sanctity of life doctrine is so enshrined as a fundamental principle of law and commands such respect from the law that I am compelled to accept that each life has inherent value in itself, however grave the impairment of some of the body's functions may be. I am satisfied that Mary's life, desperate as it is, still has its own ineliminable value and dignity …

I have to balance the welfare of one child against the other. Into each scale goes their right to life. This right is universal: we all share it equally. The scales remain in balance. I am not entitled to value the quality of one human life as worth more than another's and I do not do so. But it is legitimate to look at the actual condition of the children as they are and assess their expectations when determining whether it is worth treating them. The worthwhileness of the proposed treatment is a legitimate factor to weigh. For the reasons given, the treatment is not worthwhile for Mary for one cannot escape from the fact that Mary has always been fated for early death: her capacity to live has been fatally compromised. Though Mary has a right to live, she has little right to be alive.

The Guardian 23 September 2000

> **Q6** What different (or *whose* different) values appear to be in conflict here?
>
> **Q7** Do you agree that life is the highest value? Is there anything of equally high, or higher, value?

Mackie, J.L. (1977) *Ethics* London: Penguin Books

Equal opportunities

Legislating for equality

Article 1 of the United Nations Universal Declaration of Human Rights states that: 'All human beings are born free and equal in dignity and right'. The case of Jodie and Mary, the conjoined twins (see Concept H), illustrates the brute fact that all human beings are not born equal. One twin had a functioning heart and lungs, and the other did not. Had Mary lived, her rights would have been protected, in a formal sense, by Article 2 (and by Article 14 of the European Convention, based upon it):

> *Everyone is entitled to all rights and freedoms set forth in this Declaration, without distinction of any kind, such as race, colour, sex, language, religion, political or other opinion, national or social origin, property, birth or other status.*
>
> Article 2

Although these Articles state emphatically the rights of the individual, to be effective they needed to be enshrined in national legislation. Thus, in Britain, the following Acts of Parliament were passed:

The Equal Opportunities Commission

1971 Equal Pay Act

1975 Sex Discrimination Act (setting up the Equal Opportunities Commission – EOC)

1976 Race Relations Act (setting up the Commission for Racial Equality – CRE)

1981 Disabled Persons Act

1995 Disability Discrimination Act

How effective have these acts been? They can help to prevent discrimination on one or more of the grounds referred to in Article 2 of the UN declaration, but changing the way people think, that is, tackling prejudice, is an altogether harder task.

> **Q1** In what ways can Acts of parliament (given permanent effect in the EOC and CRE) help to prevent prejudice? What are the problems involved in doing this?

What it means to be British

In 2000, a report by the Runnymede Trust, the UK-based independent think-tank on ethnicity and cultural diversity, complained of a tendency to use the word 'British' to *exclude*, rather than *include*. Clements and Spinks in their publication, *The Equal Opportunities Guide*, make a similar point:

> *It is the white, heterosexual male majority with access to forms of power (particularly political power) in our community who have established and who continue to define what is to be considered culturally typical or normal. They hold the monopoly on British culture and what it means.*
>
> *Black people, women, people with disabilities, single parents, members of the gay community, all of these people and others can, at certain times, find themselves marginalized (pushed to the edge of our society) and isolated in some way from the majority ... This may show itself in the way that members of the majority group talk about and behave towards members of these other groups, or it may reveal itself in a closing down of opportunities enjoyed by the majority, such as poorer education, restricted opportunities for work, lack of promotion or a lack of access to services and facilities.*
>
> Phil Clements and Tony Spinks (1996)

The diagram below gives a rough illustration of how British society is made up. (It does not include every 'minority' group; nor does it show all the possible overlaps between groups.)

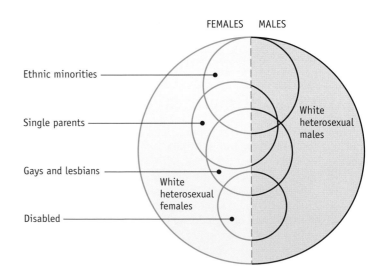

> **Q2** If the large circle represents the British people, comment on the use of the word 'majority' by Clements and Spinks.
>
> **Q3** What 'subgroups' of white heterosexual males might not have access to political power?
>
> **Q4** "We are all members of one minority or another". Discuss.

Inequality of opportunity: the evidence

Consider the following tables:

A

People in households living below 60% median income: by economic status and ethnic group, 1996–98

Great Britain						%
	White	Black	Indian	Pakistani/ Bangladeshi	Other	All
All households	17	28	27	64	29	18

ETHNIC MINORITIES

Q5 What reasons can you think of for these differences in levels of income across ethnic groups?

Q6 What are the key points arising from this table in terms of differences between (a) boys and girls (b) different ethnic groups? How far are these differences explained by inequality of opportunities?

B

Examination achievements of pupils in schools: by gender and ethnic origin, 1998

England and Wales						%
	5 or more GCSEs grades A*–C		1–4 GCSEs grades A*–C		No graded GCSEs	
	M	F	M	F	M	F
White	43	51	25	25	7	6
Black	23	35	24	42	7	7
Indian	52	55	23	28	2	3
Pakistani/Bangladeshi	29	32	29	45	6	6
Other groups	37	52	28	31	11	3
All groups	42	51	25	26	7	6

GENDER

C

Population of working age: by gender and social class, Spring 1999

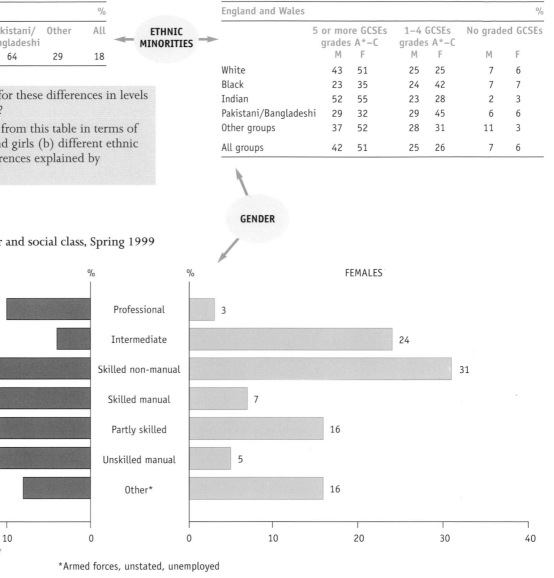

*Armed forces, unstated, unemployed

SOCIAL CLASS

D

Participation rates in higher education: by social class, 1998–99 in Great Britain

	%
Professional	72
Intermediate	45
Skilled non-manual	29
Skilled manual	18
Partly skilled	17
Unskilled	13
All social classes	31

Q7 What factors do you think explain the differences shown in Table C? How big a factor is inequality of opportunity?

Q8 What might be done to overcome the unequal opportunities seen in Table D?

Clements, Phil and Spinks, Tony (1996) *The Equal Opportunities Guide* (2nd edn) London: Kogan Page

Religion

Throughout this book, questions arise about the nature of knowledge and the sorts of evidence that underpin that knowledge. In looking at religion, this unit deals with evidence that lies firmly at the 'softer' end of the continuum described in the Introduction. The 'certainty' of religious faith is undoubtedly one of the most subjective forms of knowledge human beings can possess. This unit explores the nature of that faith and the influence it has had, both on society and on individuals.

From religious animal to secular society

As attendance at worship steadily falls and the authority of religious leaders ebbs away, few people would disagree with the claim that Britain in particular, and the 'West' in general, is an increasingly *secular* society. But just how religious have we ever been?

The Greek philosopher, **Aristotle** (384–322 BCE) said that: "man is a social/political animal"; **Edmund Burke** (parliamentarian, 1729–97) said something similar:

Man is by his constitution a religious animal.

Reflections on the Revolution in France 1790

Burke appears to have been right if he meant that human beings have always had gods. This is a point made by Karen Armstrong, in her book, *A History of God*:

Early faiths expressed the wonder and mystery that seems always to have been an essential component of the human experience of this beautiful yet terrifying world ... It was not tacked on to a primordially secular nature by manipulative kings and priests, but was natural to humanity. Indeed, our current secularism is an entirely new experience, unprecedented in human history ...
The sense of presence, ecstasy and dread in the presence of a reality – called Nirvana, the One, Brahman, or God – seems to be a state of mind and a perception that is natural and endlessly sought by human beings.

Karen Armstrong (1993)

Q1 Why, according to this account, is it 'natural' that human beings should always have been religious?

Q2 How would you account for what Armstrong calls "our current secularism"?

Perhaps, in fact, Burke meant that religion – and he would have meant the *Protestant* religion – is essential to political stability. This was certainly the view of **Francis Bacon** (1561–1626), who became Lord Chancellor under James I and had a clear interest in understanding the political role of religion:

The four pillars of government ... (which are religion, justice, counsel, and treasure).

Francis Bacon *Essays* 1597

Scottish historian **Thomas Carlyle** (1795–1881) expressed a similar view in describing civilization:

The three great elements of modern civilization: Gunpowder; Printing, and the Protestant Religion.

Thomas Carlyle *Critical and Miscellaneous Essays* 1838

Thus religion – in England at any rate – was thought of as having civilizing effects, as being part of the equipment of an English gentleman. It smoothed and polished a man's sharp edges:

Educate men without religion and you make them but clever devils.

Duke of Wellington (soldier and statesman, 1769–1852)

What we must look for here is, 1st, religious and moral principles; 2ndly, gentlemanly conduct; 3rdly, intellectual ability.

Thomas Arnold (headteacher of Rugby School, 1795–1842) *Arnold of Rugby*

A public or private matter?

There has always been something of a split in Britain between those 'enthusiasts', Catholic and Protestant, who want religion to be a public thing, and those who want to believe (or not believe) in private:

Let every Christian, as much as in him lies, engage himself openly and publicly, before all the world, in some mental pursuit for the Building of Jerusalem.

William Blake (artist and poet, 1757–1827) *Jerusalem*

It would be gain to the country were it vastly more ... fierce in its religion than at present it shows itself to be.

John Henry Newman (theologian, later Cardinal, 1801–90)
History of my Religious Opinions 1833–9

We have in England a particular bashfulness in everything that regards religion.

Joseph Addison (dramatist and essayist, 1672–1719)

Things have come to a pretty pass when religion is allowed to invade the sphere of private life.

Lord Melbourne (statesman and Prime Minister, 1779–1848)

Religion is in the heart, not in the knees.

Douglas Jerrold (English dramatist, 1803–57)

Q3 What do you think Jerrold means? Do you agree with him?

Q4 What are the dangers of organizing religion around public displays of faith, rather than encouraging private worship?

Religious affiliation in Britain today

What is the current state of religious adherence in Britain? The 10-yearly census includes questions about religious affiliation and gives 'membership' numbers of religious bodies:

Table A

Religious affiliation in the UK			Thousands
	1971	1981	1991
Christian			
Trinitarian* churches			
Roman Catholic	2 746	2 455	2 198
Anglican	2 987	2 180	1 728
Presbyterian	1 751	1 437	1 214
Other free churches	843	678	776
Methodist	673	540	478
Orthodox	191	203	266
Baptist	272	239	230
All Trinitarian churches	9 463	7 732	6 890
Non-Trinitarian churches			
Mormons	85	114	160
Jehovah's Witnesses	62	85	117
Other non-Trinitarian	138	154	182
All non-Trinitarian churches	285	353	459
Other religions			
Muslim	130	306	495
Sikh	100	150	250
Hindu	80	120	140
Jewish	120	111	101
Others	21	53	87
All other religions	451	740	1,073
All religions	10 199	8 825	8 422

* Trinitarian churches are Christian churches with a central belief in the Trinity, that is, the three-fold godhead of Father, Son and Holy Spirit. All the major Christian churches are Trinitarian.

Q5 Which Trinitarian church has suffered the biggest proportionate loss of members over the 20-year period?

Q6 Which religious group has enjoyed the biggest proportionate gain?

The certainty of religious knowledge

It was one of the non-Trinitarian churches that made the following claim to certain knowledge:

Knowledge
That Leads to Life!

Science and technology can sometimes be dazzling! Still, human knowledge has not made life secure and happy for most people. The only knowledge that can accomplish this is described in the Bible at John 17:3, which says: "This means everlasting life, their taking in knowledge of you, the only true God, and of the one whom you sent forth, Jesus Christ."

Such knowledge is found within the pages of the Bible. Although many express strong opinions regarding that sacred book, few have ever examined it for themselves. What about you?

Q7 This knowledge comes from a fundamentalist interpretation of the Bible, in other words, a belief that what is written in the Bible is the literal truth. Where might fundamentalists place their 'knowledge' on the continuum of hard/soft evidence?

What about the British public? Do they share the same certainty of faith? Respondents were asked, in 1998, which statement came closest to their belief about God. The figures are percentages.

Table B

I know God really exists and I have no doubt about it.	21
While I have doubts, I feel that I do believe in God.	23
I find myself believing in God some of the time, but not at others.	14
I don't believe in a personal God, but I do believe in a Higher Power of some kind.	14
I don't know whether there is a God, and I don't believe there is any way to find out.	15
I don't believe in God.	10
Not answered.	3

Q8 What sort of 'knowledge' is it that the Bible is said to give, and that 21 per cent of respondents say they have?

Q9 Which statement comes closest to your own position?

Q10 Does the message of Table B contradict, reinforce or have nothing to do with, the message of Table A?

Armstrong, Karen (1993) *A History of God* London: Mandarin Paperbacks

Part 1 Faith and faiths

These two pages examine what is meant by the word *faith* and gives an overview, in diagrammatic form, of some of the main faiths of the Western and Eastern worlds. Many of the names and terms may be unfamiliar to you, in which case this diagram may serve as a framework for your own research.

Christian churches

The history of Christianity is marked by two great divisions. The first was the so-called Great Schism of 1034, when the Western, Latin-speaking, Catholic (or, *universal*) Church and the Eastern, Greek-speaking, Orthodox (*right-thinking*) Church broke apart for good.

The second major division came in the Reformation of the 1500s, when reformers protested against what they called the abuses of the Roman Catholic church. Since then, one group after another has gone its separate way, following disagreement on a point of doctrine or practice. Some have even abandoned belief in the Trinity, the traditional foundation of Christian faith.

Q1 Does the branching of Christianity weaken it, or does it give it strength, allowing everyone to find something to suit them?

Christian churches

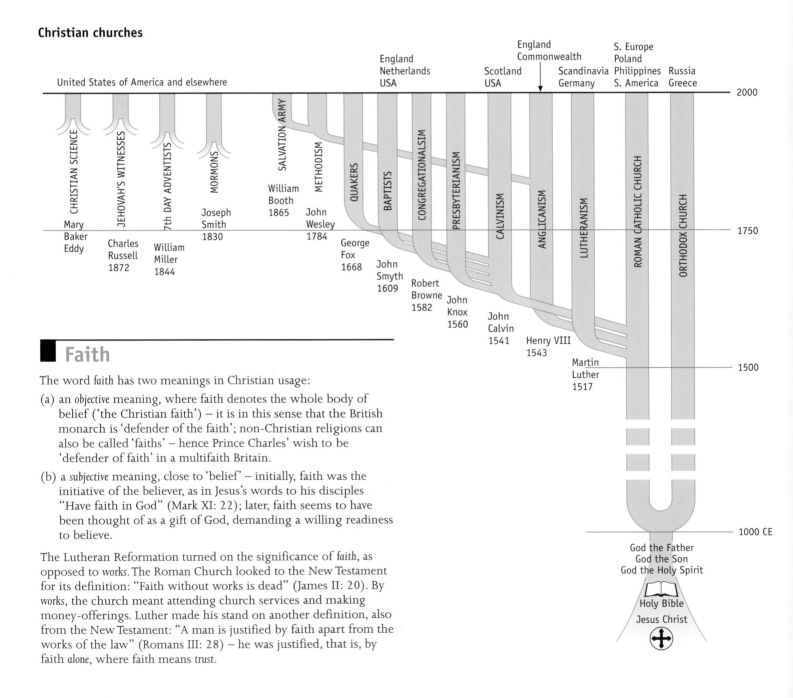

Faith

The word *faith* has two meanings in Christian usage:

(a) an *objective* meaning, where faith denotes the whole body of belief ('the Christian faith') – it is in this sense that the British monarch is 'defender of the faith'; non-Christian religions can also be called 'faiths' – hence Prince Charles' wish to be 'defender of faith' in a multifaith Britain.

(b) a *subjective* meaning, close to 'belief' – initially, faith was the initiative of the believer, as in Jesus's words to his disciples "Have faith in God" (Mark XI: 22); later, faith seems to have been thought of as a gift of God, demanding a willing readiness to believe.

The Lutheran Reformation turned on the significance of *faith*, as opposed to *works*. The Roman Church looked to the New Testament for its definition: "Faith without works is dead" (James II: 20). By *works*, the church meant attending church services and making money-offerings. Luther made his stand on another definition, also from the New Testament: "A man is justified by faith apart from the works of the law" (Romans III: 28) – he was justified, that is, by faith *alone*, where faith means *trust*.

Faith vs reason

Another long-standing debate concerns the relationship between *faith* and *reason*. The traditional view has been, in the philosopher Anthony Kenny's words, that:

… faith was not in conflict with reason but was a rational state of mind. Faith was a virtue permitting the mind access to truths which would otherwise be beyond its reach.

What is Faith? 1992

Q2 Is it your view that faith can give us knowledge?

Q3 In your view can religious faith be compared with the faith of the scientist making a hypothesis?

Eastern religions

The farther East one goes, the less there is one single god who is worshipped. Religion here is more concerned with the conduct of one's life and permeates that life more thoroughly. It then becomes much less easy (or worthwhile) to distinguish between religion and philosophy. India, the Indus River, Hindi the language, Hinduism – all have the same root in the one land. Vishnu, Rama, Ganesh, are not regarded by the more learned Hindus as separate gods, but as revelations (*avatars*) of the one spirit, Brahman.

When is a religion not a religion? One way of defining religion is as a system of faith in, and worship of, a superhuman controlling power. This definition is easy to apply to the three great *monotheistic* (that is, single-god) religions – Judaism, Christianity and Islam – but is does not sit comfortably with most of the Far Eastern religions. And where do so-called 'new-age' religions fit in? Believers in traditional religions would argue that these are simply a collection of weird, even dangerous, fads, but their type of spirituality is arguably meeting some kind of religious need.

Q4 Are socialism, humanism, consumerism (etc.) simply godless religions?

Q5 How do we square claims of growing secularism in the West with the surge in support for evangelical churches in the USA?

Q6 Is globalization (Westernization/Americanization) likely to be a threat to traditional religions? Or does it provide opportunities for them?

Eastern religions

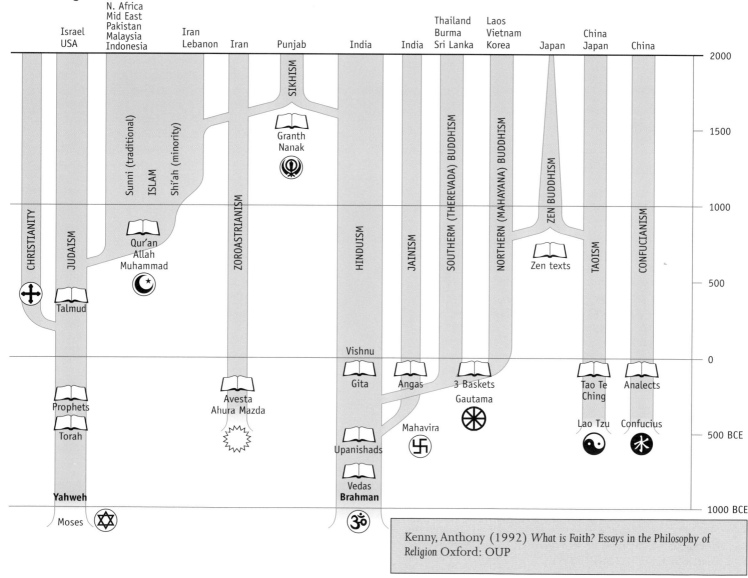

Kenny, Anthony (1992) *What is Faith? Essays in the Philosophy of Religion* Oxford: OUP

Part 2 Morals

In Concept H, values were defined as those aspects of life to which individuals and society attaches importance. What, then, are *morals* and how do they relate to values? These pages examine this question.

Values, morals and ethics

The connection between values, morals and ethics can be shown in a diagram, where *values* form an outer circle. Inside this circle is another circle representing *moral* values, in other words, values that determine the way people behave towards each other and their views about what constitutes good or bad behaviour. *Ethics* are morals that operate in particular, often professional, circumstances: thus, we speak of medical ethics, legal ethics and business ethics – moral values that govern the professionals' behaviour towards their clients.

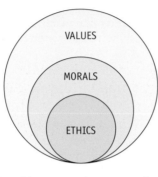

In practice, morals and ethics are often used interchangeably. Indeed, the word *morals* is used less than it used to be, perhaps because it has religious associations and, in an increasingly secular world, people are more familiar with the notion of ethics, as they have experience of these at a practical level in professional codes of conduct. Morality is now often limited to discussions of sexual behaviour – where 'bad' behaviour is considered 'immoral'.

Morals and religion

The claim has traditionally been made that the Western moral system is based on the teaching of Jesus and the Christian church. A Christian believer might say:

We have all been brought up, in the West, whether we were formally Christians or not, to believe that it is wrong to kill, to steal, to tell lies about each other; that we should respect our parents; that we should treat other people as we would want them to treat us. These are all ways of behaving that have come to us from the Ten Commandments, or from the life and teachings of Jesus. As God made us, we owe it to Him to live as He wanted us to live. To the extent that we do not do this, we make mistakes whose consequences are only too obvious. If we are lost in a moral maze, it is because we have set aside the compass that we had.

Q1 What do you make of this line of argument? Do you believe that without a Christian upbringing, people would inevitably be lost in a 'moral maze'?

Q2 How might an atheist or a humanist explain the existence of the Ten Commandments?

Q3 Think about the actions of a killer such as Hamilton who gunned down a class of schoolchildren in Dunblane, or of Robert Thompson and Jon Venables who beat two-year-old James Bulger to death. Is there an *evil* in their behaviour that can only be understood in religious terms?

The writer of the following passage was not a clergyman: he was an academic:

I suspect that ... God does not desire us to know for certain about his existence or otherwise, and believes that it is best for our moral state to remain in a measure of doubt. This is the condition of our freedom, of our having genuine and effective choice. If we knew for sure God existed and was almighty, we would not dare to oppose his will ... Accordingly, he has given us only hints of his existence. And the hints are even becoming fewer. The age of miracles (if it ever existed) is over; Charles Darwin has cast doubts upon the first chapters of Genesis; and churchmen no longer preach hellfire. The crutches of faith are being removed, one after another. We are being driven to a less naïve and more adult spirituality. Doubt is designedly part of our condition ...

We thus arrive at a curious paradox. Whereas the presence of evil seems to cast doubt upon the existence of God, it also indicates the necessity of religion. For there is no other hope of an improved ethic. In theory, one could be constructed and practised without any reference to God. An attempt to sketch one out was made by the utilitarian philosophers. But the weakness of such systems was pointed out by Plato long ago: "We cannot expect a whole nation to be philosophers". Right conduct is largely a matter of habit, and habits have to be formed early in life. We really cannot imagine young Johnny engaging in moral discourse at the age of three.

All the great religions of the world beckon us in much the same direction. The moral codes they prescribe are similar. In no case can we be sure of the truth of their theological and metaphysical bases. But we have no time to plumb controversy to its depths, either individually or collectively. Events keep moving on, and we do need to act. Are we, or are we not, on the side of the angels?

P.M. Burrows (1998)

Q4 "We cannot expect a whole nation to be philosophers." How does this demonstrate a weakness in moral systems that take no account of God, according to Burrows?

Q5 What does Burrows appear to believe that 'young Johnny' – and all other young people – really need by way of moral guidance? Do you agree?

An absolute moral law?

Is there an objective right and wrong? **Immanuel Kant** (1724–1804), a Christian and a philosopher, believed that there was. He held that we could deduce by reason alone that there are two moral imperatives or commands by which all human beings could live, whether or not they believed in God. These are:

- act in such a way that your action might be made a universal law

- treat all persons never merely as means to an end but always as ends in themselves.

So, for example, someone about to commit a spiteful or vicious act should think what the world would be like if spitefulness or viciousness were the norm. The second imperative comes close to the Golden Rule: treat others as you would have them treat you.

Q6 How well do you think Kant's moral imperatives serve as the basis for an objective, non-religious ethic?

The non-believer might be inclined to say something like the following about the relationship between religion and morals:

Every religion has had its own moral code, yet they are all fundamentally similar. This isn't surprising: we all prefer pleasure to pain; none of us wants to get hurt. Religious people might have claimed that their morals came from God – but if something's unreasonable (like giving a thief your coat as well as your jacket) or unacceptable (like sacrificing your only son), God can't make it right. We have to take responsibility for our own moral decisions, not take refuge in what 'God said'.

Q7 How far do you agree with the opinion above?

Absolutism vs relativism

A moral *absolutist* believes that there is one set of morals that is universally binding, whereas a moral *relativist* (in theory) believes that no one set of morals is better than any other.

The writer of the passage below is not an atheist or agnostic; he is a bishop – the Bishop of Edinburgh, the premier bishop of Scotland. Here he discusses the tension between moral absolutism and moral relativism:

We know that many of the systems that have used the concept of sin and unthinking obedience have been based upon structures of power and control, domination systems that have been intrinsically oppressive, so that the idea of sin itself was
5 *part of a mechanism of force designed to secure compliance to authority …*
   Morality is as much an art as a science and it calls for a certain versatility from us, that ability to improvise and respond to actual circumstances and particular situations …
10 *The challenge that faces us is to separate the basic principles that might help to guide us through what has been called the moral maze from the kind of absolute systems that claim to know the right answer to every moral dilemma that faces us …*
   When we start thinking about value systems we involve
15 *ourselves in conflicts that appear to have no simple solution. Human nature is so varied and the things we consider important are so different, that it is often impossible to do more than describe the values that are in conflict and let people make their own choices …*
20 *Most of us probably feel that somewhere beyond argument there is a unified theory of human nature and its values, and that if we all struggle hard enough we'll find it. Both experience and reflection contradict that. This, however, is not moral relativism. It is not the same thing at all as saying that*
25 *one attitude is no better or worse than any other. To say that values conflict with each other is not to say that there are no values at all, no fundamental principles that characterise us as human.*

Richard Holloway (1999)

Q8 What does Holloway mean when he says that the concept of sin was based on a structure of power and control (line 3)?

Q9 Is sin a purely religious concept? Can an atheist or humanist include a concept of sin (or an equivalent idea) in their moral system?

In Holloway's statement "when we start thinking about value systems we involve ourselves in conflicts that appear to have no simple solution" (lines 14–15), he begins to describe the difficulties behind moral relativism. It is a hard position to maintain, as few people, for example, would assert that a system of morals that allowed murder was as 'good' as one that outlawed it. However, most people would accept that both pro-abortion and anti-abortion arguments might be equally 'moral'.

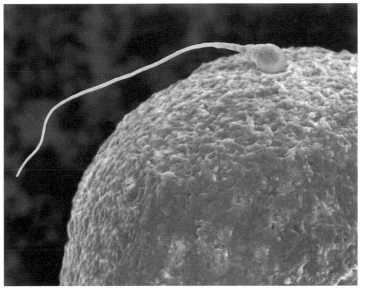

The moment of conception

Q10 Abortion is one controversial topic where people's views are determined by their moral values. Can you think of others?

Absolutism	Relativism
Objective morals	Subjective morals

Q11 Where would you place yourself on the line between moral abolutism and moral relativism?

Q12 What do you think are some of the 'fundamental principles that characterise us as human' (lines 27–28)?

Burrows, P.M. (1998) *Gospel of Doubt* Durham: The Pentland Press Ltd

Holloway, Richard (1999) *Godless Morality: Keeping Religion out of Ethics* Edinburgh: Canongate

Part 3 A balance sheet

Christianity has conferred many benefits on the Western world; it has also had many negative effects. Is it possible to weigh up the good against the bad? One way of doing this is by drawing up a balance sheet, with credits on one side and debits on the other. These pages suggest six credits and their corresponding debits. They are, all of them, open to question.

Salisbury Cathedral

CREDIT

The Bible

Above all, Christianity has given the Bible (to non-Jews), and, in particular, the New Testament. It has thus provided a history, poetry, and a stock of stories that have few rivals:

> *She brought forth her firstborn son, and wrapped him in swaddling clothes, and laid him in a manger; because there was no room for them in the inn.*
> *And there were in the same country shepherds abiding in the field, keeping watch over their flock by night.*
> *And, lo, the angel of the Lord came upon them, and the Glory of the Lord shone round about them: and they were sore afraid.*
>
> Luke II:7-9

Festivals and ceremonies

Christmas, Easter, Harvest, christenings, weddings, funerals, coronations … The Church marks the year, the life of the individual, and the life of the nation.

> *I take thee N to my wedded wife, to have and to hold from this day forward, for better for worse, for richer for poorer, in sickness and in health, to love and to cherish, till death us do part, according to God's holy ordinance; and thereto I plight thee my troth.*
>
> The Book of Common Prayer 1662

Q1 Is anything left of Christmas when 'God is dead'?

Knowledge and education

The Church fostered scholarship. **Thomas Aquinas** (1225–74) combined Christian and secular Greek knowledge. The first universities were church foundations, and the first schools were church schools. **John Colet** (c.1467–1519), **Sir Thomas More** (1478–1535) and **Desiderius Erasmus** (c.1466–1536) were churchmen and educationalists.

An ethic of love

> *You have heard that it was said "You shall love your neighbour and hate your enemy". But I say to you, love your enemies and pray for those who persecute you … For if you love those who love you, what reward have you? Do not even the tax collectors do the same?*
>
> Matthew V: 43-46

Q2 Why might churchmen have encouraged a 'simple faith' in their congregations?

Faith

> *Tis only noble to be good.*
> *Kind hearts are more than coronets*
> *And simple faith than Norman blood.*
>
> Alfred, Lord Tennyson 'Lady Clara Vere de Vere' 1842

Many hard lives were made bearable by the comforts of a 'simple faith', by the power of prayer, and the promise of heaven for those who had kept the faith.

Art

> *The new 'Gothic' style, to use the modern term, was perfected in the cathedrals of northern France, such as Laon, Senlis, Notre Dame de Paris, and Chartres, and from this region it spread to most parts of Western Europe. The churches provided a setting for worship, a processional space, and a home for the relics of the saints. Only fragments of the treasury of any great church remain from the Middle Ages, but there is enough to give a glimpse of the wealth which once accumulated there. Precious metals were used in profusion for reliquaries and altar furnishings, service-books were magnificently written and bound, and the making of vestments was a major art form.*
>
> Colin Morris in McManners 1990

Q3 List all the different arts and crafts that you can think of for which the Church has been a major patron, giving one example of each.

DEBIT

He who begins by loving Christianity better than Truth will proceed by loving his own sect of church better than Christianity, and end by loving himself better than all.

Samuel T. Coleridge *Aids to Reflection* 1825

Fundamentalism

Fundamentalism is not the same as either fanaticism or authoritarianism. Fundamentalists call for a return to basic scriptures or texts, supposed to be read in a literal manner, and they propose that the doctrines derived from such a reading be applied to social, economic or political life. Fundamentalism gives new vitality and importance to the guardians of tradition. Only they have access to the 'exact meaning' of the texts. The clergy or other privileged interpreters gain secular as well as religious power ...

Fundamentalism is edged with the possibility of violence, and it is the enemy of cosmopolitan values.

Anthony Giddens (1999)

Q4 What do you suppose Giddens means when he calls fundamentalism "the enemy of cosmopolitan values"?

Q5 What instances of fundamentalism can you think of in today's world, both Christian and non-Christian?

Ritual

I am a poor man, but I would gladly give ten shillings to find out who sent me the insulting Christmas card I received this morning.

George and Weedon Grossmith *The Diary of a Nobody* 1894

Few people find ritual as insulting as this, but it has often been emptied of meaning by unthinking repetition.

Conservatism

The church has often taken conservative – even reactionary – positions when it felt itself challenged by progress. A famous case was that of Italian astronomer, **Galileo Galilei** (1564–1642), who was forced by torture to renounce his conviction that the earth moved round the sun.

Galileo's legendary words Eppur si muove ("but it does move all the same") have stood for the essentially progressive vitality of the forces against which Rome chose to set itself, the long-term sterility of the Church of the Counter-Reformation as it degenerated into a kind of spiritual ancien régime.

Patrick Collinson in McManners 1990

Q6 What is it that draws religion and science into conflict? Is it inevitable that science should pose a threat to religion?

Persecution

The ethic of love did not extend to 'heretics'; it did not extend to 'Mohammedans' during the Crusades; and it did not extend to large numbers of women branded as witches: 'The Counter-Reformation came to its maturity with the repression represented by the inquisition...

Collinson in McManners 1990

Wealth

The Church amassed great wealth – and it was not always very scrupulous about how it acquired it. Here is an example from late 19th-century America:

The Protestant critique of worldliness was muted in fashionable churches. The immensely wealthy entrepreneurs and corporate leaders – the Rockefellers and Drews, the Fisks and McCormicks and Vanderbilts, were church members and generous donors. Many of them endowed seminaries, colleges, universities, charities. Under their influence and tutelage, of course, it became difficult for clergy or lay prophets to call into question the ruthless acquisition of wealth, even ill-gotten gain.

Martin Marty in McManners 1990

Q7 How far is the Christian church guilty of a charge of 'worldliness' today?

Q8 What did Karl Marx mean by this famous metaphor? "Religion ... is the opium of the people."

Q9 Is the balance sheet drawn up here a fair one, in your view? Are there other factors that you would add, on either side?

Detail of St Bartholomew's Day Massacre, *by François Dubois*

Giddens, Anthony (1999) *Runaway World* London: Profile Books

McManners, John (ed.) (1990) *The Oxford Illustrated History of Christianity* Oxford: OUP

Belief

Man, my Lord, is a being born to believe.

Benjamin Disraeli (1864)

So said the British 19th-century statesman, **Benjamin Disraeli** (1804–81). These two pages examine the nature of belief – what it means to *believe* in something and whether there are different levels of belief.

Q1 Do you *believe* anything that you do not *know*, or cannot know – anything for which there could not, even in principle, be evidence?

Q2 The child who says "I believe in Father Christmas" is innocently guilty of wishful thinking. How much of what we believe as adults is wishful thinking?

Belief and faith

We associate *belief* with faith. Both words appear time and again in the New Testament: faith is mentioned 194 times, and belief (or some part of the verb 'believe') is mentioned 245 times.

Disraeli appears to have meant that humans need to believe in God, or gods – that this is a part of being human. To believe, in this sense, is to make what **Søren Kierkegaard** (philosopher, 1813–55) called "the leap of faith". It is to believe not merely in the absence of *facts*, but in defiance of reason.

Thomas, one of the 12 apostles, had not been with his companions when Jesus 'appeared' to them after his death; he said that he would only believe them when he could see Jesus for himself, and touch his wounds with his own fingers. When Jesus did 'reappear', he let 'Doubting Thomas' touch him, and he said:

Have you believed because you have seen me? Blessed are those who have not seen me, and yet believe.

John XX: 29

This sort of belief is formulated in the *creed* (from the Latin *credo* – I believe) recited by Christians at Morning and Evening Prayer.

I believe in God the Father Almighty, Maker of heaven and earth; And in Jesus Christ his only Son our Lord ...
I believe in the Holy Ghost; the Holy Catholick Church; the Communion of Saints; the Forgiveness of sins; the Resurrection of the body, and the life everlasting. Amen.

The people who recite this creed have no hard evidence for their belief. God does not make himself visible; no one can really know what happens after death or what is meant by eternal life. This belief certainly involves a leap of faith, but a cynic would argue that people are willing to make it for selfish reasons – because they don't want to face the possibility that when they die, that is simply the end.

Men are nearly always willing to believe what they wish.

Julius Caesar (100–44 BCE)

For what a man would like to be true, that he more readily believes.

Francis Bacon *Novum Organum* 1620

The 'miracle' of belief

The sceptical philosopher **David Hume** (1711–76) did not believe in miracles and he thought belief was a sort of miracle. He came as close as a man dared come in his day to asserting, not merely that belief is unreasonable, but that it is absurd:

The Christian religion not only was at first attended with miracles, but even at this day cannot be believed by any reasonable person without one. Mere reasoning is insufficient to convince us of its veracity: and whoever is moved by faith to assent to it, is conscious of a continued miracle in his own person, which subverts all the principles of his understanding, and gives him a determination to believe what is most contrary to custom and experience.

Enquiry Concerning Human Understanding 1748

Q3 Could someone have a miraculous experience, and so believe in miracles, without believing in God?

Levels of belief

Belief in a god or gods is an act of faith of the most profound kind, in that it can shape a person's entire world view and way of behaving. Is the same sort of faith in evidence when people express the following beliefs?

"I believe in ghosts."
"I believe in reincarnation."
"I believe in Father Christmas."
"I believe in the healing power of love."

It is conventional to make a distinction between believing *in* (God, ghosts, the afterlife, and so on) and believing *that* (God exists, there are fairies at the bottom of the garden, and so on). The distinction has some value if 'believing that ...' merely means agreeing to a proposition on an *intellectual* level, whilst 'believing in' means *active* commitment to a belief.

Neither has much to do with *argument* (see Concept D) – whether the belief is in God (see **Newman** below) or in ghosts (**Johnson**, below):

It is as absurd to argue men, as to torture them, into believing.

John Henry Newman (theologian, 1801–90)

All argument is against it (ghosts); but all belief is for it.
Dr Samuel Johnson (lexicographer and critic, 1709–84)

Q4 Many religions see it as their duty to proselytize (to convert people to their belief). What arguments do they use to do this? What methods other than argument are used to achieve this goal?

Q5 Is it possible to believe that God exists, without believing in God? In other words, is it possible to agree to the intellectual proposition, without making the act of faith?

Expressing beliefs

Is belief mere *feeling*, mere inclination – an impulse that bypasses the brain?

A dog may believe that there is food in the bowl in front of it. Accordingly, philosophers have sought accounts of belief that allow a central role to sentences – it cannot be an accident that finding the right sentence is the way to capture what someone believes – while allowing that creatures without a language can have beliefs. One way of doing this is to construe beliefs as relations to inner sentences somehow inscribed in the brain. On this view although dogs do not have a public language, to the extent that they have beliefs they have something sentence-like in their heads.

David Braddon-Mitchell and **Frank Jackson** in Routledge 2000

Q6 Do you have any experience of an animal that suggests to you that it *believes* in something?

Q7 Do you agree with the authors above that a belief is best captured in *sentences*? Is it possible to have beliefs that cannot be put into words?

Beliefs and ideologies

May Day Parade in Moscow, 1973

A belief may be held very strongly, to the extent that it could be called an *ideology*. When an *individual* holds a belief, it is perhaps open to influence and erosion over time. Thus, an individual might say at the age of 18:

"I believe in capital punishment,"

"I believe in monarchy,"

"I believe in freedom of information,"

"I believe in the right to roam,"

and cease to believe in these things by the age of 28.

When *groups* and *societies* hold a belief, they often create resilient, long-lasting ideologies that resist attempts to undermine them. Here the unreasonableness (in the sense of 'lack of reason' involved in making an act of faith) may be dangerous as in the former Soviet Union under Stalin, where millions of that country's citizens were sacrificed on the altar of ideology.

The dangers extend not just to individuals, but to whole societies.

Beliefs begin when the facts run out. Nobody can prove that their beliefs are right to anyone else's satisfaction. But when they click with other people's sense of what is true, they can be very powerful indeed. I suspect, in fact, that the next great clashes in the world will not be between nation states, or between conflicting economic systems, but between belief systems, which sometimes get called religions (such as Islam), sometimes civilizations (India or China), and sometimes cultures (Western). If capitalism is to be our servant rather than our master, it will be because our belief systems want it that way. Beliefs are always personal but they need not be private. Shared and spread they can change the world more than governments can.

Charles Handy (1998)

Q8 How far do you agree with Handy that (a) capitalism (b) environmentalism are beliefs that "begin when the facts run out"?

Q9 What 'clashes' between beliefs (or belief-systems) are likely in Britain, in the 21st century?

Q10 Look back at the quotation at the top of the previous page. Was Disraeli accurate, in your opinion, when he said that human beings are "born to believe"?

Handy, Charles (1998) *The Hungry Spirit* London: Arrow Books Ltd.

Routledge (2000) *Concise Routledge Encyclopedia of Philosophy* London: Routledge

Language and stereotyping

Language and conflict

"It cannot be an accident that finding the right sentence is the way to capture what someone believes." So said Braddon-Mitchell and Jackson (see Concept I, Beliefs). People think in words and language. At any rate, reflective, higher-level thought is in language (people may not have linguistic thoughts about, for example, food in a bowl in front of them).

"The next great clashes in the world will [be] between belief systems." So said Charles Handy (Concept I). As belief systems are captured in language, it is not surprising that clashes have commonly occurred between peoples who speak different languages. "To understand is to forgive", said the French mathematician and philosopher **Blaise Pascal** (1623–62). Forgiveness is not possible between people who do not 'make sense' to each other.

> *"… doan' de French people talk de same way we does?"*
> *"No, Jim; you couldn't understand a word they said – not a single word."*
> *"Well, now, I be ding-busted! How do dat come?"*
> *"I don't know; but it's so. I got some of their jabber out of a book. S'pose a man was to come to you and say* Polly-voo-franzy *– what would you think?"*
> *"I wouldn' think nuff'n; I'd take en bust him over de head."*
>
> **Mark Twain** The Adventures of Huckleberry Finn 1885

Q1 Think of some examples of conflict between groups whose language (or dialect) is different. Are there other factors involved, apart from language?

Language and globalization

The number of languages in the world is shrinking, as the following extract describes. To many people, this is a cause for concern and part of the trend towards *globalization* – the domination of world finances, power and culture by an ever-smaller number of countries, companies and individuals. To some other people – such as Jim, above – it is a great pity that everyone does not speak English.

> *Ninety per cent of the world's languages may be in danger. Around 6 000 languages are currently spoken in the world. Of these, half are moribund in that they are no longer learned by the new generation of speakers. A further 2 500 are in a danger zone, in that they have fewer than a hundred thousand speakers. This leaves around 600, a mere ten per cent of the current total, as likely survivors a century from now. Of course, languages inevitably split, just as Latin eventually split into the various Romance languages. So some new languages may emerge. But the diversity will be much reduced. The splendiferous bouquet of current languages will be whittled down to a small posy with only a few different flowers.*
>
> **Jean Aitchison** (1997)

Europe needs plain English

Daily Mail
Comment

We are never going to score in Europe if we don't go on the attack and set the pace in a way that is breathtakingly and distinctively British.

How? The answer is as obvious, as the ears, eyes and mouth on our face. We must capitalise on our most priceless asset: The Queen's English. If Europe is to have a future, it needs more than a common currency, a common foreign policy and a common set of laws. It must have a common language. That language can only be English …

Most European children learn it as their second language.

Air traffic controllers of every continent recognise its sovereign value as the only conceivable common means of communication.

So in championing the case for English as the common language for the Community and all its institutions, politicians at Westminster would be surfing on the tide of progress.

Extract from front page, Daily Mail 14 November 1991

Q2 Is the reduction in the number of languages in the world a matter for regret in your view?

Q3 What do you make of the Daily Mail's proposal? Is it sensible, desirable or dangerous?

Capturing beliefs in language

If language is what captures people's beliefs (or prejudices), it may capture language-*users*, too. In other words, the words that people use may trap their thoughts, and so stop them thinking. The following lines explain how this might happen: when certain words are used closely together often enough, the brain learns to associate them automatically, in a way that bypasses thought.

Jean Aitchison again:

> *Humans subconsciously notice which words occur together. Newspapers kept reminding us that George Bush had shaken off his* wimp *image: 'President Bush has decisively buried his lingering image as White House wimp', we were told; But in so doing, they were reinforcing his negative image. The repeated* Bush-wimp *pairing ensured that he remains perhaps permanently associated with wimphood, however undeservedly.*
>
> **Jean Aitchison** (1997)

In the same way, the word 'sleaze' came to be attached to John Major's government of the 1990s, (though Major himself was called both 'grey' and 'decent'), and the words 'arrogance' and 'spin' were affixed to New Labour, when they came to power in 1997.

Stereotypes

It is this knee jerk, unthinking kind of reaction that is the basis of *prejudice*, which literally means 'judging in advance'. Prejudice is expressed in the words used to describe people. *Labels* come to be attached to individuals and groups of people based on mental short-cuts or *stereotypes*, in other words, fixed and usually inaccurate images of people.

This list of words describes some of the labels that are used to stereotype different groups of people on a sliding scale of abuse.

The words or labels people use to describe others often say more about their own attitudes and feelings, rather than describing accurately the people being labelled.

Q4 Add to this list. Look through some recent newspaper articles to see how language is used, either to praise people or to stir up bad feelings towards them.

gentlemen

WOMEN

freedom-fighters

chief executive

senior citizens/elderly/aged/old/pensioners	wrinklies/geriatrics
young people/youngsters/teenagers	youths/yobs/delinquents/hooligans
philosophers/thinkers/intellectuals	highbrows/pedants/smart-alecks/posers
unorthodox/eccentrics	cranks/weirdos
ladies/women	girls/lasses/wenches/bitches/harpies
gentlemen/men	boys/lads/fellows/blokes/louts
statesmen/legislators/leaders	politicians/demagogues
country people	rustics/yokels/peasants/country bumpkins
city-dwellers/urbanites/suburbanites	townies
nonconformists/dissenters	heretics/subversives
Conservatives	Tories/Thatcherites/right-wingers
radicals/activists/freedom-fighters	agitators/terrorists
peace-lovers/pacifists	conchies/cowards
liberals	trendies/lefties/fellow-travellers
clergy/pastors	preachers/bible-bashers
Roman Catholics	Romanists/papists
gays and lesbians/homosexuals	queers/queens/perverts
ethnic minorities/people of colour/blacks	West Indians/Negroes/niggers
allies/foreigners	immigrants/aliens
travellers	gypsies/vagrants
poor/homeless	beggars/scroungers/dossers
writers/journalists	reporters/hacks/scribblers
chief executives/employers/entrepreneurs	bosses/capitalists/fat cats
brokers/bankers/traders	dealers/hucksters/thieves

LADS

Girls

terrorists

Fat Cat

Language and propaganda

The use of labels and stereotypes is at its most blatant in *propaganda* – the organized dissemination of information by government or other source of power in order to promote its own cause. In this brief passage from Orwell's 1984, Orwell describes the reaction of the main character, Winston, to Party propaganda (you need to know that Goldstein is not a real person, but is created by the Party as a 'Public Enemy' in order to incite loyalty to the Party):

Winstons' diaphragm was constricted. He could never see the face of Goldstein without a painful mixture of emotions. It was a lean Jewish face, with a great fuzzy aureole of white hair and a small goatee beard – a clever face, and yet somehow inherently despicable, with a kind of senile silliness in the long thin nose near the end of which a pair of spectacles was perched. It resembled the face of a sheep, and the voice, too, had a sheeplike quality. Goldstein was delivering his usual venomous attack upon *the doctrines of the Party – an attack so exaggerated and perverse that a child should have been able to see through it, and yet just plausible enough to fill one with an alarmed feeling that other people, less level-headed than oneself, might be taken in by it.*

George Orwell 1984–1949

Q5 What words does Orwell use that create a negative image of Goldstein?

Q6 How far does all stereotyping boil down to a use of language?

Aitchison, Jean (1997) *The LanguageWeb* Cambridge: CUP

10 The Arts

The soft end of the continuum

... The arts speak to the imagination and spirit in all of us. They enlighten, entertain, inform, educate and move us. And they lead us into a world unknown to previous perception.

Chris Smith (1998)

In the Introduction to this book, it was suggested that all knowledge and evidence can be placed on a continuum from hard to soft, from quantitative to qualitative, from objective to subjective. The Arts are very much at the soft *value-judgement* end of the continuum, almost as far away from hard objective *fact-statements* as they can be. Evidence in the arts is as soft and subjective as it gets. This is not to devalue the arts: there is nothing trivial about perception. But everyone should be suspicious about statements about the arts that claim to tell objective truth.

All writers [on art] have a perspective on, or an approach to, what they are dealing with. This is true even if they disclaim any approach, or if they offer an account so apparently magisterial and authoritative that it appears to be universal truth rather than one of many possible arguments.

Marcia Pointon (Art historian, 1943–) 1997

Arts, culture and society

Jean Jacques Rousseau (1712–78) said that *culture* is the opposite of *nature* (see Concept F, 'Culture'). Art, too, can be said to be the opposite of nature. This does not mean though that art and culture are one and the same thing. Culture can be thought of as including the Arts. The Arts are a family of ways in which we represent and express our cultural interests and values.

Culture and *Society* mean almost the same thing; and artists have had a role to play in a number of different subcultures within society at different stages in our history.

Q1 Think of artists (writers, musicians, painters, etc.), past and present, and place each of them in a subculture in the diagram.

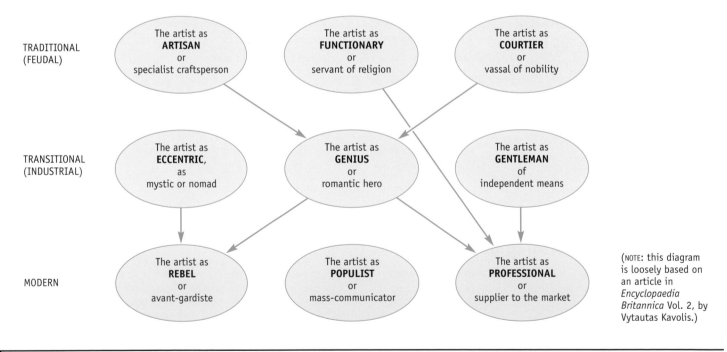

TRADITIONAL (FEUDAL)	The artist as **ARTISAN** or specialist craftsperson	The artist as **FUNCTIONARY** or servant of religion	The artist as **COURTIER** or vassal of nobility
TRANSITIONAL (INDUSTRIAL)	The artist as **ECCENTRIC**, as mystic or nomad	The artist as **GENIUS** or romantic hero	The artist as **GENTLEMAN** of independent means
MODERN	The artist as **REBEL** or avant-gardiste	The artist as **POPULIST** or mass-communicator	The artist as **PROFESSIONAL** or supplier to the market

(NOTE: this diagram is loosely based on an article in *Encyclopaedia Britannica* Vol. 2, by Vytautas Kavolis.)

Art and artificiality

The word 'arts' has two primary meanings, and a third, subsidiary meaning:

ars, artis n. f. (Latin.)

1. a practical skill, applied to the production of beauty; a branch of learning.
2. the thing produced; a work of art and creative imagination
3. cunning, trickery.

Q2 How do the different meanings of the word 'art' make for difficulties when it comes to discussing the arts?

artist, artistic, artistry
artefact (artifact) – a product of human art
artful, artless – with or without skill and cunning
artifice, artificial, artificiality.

The function of art

In pre-industrial societies, there was the *artisan* culture (of specialist craftspeople) and the *folk* culture (of non-specialist potters, storytellers and musicians). The art of both cultures was *utilitarian* – that is, art that can be said to have a specific 'practical' or social function. It is only today – hundreds and thousands of years later – that it is called *art*.

Art has also fulfilled a religious function. However, some Christian writers thought it was presumptuous to attempt to outdo God – to 'play God', indeed, since 'nature … is above all art' (**Samuel Daniel** poet, c.1562–1619).

> *All things are artificial, for nature is the art of God.*
> Sir Thomas Browne (physician, philosopher and author 1605–1682)

According to these writers, man could not better nature, but he must do something to redeem his fallen state:

> *The great design of art is to restore the decays that happened to human nature by the fall, by restoring order.*
> John Dennis (writer, 1657–1734)

After the Renaissance, artists gained in self-confidence and it was thought possible that art might tame wild nature, and so enhance it:

> *By viewing Nature, Nature's handmaid, art,*
> *Makes mighty things from small beginnings grow.*
> John Dryden (poet 1631–1700) Annus Mirabilis 1667

To a Romantic, like the poet Keats, art (often with a capital A) came near to being a substitute for religion:

> *The excellence of every art is its intensity, capable of making all disagreeables evaporate, from their being in close relationship with beauty and truth.*
> John Keats (poet 1795–1821)

For 19th century Victorians, art might not only relate to truth, but, as religious faith declined, it might *be* truth, and so have a *moral* function.

> *It is the glory and good of Art, that Art remains the one way possible of speaking truths.*
> Robert Browning (poet 1812–89) The Ring and the Book 1868-9

> *If art does not enlarge men's sympathies, it does nothing morally.*
> George Eliot (writer, 1819–80)

Q3 To what extent can the arts be said to have anything to do with nature?

Q4 How far can the arts be said to speak 'truths', or to have any ' moral' effects?

Art for art's sake

In the late 19th and the 20th centuries, *Modernism* broke with tradition, and with the idea that art has any function at all. **Victor Cousin**'s (philosopher, 1792–1867) 'Art for art's sake' was the motto of the times; and **Oscar Wilde** (1854–1900) was the prophet of things to come:

> *Art never expresses anything but itself.*
> The Decay of Lying

> *All art is quite useless.*
> The Picture of Dorian Gray 1891

The status of art

In the 20th century, painters ceased to represent nature; composers turned their backs on tuneful melodies; and poets abandoned rhyme and metre. Modernism was an essentially minority taste, that distanced itself from the art of the people – the mass. This led to the distinction that is commonly made between 'low' and 'high' art.

But is the distinction valid? Janice Street-Porter (journalist) thinks so; Chris Smith (former Culture Secretary) thinks not.

> *I believe in high art, which, by its nature, will be inaccessible to an uneducated mass. Without light and shade, the difficult as well as the straightforward, our cultural life would be bland. I worry about the current fashion which places accessibility above all else. In a discussion about arts funding on Radio 3 last week, the moral philosopher Mary Warnock argued that art could be both élitist and accessible to anyone, acknowledging that accessibility was this government's criterion for distributing money to the arts, under the banner "Arts for Everyone". This concept is both patronising and doomed. Arts funding should not be based on the number of people who visit galleries or museums. There has to be a place to value the scholarly, the small-scale and the obscure.*
> Janet Street-Porter (2000)

> *I loathe the distinction that some people try to draw between so-called 'high art' and 'low art'. What on earth counts as 'high' and 'low'? Madame Butterfly at the Albert Hall, packed to the rafters and brilliantly performed? The people of Sunderland flocking in their droves to buy Prokoviev recordings because they love the theme tune of their football club? Nigel Kennedy playing Elgar's Violin Concerto like an angel? A brilliant one-man rendition of Kenneth Williams at the Edinburgh Festival which had standing-room only at 11 in the morning? The steel bands playing at the Notting Hill Carnival? Antony Gormley's Field which attracted rave reviews and thousands of visitors wherever it went? Guys and Dolls at the National Theatre, sitting brilliantly alongside the finest rendition of King Lear we have seen in decades?*
> Chris Smith (1998)

Q5 Street-Porter calls the government's "Arts for Everyone" policy 'patronizing'? What does she mean?

Q6 Do you agree with Smith that it is meaningless to make a distinction between 'high art' and 'low art'?

Pointon, Marcia (1997) *History of Art: A Students' Handbook* (4th Edn.) London: Routledge

Smith, Chris (1998) *Creative Britain* London: Faber & Faber

Street-Porter, Janet (2000) 'You won't get far …' in *The Independent on Sunday* 17 December 2000

Part 1 Mapping the Arts

■ When is an object 'art'?

How should the arts be classified? In the medieval period, all knowledge was divided into the 'Seven Liberal Arts' (see Concept B, 'The curriculum'). Then the distinction was made between Sciences and Arts that is preserved in the names given to Bachelors and Masters degrees.

The arts as we know them tended to be divided into *Arts* and *Crafts*, or *Fine Arts* and *Useful Arts*. Just as the sciences (and mathematics)

were divided into 'pure' and 'applied'; so the arts were divided into the pure (or *aesthetic*) and the applied (or *utilitarian*) arts. There was always something rather aristocratic (or 'snobbish') – or, at least, value-laden – about this distinction. There is less inclination to make this distinction now, and to set the painter above the potter, or the sculptor above the stage-designer.

Here are some commonly used categories:

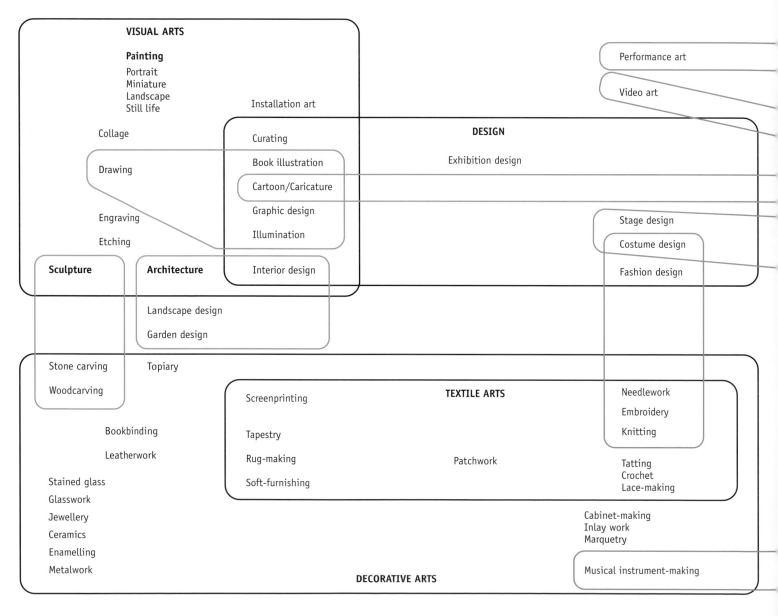

Art history addresses not only how a work by Leonardo came to be made and how it was received at the time it was produced [but why] we think of Leonardo as Art and an advertisement in a magazine as Not Art.

Marcia Pointon (1997)

Fine art is that in which the hand, the head, and the heart go together.

John Ruskin (1859)

Q1 What does Marcia Pointon mean when she says an advertisement in a magazine is 'Not Art'?

Q2 Would an advertisement be art if it had been hand-drawn, was intelligent and full of feeling?

Virtually any area of Britain … offers something worthy of
attention to the art historian, whether it is the ruins of a Norman
castle, a Second World War memorial in a Nottinghamshire village,
a set of standing stones in Orkney, an adventurously designed new
branch of Sainsburys, a local library that has inherited a collection
of objects accumulated by a former serviceman in India, a now
disused railway station in Yorkshire, or a stately home now run by
the National Trust.

Marcia Pointon (1997)

Q3 All the above items may be of 'interest to the art historian':
are they, therefore, all art?

Design, craftsmanship and artistic flair are all attributes that a
creator brings to an object above and beyond the utilitarian
approach that looks simply at the way something is used, rather
than the qualities inherent in it. Linking quality of design with
usefulness of purpose is the task of the creator, and the best
creators make it seem as if they are one and the same goal.

Chris Smith (1998)

Art has to move you and design does not, unless it's a good
design for a bus.

David Hockney (1988)

Q4 Do you agree with Smith, or Hockney, or both?

PERFORMING ARTS

Mime

Circus

MEDIA ARTS

Photography

Animation   Programming

Website design   Broadcasting

Screenplay writing

Drama

Journalism

Cinema

Directing

Acting

Puppetry

Dance

Theatre

Comedy
Tragedy
Satire

Ballet

Opera

Singing

History   Novel: Crime
                        Romance
Travel   Science fiction
                        Ideas

Essay   Novella/Short story   Poetry

LITERATURE

Epic

Dramatic

Lyric

Choral
Conducting

Campanology   Conducting

Orchestrating/Arranging

Composition

Instrumental
playing   **MUSIC**

Pointon, Marcia, op. cit.; Smith, Chris, op. cit.

Part 2 The visual Arts

What is art?

This section takes one view on the visual arts – it is a value-judgement. It could not be otherwise.

Traditionally, art was judged according to certain criteria. It:

- Interpreted some aspect of real life
- Was original
- Was a work of skill and imagination.

These traditional judgements were discarded in the 20th century in favour of new criteria. Art could:

- Challenge, disturb, even shock
- Be given meaning by the viewer
- Be whatever it chooses to be.

According to tradition, an 'artist' applied practical skill to express an idea, using certain material (the first meaning of *ars, artis* – see Unit 10, introduction) and the result was an art object, a thing of beauty (the second meaning). Some people think that the third meaning of art ('cunning, trickery') applies to much of 'modern art'.

If someone calls it art, it is art.

Donald Judd in Archer 1997

A work of art of which nothing can be said, except that it is.

Maurice Blanchot in Archer, 1997

It is the artist, purely because he is the artist, who has the power to designate something as art.

Archer (1997) reporting on Marcel Duchamp

Anything that a body, past or present, regards as art should be treated as art.

Marcia Pointon (1997)

Can anything be seen as art?

If everything is art, then nothing is art. Yet, 'anything goes' seems only to apply to the visual arts. Very few people will read 'anything goes' novels (only scholars read James Joyce's *Finnegan's Wake*, of 1939); very few will listen to 'anything goes' music (who listens to John Cage's 4'3", of 1954?). Even among the visual arts, architecture is not art merely because an architect says it is.

Q1 Where do you stand so far? Do you agree with Donald Judd, above? Is Pointon saying the same thing as Judd? Do you agree that 'anything goes' gets us nowhere?

Marcel Duchamp (1887–1968) created 'ready made' art. He mounted a bicycle wheel on a stool and called it *BicycleWheel* (1913); he inscribed a gents' urinal 'R. Mutt' and called it *Fountain* (1917). Both have been called 'art'. He explained in a lecture, in 1957, that:

… the work of art is not performed by the artist alone' and that the spectator's point of view affects the all-important 'transubstantiation' of inert matter into art.

David Hopkins (2000)

In 1973, **Michael Craig-Martin** exhibited a glass of water on a bathroom shelf, and called it *An Oak Tree*. John Ezard said of it, in *The Guardian* (23 November 2000) that it 'requires an act of faith comparable to a belief in religious transubstantiation'. ('Transubstantiation' is the word used to describe the changing of the bread and wine of the catholic mass into the body and blood of Christ. Religious faith prompts belief in the change.)

Is it uniqueness that makes it art?

A work of art is unique in the sense that, in the Michael Craig-Martin example, there is only one glass of water on one bathroom shelf that has been called *An Oak Tree*. But novels, poems, recordings of a song, performances of a play are copied in their thousands. Are they then not art? Consider the following examples:

In 1957 [Yves] Klein had a key exhibition at the Galleria Apollinaire in Milan. He showed 11 blue monochromes, all unframed and uniform in size and facture. They were sold at variable prices, established after Klein's consultations with individual buyers.

David Hopkins (2000)

Andy Warhol (c. 1926–87) produced screen-printed dollar bills, Campbell's soup tins, and Coca-Cola bottles in his 'Factory', from 1962 onwards. **Damien Hirst**'s 'spot' paintings, 'spin' paintings and pill cases are made by teams of operatives in Leyton, Vauxhall and Stroud ('An artist? I'm a brand name, says Hirst' *The Independent on Sunday*, 1 October 2000).

Q2 Does this sort of mass-production affect what we might call 'art' and what we might call 'not art'?

Controversy in art

The following examples of 20th century art were all controversial.

Yoko Ono and Marina Abramovic

In 1964, in Kyoto, Japan, in a performance entitled Cut Piece, *Yoko Ono kneeled motionless and statuesque. Members of the audience were invited, one by one, to cut away a portion of her clothing. 'It is difficult to think of an earlier work of art that so acutely pinpoints (at the very point when modern feminist activism was just emerging) the political question of women's physical vulnerability as mediated by regimes of vision'.*

Thomas Crow (1996)

In her final 'Rhythm' performance, Rhythm 0 (1974) Marina Abramovic placed herself silently in the Studio Mona Gallery in Naples next to a table holding 72 varied objects. Visitors were invited to use them, and her, as they saw fit. Proceedings were halted when Abramovic, having had all her clothing cut from her, was forced to hold a pistol, placing the barrel in her open mouth.

Michael Archer (1997)

Q3 Did Marina Abramovic know about the work of Yoko Ono, ten years earlier, when she performed in 1974? Does it matter if she did or not?

But why only pretend to fire the pistol?

The Californian Chris Burden performed a number of carefully planned but self-endangering actions. In Shoot, performed at 'F-Space' gallery, Santa Ana, California, in 1971, he arranged for a male friend to shoot him, sustaining a deep arm wound.

David Hopkins (2000)

And why use your real body?

Felix Gonzales-Torres allowed others to make free with his body only in metaphor: 'Untitled' (Lover Boy)(1990) was a stack of blue paper with the instruction. 'You are allowed, if you wish, to take a sheet from the top of the pile, to consume not only the body of art, but also the body of the artist. The overtones are religious, sacramental, since the stack, constantly replenished, will not be exhausted.' (Archer, 1997)

Can a stack of bricks be art?

In 1976, the revelation that the Tate Gallery in London had bought part of [Carl] André's brick work Equivalents I-VIII, as orchestrated by Britain's popular press, led to philistine attacks on the spending policies of Britain's public galleries from general public and the art establishment alike.

David Hopkins (2000)

Q4 What are 'philistine attacks'?

To read histories of 'modern art' is to be confronted by one challenge to 'faith' in art after another. Perhaps most challenging of all is that an all-white painting might have been painted by any one of three different artists, and an all-black one by one of four.

Robert Ryman, c. 1958
Robert Rauschenberg, c. 1951
Kasimir Malevich, c. 1918

Ad Reinhardt, c. 1958
Robert Rauschenberg, c. 1952
Yves Klein, c. 1955
Andy Warhol, c. 1963

Q5 'The so-called "fine" arts are played out. There is nothing more worth doing. It has all been done.' Discuss.

■ Is art a business?

Some might argue that art works have become *commodities*. Artists, together with critics, collectors and gallery-owners, have commodified art.

The critical parameters set up by [Clement] Greenberg ... to legitimate Post-Painterly Abstraction had the effect of marginalizing other practices of abstraction.
David Hopkins (2000)

... the gallery system with its hunger for artistic 'commodities'
David Hopkins (2000)

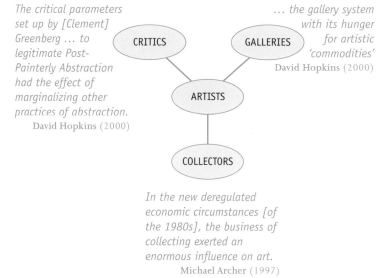

In the new deregulated economic circumstances [of the 1980s], the business of collecting exerted an enormous influence on art.
Michael Archer (1997)

This perceived commodification of art has led to criticism of the art business. When the public sees 'inert matter' (for example, bricks) transubstantiated not into 'art' but into fortunes paid to artists by gallery-owners and collectors with more money than taste, it is no wonder that many lost faith.

Q6 Do you agree that art is commodified?

Archer, Michael (1997) *Art Since 1960* London: Thames and Hudson

Crow, Thomas (1996) *The Rise of the Sixties* London: Weidenfeld & Nicolson

Hopkins, David (2000) *After Modern Art 1945–2000* Oxford: OUP

Pointon, Marcia (1997) op.cit.

Part 3 Art as entertainment

Mass entertainment

There was much talk, before and after the turn of the millennium, about 'dumbing down'. It was feared that the arts, the news, education, politics – all things 'serious' – were subject to the pressures of populism, mass taste and 'tabloidization'. It was suggested in part 2 of this unit that the visual arts have had more to do with 'sensation' and with money-making than with enlightenment.

One factor in this debate has been the intimate connection between the *Arts* and the *Media* – or perhaps between the arts (and the news, and education, and entertainment) with *technology*. Access to domestic media technology has grown by leaps and bounds.

Households with selected consumer durables

Great Britain				%
	1972	1981	1991–92	1998–99
Television	93	97	98	98
Video recorder	–	–	68	85
CD player	–	–	27	68
Home computer	–	–	21	34

Adapted from Table 13.2 Social Trends 30, 2000

Q1 By what percentages did the ownership of (a) video recorders, and (b) CD players rise during the 1990s?

Q2 What are the likely future trends where domestic media technology is concerned?

Children and the media

Of interest to commentators on these matters is the access that children and young people have to this technology. In 1999, the London School of Economics published a report *Young People, New Media*. These were some of the findings (reported in *The Independent*):

A generation of British children are locking themselves away in their bedrooms where they are increasingly turning to television and computer games as their sole sources of entertainment, an extraordinary new survey has found … Today's children are indeed the media rich. One in five has their own VCR, two-thirds play on computer games, while 68 per cent have a personal stereo.

Coupled with such access to technology is the trend towards the bedroom being the sole private space for children. While teenagers sulking in their bedrooms is nothing new, the study finds that children from the age of nine are turning to their bedrooms as a place to socialise. Most striking are the two thirds of all children who have a television in their rooms (a figure which rises to nearly three quarters among working-class families).

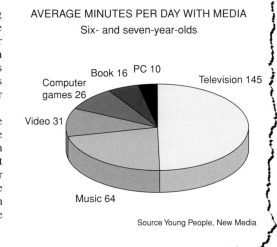

AVERAGE MINUTES PER DAY WITH MEDIA
Six- and seven-year-olds

Book 16 PC 10
Computer games 26
Television 145
Video 31
Music 64

Source Young People, New Media

Rhys Williams and Andrew Buncombe (1999)

Q3 What is the total average time spent daily, by six- and seven-year-olds, accessing electronic entertainment?

Q4 What proportion of this time is accounted for by television and video together?

Q5 While accessing the various forms of electronic entertainment shown in the pie chart, are children likely to be doing anything else at the same time? If so, what might children be doing, and which forms of media aid this activity?

Q6 If children aren't doing anything else, is this a problem?

Soap operas

Television is the means by which most people will access the 'arts', and of the arts, drama is represented most on television – and drama, for the most part, means the soap opera.

In assessing soap, it is important to remember its original (and continuing) function – to deliver mass audiences to advertisers, or, in the case of public-service television, to justify continued public subsidy. In this sense, soap opera – a story without end, broadcast regularly (on a daily basis if possible) to large and loyal audiences – is the perfect television format.

David McQueen (1998)

This said, there is an argument that there is 'bad' soap, and 'good' soap:

Co-operation between channels – for whom a ratings war on soaps would be counter-productive – allows viewers to get several uninterrupted 'fixes'. Effectively, such guaranteed, massive daily 'doses' offer an escape from the viewer's own life and worries through the problems and 'lives' of fictional characters, no matter how vacuous these may be …

Soap's appeal to a mass audience is, its critics argue, too often maintained by insisting on the obvious, the bland, the grindingly unoriginal. At its worst, soap deadens the mind to any sense of possibility. Brookside's regeneration of soap – particularly the sense of social awareness it encouraged – has forced a critical reconsideration of the genre. Eastenders and Brookside continue to raise issues and reflect something of the cultural and ethnic diversity of contemporary Britain. Neither is afraid of provoking a degree of controversy, whether it be stories of lesbianism, domestic violence, heroin addiction or AIDS. They address problems which other television forms ignore and they allow time and space to explore the complexities and repercussions that such problems can involve. Soap is, therefore, at least potentially, a progressive television form.

David McQueen (1998)

Q7 Would you be inclined to take a negative or the positive view of soap opera? On what grounds?

Q8 In what sense might soap opera, at its best, be 'art'?

◼ Entertainment outside the home

Television is easy because immediately available; 'going out' is more difficult – at least for home-owning adults. Nevertheless, television does not have a monopoly of cultural events.

Attendance at cultural events

Great Britain			**%**
	1987–88	1991–92	1997–98
Cinema	34	44	54
Plays	24	23	23
Art galleries/Exhibitions	21	21	22
Classical music	12	12	12
Ballet	6	6	6
Opera	5	6	6
Contemporary dance	4	3	4

Q9 What conclusions can validly be drawn from these figures?

Q10 Why do you think the cinema is increasing in popularity?

'Special effects' have come to the theatre, as well as to the cinema – and it is perfectly possible to hold two opposing views about the theatre in Britain, at one and the same time.

In 1984 Starlight Express *took up residency at the Apollo Victoria. It was this work that critics cited as a regrettable triumph of bravado and glitz over substance and sense. A paean to the age of steam, the work required that the auditorium be fitted with a track that swooped and dived around the auditorium, allowing the performers dressed up as trains to roller-skate at frightening speeds. The production cost alone was £1.4 million. The combination of John Napier and Trevor Nunn resulted in several breath-taking races, large video screens that allowed the audience to follow the performers' progress and pounding disco beats designed to enhance the excitement. Most critics found the frenetic pace of the production less effective than the feline grace of* Cats.

Dominic Shellard (1999)

Seldom has the British theatre been in such a period of regeneration … the National Theatre (now a Grade 2 listed building) is having its first face-lift … money has been made available to improve the facilities of the Royal Court, fine new regional theatres like the West Yorkshire Playhouse in Leeds have been built, impressive arts complexes planned, as in Salford, and the old London Lyceum has been restored to its splendour … Throughout the country, successful regional tours by professional companies now take quality theatre to the local authority theatres put up during the wave of creative optimism which followed the end of the war. We have a Theatres Trust to watch-dog theatrical provision, … and greatly improved facilities for training in a number of University Drama departments and several drama schools.

Dominic Shellard (1999)

Q11 Write about the extent to which any play that you have seen was a 'work of art'.

Q12 Michael Jackson, former chief executive of Channel 4, has said: "I think a lot of the barriers between high and low culture, the serious and the trivial, have been crossed." Is it the business of art to do this, in your view?

McQueen, David (1998) *Television: A Media Student's Guide* London: Arnold

Shellard, Dominic (1999) *British Theatre Since the War* London and New Haven: Yale University Press

Rhys, Williams and Buncombe, Andrew (1999) 'Our generation of couch potato kids, stuck in their rooms and glued to TV' *The Independent* 19 March 1999

Criticism

Criticism as judgment

Education at an 'advanced' level is about *critical thinking*. Throughout this course you will have been 'critical' – you will have engaged in 'criticism'.

The root word is Greek:

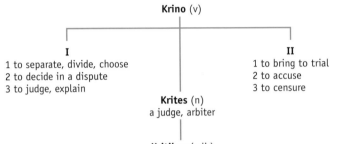

Krino (v)

I	II
1 to separate, divide, choose	1 to bring to trial
2 to decide in a dispute	2 to accuse
3 to judge, explain	3 to censure

Krites (n)
a judge, arbiter

Kritikos (adj.)
able to discern; discriminating; critical

A *critic* is a judge; *criticism* is judgment; and a *critique* is an act, or product, of judgment. It is a pity that, of the two meanings of 'criticism' – *judgment* and *censure* (or fault-finding) – it is the latter which is more often used.

Discriminating judgement

This course is concerned with criticism as *impartial, discriminating judgement*. That is, judgement that is objective, and that is able to appreciate fine distinctions and differences.

> **Q1** The word 'discriminate' has undergone a shift of meaning in quite recent times. Find out what its underlying, and (sometimes negative) modern meanings are, and use each in a sentence to illustrate its meaning.

Criteria

Perhaps it is as well to bear in mind that another word from the Greek root verb is:

Kriterion (n)
a standard; a means of testing; a test
a court of judgement; a tribunal

Our word *criterion* means much the same: it is *a standard by which to judge something* (its plural is 'criteria'). Ideally, a critic should be clear about the *criteria* on which a *criticism* is based – otherwise it is no more than an opinion.

Criticism of the arts

It is odd, given that critical thinking is the most balanced, discriminating kind of thinking, that criticism should have come to be associated with the arts. People speak of art-criticism, literary-criticism and music-criticism, but not of physics-criticism or economics-criticism. **Matthew Arnold** (1822–88) was partly responsible for this: just as culture, for him, meant 'acquainting ourselves with the best of that has been known and said in the world' (see Concept F, 'Culture'), so he wrote:

> *I am bound by my own definition of criticism: a disinterested endeavour to learn and propagate the best that is known and thought in the world.*
>
> Essays in Criticism 1865

And for Arnold, he meant 'arts' and 'letters' (or literature) as 'the best that is known and thought in the world', rather than the sciences.

Criticism had generally been associated with writing. Writers have tended to dislike critics. **Francis Bacon** (1561–1626) reports **Sir Henry Wotton** (poet 1568–1639) to this effect:

> *Critics are like brushers of nobleman's clothes.*
>
> Apophthegms, 1625

Other writers have followed suit:

> *Reviewers are usually people who would have been poets, historians, biographers, etc. if they could; they have tried their talents at one or at the other, and have failed; therefore, they turn critics.*
>
> **Samuel Taylor Coleridge** (poet 1772–1834)
> Letters on Shakespeare and Milton 1888–9

> *A man must serve his time to every trade*
> *Save censure – critics all are ready made.*
> **Lord Byron** (poet 1788–1824) English Bards and Scotch Reviewers 1809

> **Q2** Explain what you think (a) Sir Henry Wotton, and (b) Lord Byron meant.

Critical bias

In the same satire (*English Bards and Scotch Reviewers*), Byron wrote:

> *As soon seek roses in December – ice in June; hope [for] constancy in wind, or corn in chaff; believe a woman or an epitaph, or any other thing that is false, before you trust in critics.*

Why, though, should a reader trust a poet/satirist who refuses to believe what women say merely because they are women? It is a critique which should alert us to the fact that writers, readers and critics all have a point of view. None of them is a god.

Literary criticism has fastened upon one or more of three stages in the creation of meaning – and each of these stages is a *construct of a particular time and a particular place*:

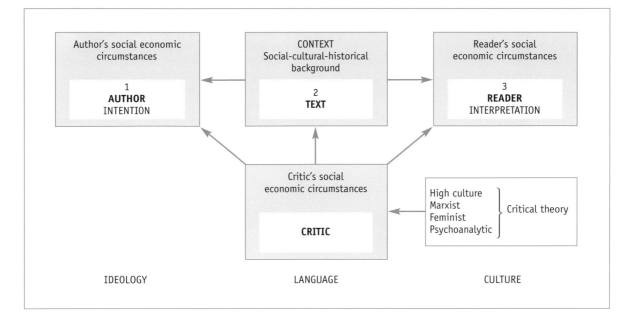

Academic literary criticism

Early academic literary criticism was very sure of itself. **F.R. Leavis** (1895–1978) was a prominent representative of 'High-Culture' criticism:

> *F.R. Leavis asserted that the competent critic's primary concern was with questions of evaluation, that is to discover the universal truth behind the language of the text.*
>
> **Marion Wynne-Davies** (1989)

Even into relatively modern times, there was an expectation that criticism would yield more or less universal truths:

> *In 'A Theory of Literature' (1963) René Wellek and Austin Warren define literature as 'creative, an art', whereas literary study is 'not precisely a science', but is nonetheless, ' a species of knowledge or learning'.*
>
> ibid.

Jacques Derrida (1930–) and 'deconstruction' undermined this confidence in criticism and its seeking out of truth. He showed that a text has no one meaning, but multiple meanings – and one meaning may contradict another. Even the *author* has no ultimate authority to impose a meaning on a text; certainly, no one reader, no one critic, can do so, because no one can put a stop to all the possibilities of new and different readings.

Comparative criticism

If criticism is to be more than the expression of subjective opinion, it will still need to involve *comparison* of like with like; and there needs to be some criteria by which to make the comparison. For example, Kenneth Tynan, the theatre critic, wanted a play to change his mind.

> *Drama criticism [is] a self-knowing account of the way in which one's consciousness has been modified during an evening in the theatre.*
>
> **Kenneth Tynan** *Tynan Right and Left 1967*

According to Tynan, a play that changed his mind, however minutely, was 'better' than one that did not – or could not.

Q3 Draw up some criteria by which you might compare one novel (or play, or film, or piece of music, or architect-designed building, or painting, or poem, or photograph) with another.

Q4 What do you find is the 'problem' that you face when you compare one film with another, or one piece of music with another?

Wynne-Davies, Marion (Ed.)(1989) *Bloomsbury Guide to English Literature* London: Bloomsbury

Literature

What is literature?

As 'criticism' has come to mean, in practice, criticism of the arts, so 'literature' is a term often applied to *fiction* only: to the novel and the short story (or novella), to drama, and to poetry. It is perhaps odd that autobiography, biography (both might be called 'literary'), history, travel-writing, books about the arts and sciences, books about books – all the shelves of books about what we call 'the real world' – should be given a negative name: *non-fiction*. It is as if poetry and prose fiction are what really count, and everything else that is not poetry and prose fiction – is not *literature*.

The rise and fall of literary forms

Different literary *genres* have risen and fallen in public esteem. What might once have been a *minority* interest grew in popularity until it was the *dominant* literary form. In the diagram, the rise and fall of five genres are charted over a 500-year period, in Britain. This diagram is offered as a subjective judgement rather than a feat of factual accuracy.

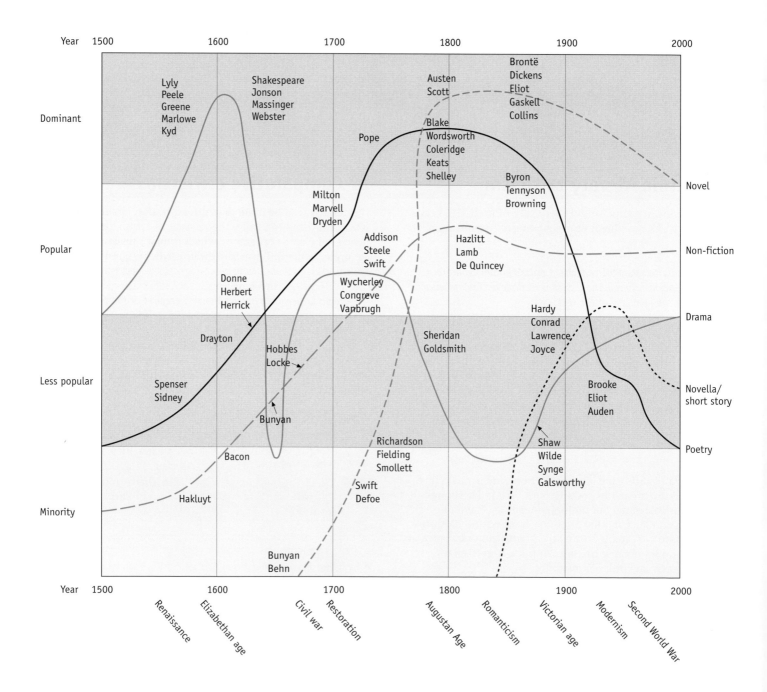

Q1 Why should drama have been so popular at the end of the Elizabethan period?

Q2 Why did drama fall out of favour in the middle of the 17th century?

Q3 Why do you think the novel came to be such a popular form of literature in the 19th century?

Q4 What do you think are the likely trends into the 21st century, where the above genres are concerned?

Marion Wynne-Davies refers to two changes taking place:

> The ... blurring of the division between the literary canon and other forms of writing has had a long-term effect. Today genres regarded as 'popular', such as science fiction are admitted into the canon, and literature as a field of academic study is often integrated into the broader framework of 'Cultural Studies'.
>
> **Marion Wynne-Davies**, op.cit.

In an article written shortly after the death of the Welsh poet **R.S. Thomas** (1913–2000), the novelist Malcolm Bradbury wrote:

> Like everything else in our current post-culture, poetry seems to have adapted to flimsiness, triviality, to the age of the book as commodity, the writer as would-be celebrity, the text as seductive object of play ... What has changed most is our expectations of the poet. The entire 20th century saw an erosion in the public meaning of poetry, its capacity to speak general truths. The post-modern turning of the century has seen the fading of art's private and avant-garde seriousness too. Poetry has become just another show on the road.
>
> **Malcolm Bradbury** 'Let's not lose his art of being awkward',
> The Independent on Sunday 1 October 2000

Q5 How far do you agree that poetry has a "capacity to speak general truths" that, perhaps, other genres do not?

Broadening the definition of culture

If art has lost its 'seriousness' (see Unit 10); if, according to Bradbury, literature, like art, has been 'commodified', could it be that people today are turning elsewhere for 'general truths' than to fiction? There is a lot more to culture than literature and the arts:

> Edinburgh is the place where disgruntled or superannuated broadcasting folk sound off. The latest salvo is from Sir John Drummond, once controller of Radio 3 and director of the Edinburgh Festival. He trundles out the heavy cavalry with the word "Philistinism", which in the acute gradations of cultural snobbism is used to refer to anyone who has never sat through the Ring Cycle and doesn't know any Greek ...
>
> Are we in mourning for a society of posh chaps who knew a lot about everything except the real world or are we trying to produce

> an undemanding serviceable education that will equip most people for life as they find it? Drummond's charge is that in TV, radio and politics, the choice has already been made of the undemanding and the superficial.
>
> I did note that when he poured scorn on University Challenge, his criticism was of the failure of undergraduates to recognise Hamlet; no doubt he, like me, hasn't a clue about the science questions, but of course ignorance of science is not philistinism, merely breeding.
>
> **Justin Cartwright** 'Justin Cartwright's Diary' The Guardian 12 August 2000

Scientists, such as **Richard Dawkins** (1941–), **John D. Barrow** (1952–), **Steven Rose** (1938–), **Richard Feynman** (1918–88) and others have written scientific 'literature' which is accessible to the non-scientist. These scientists are consciously harnessing literature to science. The result is not science fiction; it is what **Carl Djerassi** (chemist 1923–) calls 'science in fiction'. The novelist **David Lodge** (1935–) has said of Djerassi:

> He sees fiction as a means of communicating information about science and its moral and ethical implications. There is an explicit programme to bridge the two cultures.
>
> The Guardian, 26 August 2000

Another scientist, with the same programme, is the biologist **E.O. Wilson** (1930–). He wrote the following about his objectives:

> Thanks to the continuing exponential growth of scientific knowledge as well as the innovative thrust of the creative arts, the bridging of the two cultures is now in sight as a frontier of its own. Among the greatest challenges, still largely unmet, is the conversion of the scientific creative process and world view into literature ...
>
> The linkage of science and literature is a premier challenge of the 21st century, for the following reason: the scientific method has expanded our understanding of life and the universe in spectacular fashion across the entire scale of space and time, in every sensory modality, and beyond the farthest dreams of the pre-scientific mind. It is as if humanity, after wandering for millennia in a great dark cavern with only the light of a candle, can now find its way with a searchlight.
>
> **E.O. Wilson** 'Wings across two cultures' The Guardian 8 July 2000

Last thoughts

This coursebook has come full circle. It began with mathematical facts. Here are two more, to do with 'science' and 'literature'.

- 50 per cent of people in the world are under-nourished
- 70 per cent of people in the world cannot read.

Q6 If concerted international food and literacy programmes proved to be successful, what would you want the newly-literate to read first, and why?

Skills: Writing an essay

The structure of an essay

An essay is the laying-out of a case. When journalists, academics and writers – in fact, persuaders of all sorts – want to make a case they, in effect, write an essay. An essay is still the main means by which an A-level, undergraduate or post-graduate student demonstrates understanding of a topic. It is difficult to see how it could be otherwise. Multi-choice and short-answer questions can test understanding of information, and comprehension questions can test understanding of an argument – but an essay (however short) can test understanding of a complex issue.

A good essay consists of **content** and **comment**. The content takes the form of relevant **facts** and **findings** from one's own experience and research. Comment is just another word for opinion, or judgement.

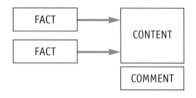

Here is a very brief example: *What lies behind Britain's reluctance to adopt the Euro?*

Content	Facts: 1 The euro lost $\frac{1}{3}$ of its value against the dollar in its first two years of trading. 2 Britons have already had to surrender familiar weights and measures. 3 Entry into the ERM in 1992 was an economic and political embarrassment. 4 The Danish people rejected the Euro in 2000. Findings: 1 Older people still have unfortunate memories of decimalization in 1971. 2 The pound has come to be a last-ditch symbol of British sovereignty.
Comment	Europe in general, and the Euro (or 'Brussels') in particular, represents unwanted bureaucracy. Britons are essentially conservative and want to protect their uniqueness.

It might help to distinguish between two kinds of essay: the exposition and the discussion. An exposition is a 'showing', and an expository essay is a response to a closed question. The above question about the Euro is a closed question: it is assumed that Britain is reluctant to adopt the Euro; all the respondent has to do is to say why.

If it had been an *open* question:

e.g. *What is the attitude of Britons towards the Euro?*

or it had not been a question at all, but had been an open assignment:

e.g. *Discuss the benefits and drawbacks of Britain's adoption of the Euro.*

or: *'Britons will never willingly give up the pound.' Discuss.*

it would be up to the respondent to consider more than one argument and a discussion essay would be required. Let us look at each of these two types of essay in turn:

The exposition essay

This book has an introduction that explains what, and who, the book is intended for, why the book had been written, what it would contain, and how this content would be laid out. Similarly, an essay needs a brief introduction that is:

1   a definition of terms (if necessary)

2   a statement of intent.

A good introduction is concise: in it – probably in one paragraph – the writer should announce what is coming: the writer should not start by immediately answering the question.

e.g.   *Give reasons for the steady decline in the sales of newspapers in Britain.*

Introduction   For the purposes of this essay, 'newspapers' will be taken to refer to national daily newspapers.   } definition of term

Several reasons will be given for declining sales over the past thirty or forty years.   } statement of intent

What follows the introduction will be something like a list of reasons. In practice, there may be little difference between 'facts' and 'findings', but a good rule to follow is to present the hard evidence first. Each reason might have a paragraph to itself.

Here is a digest of possible content, but note that at this stage none of the points has been expanded or developed as they would be in an essay:

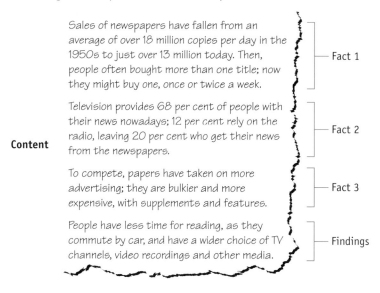

Content

Sales of newspapers have fallen from an average of over 18 million copies per day in the 1950s to just over 13 million today. Then, people often bought more than one title; now they might buy one, once or twice a week.   — Fact 1

Television provides 68 per cent of people with their news nowadays; 12 per cent rely on the radio, leaving 20 per cent who get their news from the newspapers.   — Fact 2

To compete, papers have taken on more advertising; they are bulkier and more expensive, with supplements and features.   — Fact 3

People have less time for reading, as they commute by car, and have a wider choice of TV channels, video recordings and other media.   — Findings

The comment will often come at the end, as a conclusion (though there is no reason why comment should not be scattered across the essay). It will often be in the form of a summary of what has gone before – but:

1   if a question is asked, the conclusion is where it must be answered

2   if an opinion is asked for, the conclusion is where it must be given.

And this is where the statement of intent must be cashed in.

Comment   Newspapers have faced fierce competition from visual news media in recent years. As they have found a new role for themselves, so they have lost the steady readership that they used to have – and the decline is likely to continue as internet access grows.

The discussion essay

Example 1 – The monarchy

A closed question assumes a certain kind of answer (as shown earlier); an open question has at least two possible answers. A discussion is essentially a comparison of one **argument** with another – and both arguments need to be represented. The closed question:

e.g.   *Why is it that the British monarchy enjoys less public esteem in the 21st century than it did in the 1950s?*

can really only be answered in one way: in a **list** of reasons. To the open question:

e.g.   *How far do you agree that the monarchy has no place in the 21st century?*

there are at least two possible answers: it does have a place; it does not have a place.

In arguing that the monarchy does have a place in the 21st century, the anti-monarchy argument should be represented first. In so doing, you:

1   acknowledge that there is more than one point of view – that yours is not the only possible position

2   define, and set aside, the position that you will oppose

3   ensure that you can go on to support your own position with facts and findings, by way of **evidence**.

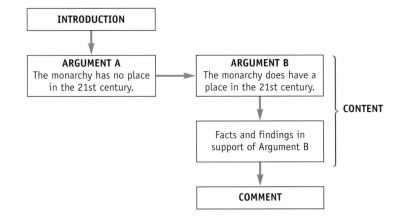

It is worth developing this example, since this will be the pattern of most AS/A-level General Studies essays:

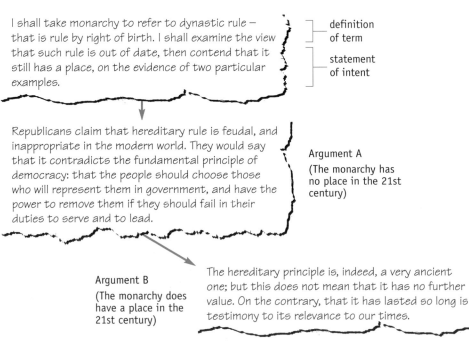

Fact/finding/item of evidence 1	Monarchy is perfectly compatible with democracy. This is proved in the case of Great Britain, where the monarch is said to reign, but not to rule. The Queen has the pomp, and the Prime Minister in Cabinet has the power. The British people would no longer tolerate a powerful Queen than they would a pompous prime minister. The Royal Family is looked up to as the guardian of tradition — and for this, it is best that they be trained from birth.
Fact/finding/item of evidence 2	Monarchy also works well in those, particularly Islamic, countries where strong leadership is respected, and where, if this leader is not royal, there is otherwise a tendency to dictatorship. One only has to compare Jordan with Iraq to make this point.
Comment/ conclusion	We see, then, that monarchy does have a place in the modern world. It is not only compatible with democracy, it may even be the best guarantee of democracy yet devised.

Example 2 – Tourism

Suppose that, in class, you have looked at a number of sources of information and opinion about tourism. Suppose, also, that you have holidayed in the Balearic Islands/Italy/Greece/Turkey, and seen for yourself the impact – both positive and negative – that tourism can have on a coastal community and ecosystem.

These are the sources at your disposal:

Source A

San Feliu de Mar

This was a village that, until the 1960s, depended for its livelihood on fishing and the supply of cork to the wine-bottling industry. There was only one hotel of any size, the Cataluña, that had attracted the custom of well-heeled Britons and Germans for some years. As these visitors had begun to take their holidays farther afield, however, it had become necessary to broaden the appeal of the place to operators of package tours. San Feliu had good transport links and access to urban amenities, so it was well-placed to take advantage of the larger numbers of, particularly, Britons who could afford an 'all-in' holiday by the Mediterranean.

Two new hotels were built and leisure facilities were provided to meet this new demand – an 18-hole golf course, an open-air swimming pool and the beginnings of a yacht marina; nightclubs would come later. It is as well that these developments took place, since cork-production was shifting to Portugal, where economies of scale could be realized, and since the income from fishing was in steady decline. Inshore waters were subject to pollution from sewage outflows, and over-fishing was depleting stocks farther out to sea.

By the mid-1970s, therefore, the tourist trade was opening up labour opportunities – in hotels and restaurants, in painting and decorating, and in small retail outlets – to men and women who had worked in primary industry until then. It was seasonal employment, of course – but then so had much employment been, in these coastal villages. Now they were villages no longer: they were resorts, tempted at first to sacrifice quality in favour of sheer numbers of visitors with pesetas to spend on cheap thrills and chips-with-everything meals, that learned to set limits to hotel-building. San Feliu de Mar could have gone the way of many noisy, brash resorts – but the local council was strong enough, and enlightened enough, to preserve the features of the town that the more discerning holidaymakers enjoyed: the street-markets, the sandy ramblas, the palms, and the rocky paths among cork-oak trees behind the town.

R.K. Allenby (1998)

Source B

Holidays abroad by destination				%
	1971	**1981**	**1991**	**1998**
Spain	34.3	21.7	21.3	27.5
France	15.9	27.2	25.8	20.2
United States	1.0	5.5	6.9	7.0
Greece	4.5	6.7	7.6	5.3
Italy	9.2	5.8	3.5	4.0
Portugal	2.6	2.8	4.8	3.6
Irish Republic	–	3.6	3.0	3.5
Turkey	–	0.1	0.7	3.0
Netherlands	3.6	2.4	3.5	2.7
Cyprus	1.0	0.7	2.4	2.6
Belgium	–	2.1	2.1	2.3
Germany	3.4	2.6	2.7	1.8
Malta	–	2.6	1.7	1.3
Austria	5.5	2.5	2.4	1.3
Other countries	19.0	13.7	11.8	13.9
All destinations (100%) (thousands)	4,201	13,131	26,788	32,306

NOTE: this is the complete table of which that on page 72 is an extract.

Source C

A nation of servants

Perhaps we need not be too romantic about the life of the New Britain islanders. They were never quite as battle-prone as their countrymen on the mainland, where clan-fighting was the norm, but they were a proud people, with a fierce attachment to the land.

They were no match though for the multinational real-estate companies and hotel chains. Big money played one clan off against another, and made all sorts of promises of the good times ahead – and, to be sure, the islanders do have money in their pockets as never before. But, at what cost!

The Club Med-style hotel complexes and imitation coral-atoll swimming pools have made some aesthetic concessions to the landscape; but the lives and customs of the people themselves have been bought. They are dressed in colourful laplaps to serve at table, where they might have preferred to wear jeans. They wear laundered shirts and hibiscus blooms behind their ears, where they would normally have worn nothing but pigs' tooth necklaces above the waist at all. They clean bedrooms and bathrooms of a sort to which they could never themselves aspire. They mow and water golf links on which they will never themselves play – indeed, the hotels and golf clubs use so much water, that the islanders regularly go short.

Their weddings and initiation ceremonies have become public performances; their singsings are the property of the tour-companies; even their clan stand-offs, their spear-carving and their bow-and-arrow making skills are commissioned by hotel managements. Bare breasts and torsos gleaming with pigs' fat are much in demand when the cruise-ships anchor in Rabaul.

Ian Partridge (1999)

The essay title that you have been assigned is as follows:

Comment on the view that tourism does more harm to a host community than good.

To write a response to this title, it is enough to scan the sources to judge that tourism does more good in some places and more harm in others. It isn't a black or white issue. Few issues are, that give rise to truly open questions.

Sources A and C, and common sense, would suggest – and your own experience might confirm this – that tourism is likely to benefit communities that are, or need to, develop and modernize; and it may harm communities where change is disruptive and the pace too swift. This is the line taken in the following essay.

According to the figures for 'overseas visits' published by the Office for National Statistics, just over 50 million Britons went abroad in 1998. The number of holidays abroad for the same year is given (ONS, 2000) as 32 306. It is these visits that are what we generally mean by tourism, not the visits – short-haul business trips in the main – that make up the balance. Tourism will do harm if it undermines the cultural stability and well being of a community. If it adds to the economic security and cultural diversity of a region it may well confer net benefits. Both possibilities will be examined here.

<table>
<tr><td>← INTRODUCTION</td></tr>
<tr><td>← definition of term 1</td></tr>
<tr><td>← definition of term 2</td></tr>
<tr><td>← statement of intent</td></tr>
</table>

It is evident (ONS, 2000) that the vast majority of foreign holidays taken by Britons are to developed countries, mainly in Europe. Only Turkey and Cyprus among the named countries in this table might be called less developed, or non-industrialized countries – and even these are applicants for EU entry. Tourism can bring significant benefits to a country, particularly in terms of foreign-exchange revenue. If 54 million Britons travelled abroad in 1999 (Carvel, 2000) 25 million foreigners came to Britain. Had they not done so, the balance of payments would have been in a sorrier state.

← ARGUMENT A
(Tourism does more good than harm)
← fact 1
← fact 2

Tourism plainly brought benefits to countries like Spain (Allenby, 1998) at a time when new employment opportunities were needed to replace those being lost in primary industry. The tourist industry developed sufficiently gradually for it not to be socially destabilizing; on the contrary, communities on the Costa Brava and the French and Italian rivieras have adapted to tourism – and have adapted tourism to themselves – as happily as the Swiss and the Austrians have accommodated skiing. Countries like the USA, – to which holiday-visits by Britons have increased sevenfold over 30 years – Britain, France, and Germany can easily absorb large numbers of foreign holidaymakers without ill effects. Indeed, in each of these countries, foreign tourists will make many amenities viable that might otherwise not be.

← fact 3
← fact 4

The situation might be quite different in developing countries. In Papua New Guinea (Partridge, 1999), for instance, communities have only recently emerged into the age of radio, television, powered flight and automation. Their cultural evolution has been sudden – even traumatic. They have achieved independence, yet they are second-class citizens in their own land. The few will have had their pockets filled, and will have grown away from their roots; but the many will have been employed in menial jobs, or been gazed at and photographed like tropical fish in a bowl. Their water will have been siphoned off, and their beaches will have been privatized. They cannot hope to live on anything like equal terms with foreign visitors; and their culture is bound to seem inferior to that of free-spending tourists. My experience in Egypt bears this out: foreign tourists either stimulate unrealistic expectations among the poor; or they cause resentment among the young and militant.

← ARGUMENT B
(Tourism may do more harm than good)
← fact 1
← fact 2
← finding 1
← finding 2

With globalization, and rising standards of living, will come international tourism. When the host community is already developed, or is developing, economically, it will benefit from such tourism. Theirs will be a genuine exchange relationship with the tourists. Where the relationship is grossly unequal, tourism may be exploitative and culturally destructive, unless it is introduced on the host community's own terms.

← COMMENT/
CONCLUSION

References

1 Allenby, R.K. (1998) *Spain in Transition* London: HarperCollinsPublishers*

2 Carvel, John (2000) 'Britons go abroad in record numbers' in *The Guardian*, 23 November 2000

3 Office for National Statistics (2000) *Social Trends 30*, London: The Stationery Office

4 Partridge, Ian (1999) 'A Nation of Servants' in *General Studies*, April 1999*

* Sources A and C were written specifically for inclusion here. Fictitious publishing details have been added to indicate how references should be made in the text, and how complete publishing details should be given in a bibliography. Both in-text, and end-of-text references are equally, and mutually necessary.

Skills: Solving a problem

Approaching problems

There is not one sort of problem, and there is not one way of solving it. There are certainly as many sorts of problem as there are subjects in the academic curriculum: so there are mathematical problems, and physical science problems, and sociological problems, and historical problems, and philosophical problems – and some of those problems are reviewed in this book. Each 'subject' has its own focus of interest, and each has devised its own techniques for sharpening that focus and testing its findings.

It would be too much to say that we can generalize across all these techniques and say: *this is the way to solve problems; these are the steps you should take in all cases.* There is no one set of 'thinking skills', any more than there is one set of 'living skills'. What we should be doing when solving problems – and this is the real business of General Studies – is to make sure that we:

- establish the facts in the case
- examine our own and other people's assumptions
- decide how hard or soft the evidence is
- come to measured conclusions.

What is a problem?

The word *problem* is used on a daily basis, in one of three ways.

(i) a problem is a sort of *puzzle*. All the necessary information is available: the solution just has to be puzzled out, as in a maths problem, or a logical problem, or a crossword problem.

 e.g. (a) If $x = \dfrac{10.015}{0.075}$, what is the value of x?
 (b) Every x is y
 No y is z
 Therefore no x …
 (c) 5 DOWN: Americanized by force (6)

(ii) a problem is a sort of *question*. Information is missing. Some empirical enquiry is called for, as in an historical problem:

 e.g. When the *Titanic* went down, the *Californian* was the nearest ship. Stanley Lord was its captain.

 (a) Was Lord on deck when the *Titanic* fired distress flares?
 (b) If so, would he have been able to see them from his position?
 (c) Were the wireless operators on duty or not?

> **Q1** Give one further (non-mathematical) example of a *puzzle*; and one further example of a *question* whose solution depends on the supply of one or more pieces of information.

(iii) a problem is a sort of *dispute*, or conflict of interests. As in the puzzle, all the necessary information is available; what is wanted is a *reconciliation* of conflicting interests and values, and a judgement that is as objective as possible.

 e.g. it is proposed that a corner house be converted into the offices of a small computer company, and that its back garden be made into an eight-space carpark. The purchasers of the house mislead the council and neighbouring house-owners as to the impact of the development.

It is this sort of 'problem' – an ordinary situation that grows into a dispute – that is the most likely candidate for a problem-solving exercise in General Studies.

Example 1 – planning dispute

What follows is a further examination of the case above.

Home-owners up in arms

The neighbourhood of Chase Common Road and St Andrew's Road has been largely residential – until recently. The houses in these roads were built in the second half of the 19ᵗʰ century. Being close to the town centre, with small gardens front and back, they have been popular and command high prices. Some of the houses on Chase Common Road are rather bigger – but these, too, were built before garage space became standard.

As Chase Common Road has got busier, so some of the properties have been turned over to commercial use. The building of a Texaco filling station and the conversion of what was St Andrew's Baptist Chapel into offices have accelerated this development.

The residents of St Andrew's Road have already had to contend with staff parking as a result of that conversion, so the council made it a condition of the conversion of the house on the corner for occupation by A.P. Scott Partners, that parking be provided. Residents at nos. 1–7 and 2–4 St Andrew's Road lodged no objection to the garden of the corner-house being surfaced for car parking – indeed, the partially-handicapped Mrs Parker, at no. 1 St Andrew's Road, was permitted to park her specially-adapted Toyota Yaris in one of the new spaces.

But A.P. Scott, it turns out, uses many more than the seven parking spaces left. "We have nowhere to park our cars now," says Mr Stuart at no. 2. "Scott's park white vans in the road, and they put cones there when the vans have gone, as if they own the road. And they must have ten or a dozen employees who fight for space every morning."

The council is looking into the problem as we go to press.

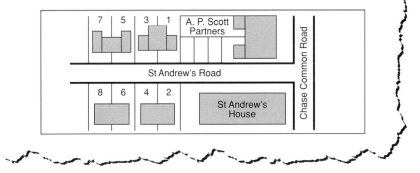

This is a very small-scale issue; but it is typical of the sort of problem that occurs in urban areas where there is competition for limited space, and where there is conflict between residential and commercial interests.

Q2 As a General Studies student, you would probably be asked to do something like the following:
  (i)   Identify the problem that has given rise to this newspaper article.
  (ii) Define the rights and responsibilities of the main parties to the dispute.
  (iii) Make recommendations to the council for action that it might take.

You may want to answer these questions yourself, before considering the 'solution' offered below.

Solution

(i)   There has been a gradual build-up of pressure on parking space in roads close to the centre of the town. Car ownership has probably grown among residents at a time when staff at offices in St Andrew's House need to park their cars. Evidently, when this conversion from a chapel was undertaken, no stipulations as to car space were made.

A.P. Scott appear to have persuaded the council that, when it applied for permission to convert the corner house to office space, the eight car spaces on what had been garden would be sufficient to its needs. Instead, and in spite of the concession made to Mrs Parker, the residents of St Andrew's Road found themselves competing for parking space with A. P. Scott employees, and with the drivers of white vans.

(ii)

Rights	Responsibilities
A.P. Scott: To allocate the eight spaces in its own car park to employees or whomsoever else.	To limit any other parking in favour of the residents of St Andrew's Road.
Residents: To park their own cars outside their own houses. (This is a right assumed rather than enshrined in law.) Not to be prevented from doing so by cones placed by A.P. Scott employees.	To make their complaints to the council; to be moderate in their defence of what they perceive to be their rights.
Council: To full and honest information from those requesting change of use, and planning permission.	To take up the case on behalf of residents and require that A.P. Scott adhere to the terms of its permission.

(The business(es) in St Andrew's House may be thought to be a fourth party in this dispute.)

Q3 Do you agree with this allocation of rights and responsibilities? Do any other parties come into the picture?

(iii) The council should ask the residents of St Andrew's Road to put their complaints in writing, being as specific as possible. If this is considered unduly bureaucratic, a group of them, including Mrs Parker and Mr Stuart, should be asked to make representations in person, either in the council offices or in the residents' own homes.

The council should then draw up a formal notice of complaint to A.P. Scott, asking for their considered response within a reasonable period of time.

If parking is then confined to the seven spaces in the company's own car park, the dispute would be reckoned to have been satisfactorily resolved.

If the company did not reply, or the situation remained unchanged, the council should (i) mark spaces on the street in St Andrew's Road for 'Residents Only' parking; (ii) prohibit the unauthorized use of cones by A.P. Scott employees, with a warning that this is a matter for the police; (iii) in the longer term, look into the possibilities of charging for non-resident on-street parking, and encouraging the owners of businesses to use alternative modes of transport to work.

Q4 Do you agree with these recommendations? Are there others that you would want to make?

Example 2 – Road building

The above example is a small-scale version of a countrywide (more or less worldwide) problem: the competition for land. The two great pressures on land in Britain, in the second half of the 20th century, were roads and housing. Both add to the 'built environment', and impinge on ever more precious 'green' space.

Road building – and particularly motorway building – has been a contentious issue for a long time. It came to a head in the early 1990s, at a time when new motorways were being built through some particularly sensitive landscapes.

Consider these two press cuttings:

Hard shoulders to cry on

John Vidal

In the next 15 years the Department of Transport intends to spend £20 billion redrawing the map of Britain, and yesterday's announcement that £2.1 billion of road programmes are to be brought forward to create 30 000 jobs in the construction industry is only a taste of what is to come.

Thousands of miles of motorway are to be widened, new ones built and more trunk routes widened or upgraded to dual carriageways. Six hundred towns and villages are queueing for bypasses, many feeder and link roads are planned and the Government's suggested 'trans-Europe' strategic routes may demand that great stretches of road be upgraded to motorway standard.

For a motorist sitting for the fourth time in a week in stationary traffic outside Birmingham or London, or contemplating a cross-country journey, £20 billion of road building might seem justifiable. Bypasses and roads are popular with the public and with the DoT, which values time saved off journeys above all other criteria. They help 'free' the country for economic progress ... Critics argue that the department's cost-benefit analysis of roads is environmentally, socially and economically flawed. They question statistics that suggest a doubling of road traffic in the South East within 35 years. They maintain that many new roads will save no more than minutes off long journeys, will devastate land and exacerbate congestion.

The Guardian 5 February 1993

Restraining the Zealots

An American charity has awarded £47 000 to Emma Must, 29, one of Britain's leading campaigners against new roads. She has spent two years organizing demonstrations on various construction sites around the country, and in 1993 spent a month in Holloway for defying injunctions to stay away from the M3 extension in Hampshire. On the other side of that coin, it appears that some £26 million of the taxpayers' money may have to be spent on protecting the four-mile M11 extension in north London from demonstrators. Millions more are having to be spent on the security of other roadworks. Yesterday, there were scuffles at the M65 extension near Blackburn, when 300 police started to clear campaigners who have been occupying tree-houses at the site for nine months ...

What is so often omitted from the argument over motorways is the perpetual necessity for this country to remain competitive in order to earn its living. It is a point that never seems to enter the heads of the protesters. But if we are to keep abreast of our European neighbours, with whom we must compete, we need an infrastructure that at least approximates to theirs. All environmental issues are today a matter of public concern, but there is a balance to be struck. Flying protesters, who contribute nothing to our economy, cannot be allowed to prevent those striving to keep this country competitive from going about their lawful business. If they do, the law has a duty to restrain them.

The Daily Telegraph editorial 2 May 1995

Q5 There are two problems here: the one that John Vidal of *The Guardian* focuses on; and the one highlighted in the *Telegraph* editorial.
(i) What are the problems identified by these two writers?
(ii) Identify those who favour road building and give an account of how they benefit by it; and explain the objections of those who oppose it.
(iii) Suggest a solution to the two problems that might reconcile what appear to be diametrically opposed positions.

Example 3 – Urban environment

To some extent, the heat has been taken out of the dispute about road building by the realization on all sides that the old 'predict and provide' policy was unsustainable. As soon as new roads were built, they were congested.

'Predict and provide' has been the policy of the planners of housing, too. Are households getting smaller, as a result of divorce and other 'lifestyle' choices? If this is the case, 4.4 million new, small houses will be needed by the year 2016. Is the trend for one quarter of all new households in Britain to locate in the South East? If so, 1.1 million new, small houses will be required in the Home Counties (excluding London) within a generation.

These projections were received, and largely accepted, by the Major government. The Blair government was initially sceptical, and laid emphasis on the need to build 60 per cent of all new houses on 'brownfield' sites. The threat of the JCB in green fields – even in the 'green belt' – was not removed. Deputy Prime Minister John Prescott commissioned two enquiries: that of Professor Stephen Crow into urban planning in the South East; and that of Lord (Richard) Rogers into the regeneration of Britain's cities. The former recommended that the proposed 1.1 million new houses be built – that the needs of the economy be placed above the supposed needs of the environment. The latter advised that cities would only enjoy a 'renaissance' if they could be made fit, not merely to commute to and to work in, but to live in.

Consider these sources, and respond to the 'problem-solving' questions below:

Towards an urban renaissance

Many of the visionaries of the 19th and 20th centuries – from Ebenezer Howard to Le Corbusier – have sought to provide us with an escape from the city … We have increasingly lost ownership of the places and spaces which were once deemed to be the heart of civilized society.

The English suburban experience continues to be characterized by heavy dependence on separate zones for different uses, undermining its economic and social cohesion, as well as impacting negatively upon the natural environment.

This trend has been fuelled by private property investment activity over the last twenty years which has tended towards a pattern of dispersal. House-builders have responded to the demand for suburban housing by providing new estates in peripheral locations. Retailers have developed larger and larger edge-of-town shopping centres for a predominantly car-borne public. Industrialists have moved out of congested urban centres to peripheral sites to take advantage of good motorway access …

How will we know that we have achieved an urban renaissance? More people will be living in our cities, in better-managed, compact urban neighbourhoods. They will be able to access a wider range of local facilities without resort to the car; be better linked both physically and electronically; and be enjoying an improved standard of public services, and a cleaner and safer living environment.

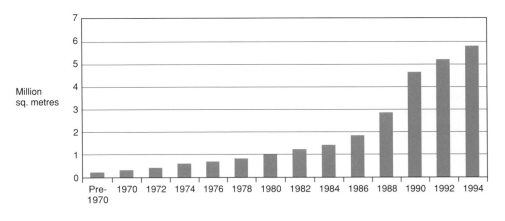

Source: Department for Transport, Local Government and the Regions (DETR), 1999
(final Report of the Urban Task Force, Norwich, HMSO)

Field of dreams

The Government wants to see cities enjoying a renaissance. But there's a long way to go. Nicola Baird wonders why we still don't have a love affair with big cities.

Half the world's population lives in cities, yet millions of people – and particularly the British – are convinced that *the* place to live is the countryside. Bizarrely, these country hopefuls are even prepared to concrete over the existing countryside in order to have their own front door choked by rambling roses and an address that hints of green lanes. All too often they are trapped in pretend countryside on an estate with no shops or public transport.

But Britain's cities are not great either. The posh areas are too expensive and the affordable sections too far from jobs, shops and entertainment. Even heritage cities, such as Canterbury and York, contain run-down areas, gridlocked roads, and bad air days. Litter and crime are endemic …

When Millennium Dome architect Richard Rogers gave the Reith Lectures in 1995, he challenged listeners to see cities in a new light. Rogers recognized that cities helped cause climate change, that their population was demanding too much food from overseas to be shipped in and producing too much waste. He admitted that: "Our cities are driving this environmental crisis," but he believed that they could be fit places to live.

"Achieving an urban renaissance is not only about numbers and percentages, it is about creating the quality of life and vitality that makes urban living desirable," says Rogers. "We must bring about a change in urban attitudes so that towns and cities once again become attractive places to live, work and socialize."

Friends of the Earth *Earth Matters*, Summer 2000

Developers of derelict sites to get tax relief

by *Clayton Hirst*

Gordon Brown is set to bow to Cabinet pressure to provide incentives to regenerate Britain's run-down areas by announcing a cocktail of measures in his November pre-Budget statement.

The *Independent on Sunday* has learned that central to the Chancellor's announcement will be a plan to give property developers capital gains tax relief when building in derelict areas …

It is understood that Mr Prescott and Mr Brown have for months been at loggerheads as to how to promote urban regeneration, with the Treasury preferring capital spending and the DETR favouring incentives. But Mr Brown has softened, and has held a series of discreet meetings with property industry bodies to thrash out ideas.

The move will also be cheered by Lord Rogers of Riverside, designer of the Millennium Dome and the Lloyds Building in the City of London. Last June Labour's favourite architect produced a government-sponsored report into ways of regenerating Britain's poorest regions. Central to the hefty document were proposals to give property developers incentives to build on urban sites and to re-use derelict buildings …

The Treasury's interest in urban regeneration is timely. New research reveals the number of derelict sites in Britain could be much greater than previously thought.

According to law firm Addleshaw Booth, in many regions the Government's official figures seriously underestimate the actual proportion of 'brown field' land.

Independent on Sunday 1 October 2000

Q6 (i) Summarize the present-day problems of city living.
(ii) Might there be groups of people who would not benefit from an 'urban renaissance'? Who would they be, and why?
(iii) By which of the above means – and others – is an urban renaissance most likely to be brought about? Give reasons for your choice.

Skills: Making a presentation

Information technology

Within a very short time, life without information technology has come to seem unimaginable. Estimates reckon that between 20–25 million people have access to a PC at home, and around 40 per cent of UK homes are connected to the internet. There are many websites that students of General Studies might be advised to consult, and some of these are given on page 139.

Key skills opportunity

One of the requirements specified in key skills Communication is that students make a presentation to others; one of the requirements specified in key skills ICT is that students present information they have acquired. It is this overlap that is the focus of this section.

In order to present information to others successfully it is necessary to:

● choose items to be presented, and set them in a logical order

● consider what will be of interest, and how that interest might be whetted and sustained

● select key dates and some telling visual images to achieve maximum impact and meet audience needs

● ensure that the presentation as a whole carries a clear, coherent message.

Microsoft PowerPoint

The PowerPoint computer program was designed specifically for the purpose of making an effective presentation. The program comes as standard with most versions of Microsoft Office, though the specifications will vary.

● Click on **Start** and then on **Programs**. Double-click on the PowerPoint icon (see A).

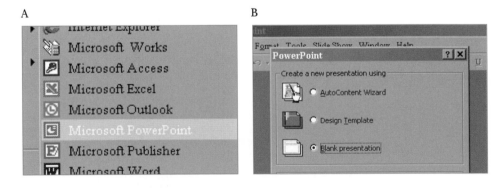

● Select 'Create a new presentation using…Blank presentation' (see B). This option offers a wide range of possible layouts or 'slides' (see C) and the program takes you through them in a logical sequence.

The first slide provides a title layout, and subsequent slides offer the opportunity of presenting text in bullet form; of combining text with bar charts or with images; and of starting from scratch with a truly blank screen.

It is easy to change your mind should you choose a format that does not suit your purpose.

C

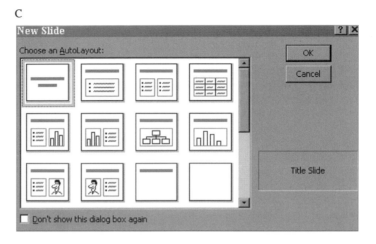

To help see the program in action, this guide will take you through an example presentation: 'Information Technology: Brave New World'. This presentation looks at the beginnings of information technology and its fundamentals: its newness and the promises made on its behalf.

● Click on **OK** to select the title page. Using 'Information Technology' as the subject of this example presentation, type the title 'Information Technology' in the hatched-sided box provided, and then add the subtitle 'Brave New World'. This helps to specify what aspect, or aspects of information technology you will cover in the presentation. Notice that the words you type are repeated in list form in the left-hand panel (see D). Use this to help you keep track of your presentation.

D

![Microsoft PowerPoint window showing the title slide "Information Technology" with "Click to add subtitle" placeholder and "Click to add notes" area.]

● Just below the word **Format** is the icon for a new page. Click on this icon to return to screen C (see above). This time the program suggests you select the second layout: the bulleted list (notice these words appear in the box at the bottom right-hand corner of the screen). Select this layout if you wish to summarize your message at this stage so that your audience knows what to expect; but you may prefer to keep them guessing about what you intend.

Slides as cues

The slides you are creating are your 'props'. They provide the structure of your presentation so the order of the slides should follow the order of the points you wish to make. Each slide should also be a cue for the next point.

The slides should not, however, contain all that you wish to say: simply reading aloud the text from the slides would make a very dull presentation.

Important points are:

- there should not be too much text on any one slide, just the salient information
- each slide should follow from the last in a logical sequence
- a slide that is purely pictorial, or that presents a graph or other diagram, will need some explanation
- a slide that presents self-explanatory text will not need much verbal support.

Suppose that these are your first two slides:

1   2

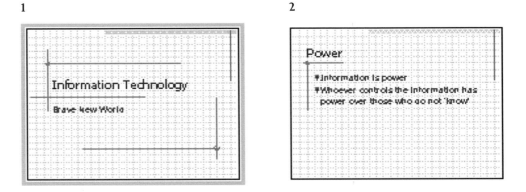

There is no need to read the title (see 1) – the audience can read it for themselves – but you may add something to each. As the audience is reading the title slide, you could read from your notes:

1 'O brave new world, that has such people in it!' This is from Shakespeare's *The Tempest*. Aldous Huxley used the phrase as the title of his 1932 novel about scientific socialism.

And as you show the 'Power' slide (see 2), you might say:

2 Francis Bacon said '*Knowledge* is power'. What power might information have? (The police seek *information* from the public about an accident or assault.)

It is often a good idea to ask a rhetorical question: the audience has to work a little, and you invite them to share your uncertainties.

Background

- Returning to PowerPoint, click on **Format**, then **Apply Design Template** to reveal a choice of backgrounds for your slides. (These vary across the versions of Windows.) Try to match the background to the subject matter of the presentation. Also, experiment with light and dark backgrounds – some can be quite difficult to read in a bright room. (The slides shown above have a 'Blueprint' background.) Above all, the slides must be legible to your audience.

Animations

- Depending on your version of PowerPoint, the program comes with a number of tricks for moving words about the screen. Find these under **Slide Show**, then **Custom Animation**. Moving text can add interest to a presentation, but it can also be distracting. The simplest, and perhaps most effective, is 'fly from the right'. Letters can be made to fly in one by one, which works well if you don't want your audience to view a statement in one go, or if you want to spring a surprise. Alternatively, you can have text crawl slowly up the screen from below.

Some variety is welcome, but it should be appropriate and not overdone. Experiment first to see what works best.

Images

Slide after slide of bullet points can be unrelenting and you may wish to add variety by using images.

The easiest way to obtain images is from a **Clip Art** file (see below). More original and realistic images can be found on the internet. Find a relevant website; choose a picture, then right-click on it to save it. This is relatively easy for a subject such as Information Technology. There is a website, for example, which consists entirely of maps of the internet as it grew from its early days as a tool of the US army. Here is a small part of this sequence:

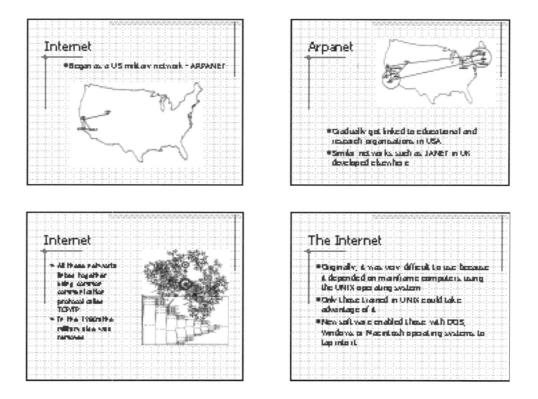

In addition to the vast numbers of images available on the internet, there are numerous CDs on the market containing thousands of pictures. But use these sensibly – there might just be too many images to choose from.

- Return to PowerPoint, and click on **Insert**, followed by **Picture**. You will then be given the choice of **Clip Art**, or one of your saved files (which is where your saved internet image will be). You might like to store useful images on floppy disks.

Further refinements to your presentation can be made by using a CD containing video clips of moving images. You might also consider playing appropriate music while one or more slides are displayed.

Other means of presentation

Of course, you might not have PowerPoint available, but this does not mean that you cannot produce an interesting and visually arresting presentation. There are many ways to present information to an audience:

- **boards/flip charts/OHPs** These can be prepared in advance, in a similar way to the PowerPoint slides, and then revealed one by one, supported by your verbal commentary.
- **handouts** Check whether you can make use of the school photocopier to make enough copies of handouts for the class. These can contain the salient points that you wish to put across, plus any diagrams and charts.
- **video clips** If appropriate, make use of the school VCR to show relevant video clips.

Bear in mind that the guidelines at the beginning of this section apply to all presentations, whether you make use of PowerPoint or other methods.

The presentation

Once you are ready to make your presentation, ensure you have prepared in advance:

- a clear structure of the points you wish to make
- the collection of slides, boards, OHPs and so on, to match this structure (24 will probably be the maximum you would need for a presentation of between 10 and 15 minutes)
- your notes of what to say as each slide, board or OHP is displayed
- any equipment you will need (PC, PowerPoint, OHP, VCR, flip chart, video projector).

Make sure that any equipment is ready to use and fully functional. Use the largest monitor you can find, or a video projector, if using a PC. Do not use any equipment that you are not fully confident with.

Once you are ready to begin your presentation, remember to:

- speak slowly, at about one half the speed of your normal speaking voice
- look at your audience from time to time – they will feel shut out if you stare fixedly at your notes, or at the screen or flip chart
- speak to, and look at, different parts of the audience, front and back, left and right – in this way they feel included in your talk, and are more likely to pay attention
- keep reasonably still – too much movement or gesticulation is distracting.

Be prepared to answer questions, particularly where information contains technical terms. Make sure you know what all the technical terms mean as these are the ones the audience are most likely ask you about.

Perhaps ask rhetorical and open questions – you might like to end your presentation on a questioning note. A presentation that leads to a genuinely open debate is the best kind of presentation.

Planning your presentation

In summary, here are the stages you will need to address when preparing your presentation:

- select a topic area
- research the topic
- consider what will be of interest
- decide how to start in order to whet the audience's appetite
- choose items to be presented, and the order in which to present them
- select salient points such as key dates
- select key visual images
- write notes that support and expand your visual presentation
- consider how you will end the talk
- decide how you will present the information and what equipment you will need
- ensure that the presentation is coherent
- make sure you are well prepared on the day.

Websites

On the following page is a representative selection of internet addresses that might be useful to General Studies students.

Acknowledgement should always be made, and the website address be given, when internet material is quoted in a presentation or an essay.

Websites

Government

House of Commons   www.parliament.uk/commons
Ministry of Agriculture, Fisheries & Food   www.defra.gov.uk
United Kingdom Government   www.ukonline.gov.uk

Press

The Big Issue   www.bigissue.com
The Guardian   www.guardian.co.uk
                                                           www.educationunlimited.co.uk
                                                           www.societyguardian.co.uk
The Independent   www.independent.co.uk/links
                                                           www.independent.co.uk/news/world
The New Internationalist   www.newint.org
The Observer   www.observer.co.uk

Broadcasting

British Broadcasting Corporation   www.bbc.co.uk/newsnight
                                                           www.bbc.co.uk/radio4/today
                                                           news.bbc.co.uk
Independent Television Commission   www.itc.org.uk

Organizations

Advertising Standards Authority   www.asa.org.uk
Amnesty International   www.amnesty.org.uk
Barnardos   www.barnados.org.uk
Community Service Volunteers   www.csv.org.uk
Confederation of British Industry   www.cbi.org.uk
Electoral Reform Society   www.electoral-reform.org.uk
Electricity Association   www.electricity.org.uk
Environmental Transport Association   www.eta.co.uk
Friends of the Earth   www.foe.co.uk
Greenpeace   www.greenpeace.org.uk
Homecheck (Pollution, Waste Disposal)   www.homecheck.co.uk
Humane Genome Mapping Project (UK)   www.hgmp.mrc.ac.uk
Human Rights Watch   www.hrw.org/wr2k1
Imperial Cancer Research Fund   www.icnet.uk
Institute of Economic Affairs   www.iea.org.uk
Life   www.lifeuk.org
Oxfam   www.oxfam.org.uk
Recycle (recycling waste)   www.recycle.mcmail.com
Understanding Energy   www.energy.org.uk
Voluntary Euthanasia Society   www.ves.org.uk
Voluntary Service Overseas   www.vso.org.uk
Waste Watch   www.wastewatch.co.uk
Worldwide Fund for Nature (UK)   www.wwf-uk.org

Examining boards

Assessment and Qualifications Alliance (AQA)   www.aqa.org.uk
Edexcel (London University)   www.edexcel.org.uk
Oxford, Cambridge, RSA Examinations (OCR)   www.ocr.org.uk

Answers

Answers are given to all closed questions. Suggestive pointers are also given towards answers to most open questions; but the reader is free to disagree with any of these. None should be considered sufficient.

Pages 2–3

1 Handling money; counting the days; checking speed; making sense of news.
2 Levels of significance in psychology; rates of growth of GDP in economics, etc.
3 When testing theories, and expressing and demonstrating knowledge.
4 Social sciences will never be as objective as traditional sciences because they measure subjective factors rather than objective ones.
5 It may show how much regularity there is in the workings of nature.
6 *Some* maths probably should be – particularly basic statistics.
7 One example could be investigating blood groups. If a child is … And their mother is …, then the father must be … because a child's blood group is determined by those of his or her parents.
8 This book aims to cast doubt on the possibility.

Pages 4–5

1 Unity, union, unique, single, singular, etc. Duo, dyad, dual, binary, brace, twins, couple, pair, double, etc. Trio, triple, trinity, treble, trilogy, etc.
2 House numbers, birthdays, ages, times, etc.
3 E and 7
4 You sniff the drink of the under-age student and check the card of the beer drinker.
5 Advanced mathematics uses our natural pattern recognition skills. Elementary mathematics uses skills that do not come naturally to humans.
6 Children are no longer taught how to perform even the basic mathematical functions – they are taught how to operate a calculator.
7 Devlin believes our difficulties with mathematics are caused by our lack of natural skills to deal with precise manipulations of information. Philips believes our difficulties are caused by poor training – that is, nature versus nurture.

Pages 6–7

1 Wonders of the world, planets, seas, heavens, tones per octave, liberal arts, deadly sins, etc.
2 Zodiacal signs, lunar phases per annum, Olympian gods, tribes of Israel, disciples, northern and southern stars, etc.
3 Hours per day and/or night; months per year.
4 It is divisible by 2, 3, 4 and 6.
5 One trillion metres; 1 000 000 000 000 m
6 Ten to the power of minus 12 metres; 0.000000000001 m
7 $\tan 44° \times 20 = 19.3$
8 31 556 925 astronomical seconds.
9 We *could*, but at the expense of observable reality, and of custom.

Pages 8–9

1 They are self-selected listeners to one programme in one town.
2 The sample is of fewer than 50 people; even percentages for Huntsville residents cannot be safely extrapolated.
3 It does. Left to themselves, respondents might have thought of different categories.
4 'Crime' is a very inclusive category; doesn't 'vandalism' include 'graffiti'? Mightn't 'noise' include neighbours?
5 Ratios may not be accurately represented; a pie chart might have been clearer.
6 The mean adds up each figure and divides by the number of incomes (6). In this case the striking figure of £985 has a high impact, appearing to increase the average. £210 is the most common figure, thus giving us the mode. Arranged in ascending order the middle figure (median) is also £210.
7 If it is the mean, the 'average' might be inflated by huge rises at the top; if the median, then 'real' inequality has grown.
8 The decline would look less dramatic.
9 What do the seven horizontal segments represent? A drop from the £10 000 to £6 500 is of 35%, not 20%.
10 The mean of the depreciation is 32%, so 30–40% is what one would expect.

Pages 10–11

2 Thursday follows Wednesday; ace trumps king; Charles is heir to the throne, etc.
3 Solar UV rays can burn the skin; salmon swim upstream to spawn.
4 Rabbits, bears, mice, dogs and bats all suckle their young. We call all such animals 'mammals'.
5 Any mammal will suckle its young; an animal that does not is not a mammal.
6 It is 'value' itself, based on experience.

Pages 12–13

1 In this case it is the mean, but the median and mode are almost identical.
2 24% (83−59). Smaller, perhaps: one might have thought the Metropolitan figure would be lower than 59.
3 A more powerful car is a common aspiration.
4 Pressure of advertising; keeping up with the Joneses; higher disposable incomes.
5 No, they are extrapolations from facts.
6 (a) 77% (b) 120.8%
7 Males 26%, females 27%.
8 More journeys are undertaken by car/train, as people live farther from their work.
9 Parents transport children because roads are congested and are perceived to be dangerous.
10 Check the graph correctly reflects the information given.
11 44.6%
12 (a) 61.2% (b) 7.5% (c) 27.4%
13 (a) Car manufacturers and salesmen, mechanics, car parts shops, driver convenience, government tax.
    (b) Parking, overcrowding, pollution, traffic speed, reduced public transport services.

Pages 14–15

1 It challenges our over-narrow definition. We define it as what (only) scientists do. Our definition ought to be more inclusive.

2 It suggests that 'science' is essentially different from non-mathematically certain areas of knowledge.

3 Rutherford meant that physics is the only mathematically certain science – others merely sort entities into classes. Based on this very exclusive definition he was being objective, but such an exclusive definition is not necessary.

5 They confirm physics as an exact science.

6 **Einstein**: formulated theories of relativity and contributed to quantum theory; **Planck**: first formulated quantum theory; **Bohr** (Aage Niels): worked on nuclear structure, his father (Niels Bohr) explained spectral lines; **Schrödinger**: contributed to the beginnings of molecular biology and formulated 'Schrödinger Cat'; **Heisenberg**: formulated the uncertainty principle.

7 The atomic and hydrogen bombs; nuclear energy; cost of particle accelerators, etc.

Pages 16–17

1 Check the pie chart correctly reflects the table.

2 The opening up of the North Sea oil field, and government preference for private industry.

3 It is not possible currently. No one looks to the future enough to consider it a viable way of life.

4 Uranium seemed inexhaustible and the energy seemed to be clean and cheap. It does not use fossil fuel, nor does it emit greenhouse gases.

5 Yes, they are viable arguments. Maintaining an interest in nuclear power means we can develop better safety procedures. Waste is the main problem.

Pages 18–19

2 3 MHz = 3×10^6 Hz; 30 MHz = 3×10^7 Hz; 300 MHz = 3×10^8 Hz; 3 GHz = 3×10^9 Hz; 30 GHz = 3×10^{10} Hz

3 (a) A microwave re-transmitter launched from the Earth, in orbit but in constant location relative to Earth.
(b) A signal having a wavelength of between about 10^{-2} and 10^{-4} m.
(c) A division of the radio wave section of the spectrum from very low to super-high frequency.
(d) The distance in metres between maximum or minimum points on an alternating wave.

4 Vacuum cleaner, dishwasher, washing machine, tumble dryer, food processor, electric carving knife, hairdryer, etc.

5 Wind turbines, wave power, hydroelectric falls.

Pages 20–21

1 Humans burn fossil fuels; grow rice; keep cattle; use fertilizer; dump waste; and remove forest.

3 Check the bar graph correctly reflects the information given.

4 'Developed countries' contribute 67.7% (2/3); 'developing countries' contribute 32.3% (1/3).

5 China and India; both are industrializing and have huge populations.

Pages 22–23

1 Sense-experiences come first; reasoning follows after.

2 We are taught the relationship, often in practical terms; thinking may help in the seeing of patterns of relationships.

3 We cannot be sure that relationships that have held in the past will do so in the future.

4 They imagine that they have a special knowledge of what counts for knowledge.

6 The facts, feelings or experiences known by a person or group of people; the state of knowing; awareness, consciousness or familiarity gained by experience or learning.

Pages 24–25

1 'A healthy mind in a healthy body'; how to be effective in debate; and how to distinguish between the 'educated' and the rest.

2 Other foundation subjects appear to be second class; a modern foreign language imposes a limited obligation; and RE is something of an afterthought.

3 They are 'fringe' subjects left to schools' discretion and what time remains.

4 The aim is to reflect a more diverse British population.

5 There are many opinions and perspectives to consider.

Pages 26–27

1 There is no reason why we should not achieve knowledge of most things. However, constant improvements in technology allow us to investigate things previously out of our reach. The mind and the universe will keep scientists busy for a while.

3 We are a part of nature and cannot detach ourselves from it.

4 If not the 'psychology' then, perhaps, the neurology of human beings.

5 Genetic engineering (especially cloning); experiments on animals; biological weapons, etc.

Pages 28–29

1 Yes, if the phrase means anything at all.

2 No. To an atheist, there is no being that has ethical oversight of humans.

3 Life is a slippery slope – but we are never at the top of it; we are on it, and we throw salt on it.

4 The benefits are too great to deny; the risks too great to discount.

5 They permit it – but they rule out eugenics.

Pages 30–31

1 The competition for resources from diverse species may mean that not all can be sustained.

2 Rainforests benefit from good growing conditions: heat and humidity. They are old and (hitherto) extensive. Diversity feeds on diversity. They are found in Brazil, Colombia, Peru; Indochina, Malaysia, Indonesia; Zaire, Angola, Central African Republic.

3 Meat eating has led to the near-extinction of certain species, e.g. whales; the loss of food energy as the chain lengthens; the instability of food chains.

4 Rainforest loss for farming, Brazil; depletion of sparrow population owing to traffic fumes, UK; poaching of male elephants for ivory, South-East Asia; loss of cod in the North Sea; grey squirrels wiping out red squirrels, UK; encroachment on green-belt land, UK.

5 Mammals 25.4%; birds 11.5%; reptiles 3.9%; amphibians 2.7%; fishes 2.6%; invertebrates 0.2%; plants 5.2%.

6 Developing countries do not wish to be constrained in their use of resources; they want to catch up with the wasteful West.

Pages 32–33

2 The rewards given depend on what each culture considers of value. They can be financial, a gift, increased status, a day trip, cuddles and affection, or even an extra portion of food. They motivate most when they are something the child craves.

3 Treat others how you wish to be treated yourself; inappropriate behaviour will be punished; look after family and friends; try to be as good as you can be, etc.

4 Freudian theory can not be measured objectively.

5 In a job interview you present yourself as likeable, confident and capable so that you will get the job.

Pages 34–35

1 It is white light diffracted into seven colour bands; it represents the visible part of the electromagnetic spectrum, with frequencies of between 400 and 700 nm.

2 They are frequently large and consist of blocks of soft-edged colour.

3 It is both. Criteria of success or failure would need to be clear, and there would need to be a definition of 'widely' for this to be a truly objective statement.

4 (a) They thought the sun was moving, and appreciated its divine, life-sustaining powers; (b) They thought they were inherent in substances, divinely given properties; (c) They supposed they were being blessed or bewitched.

5 Diamonds are precious stones. Diamonds grace an engagement ring.

Pages 36–37

1 (a) Differential or integral calculus.
(b) Speed, acceleration, velocity.
(c) The periodic table of elements.
(d) Phylum, genus, species.

2 History: classical/medieval/modern.
Geography: human/economic/physical.
Economics: micro-/macro-economics.
Psychology: cognitive/social/individual.

3 (a) Sociologists; demographers; social service providers, etc.
(b) Knowing who is in need of services; who to target products at; who to conscript in time of war, etc.

4 It requires definition of the 'head'; it discounts female roles; it over-emphasizes economic status.

5 Educational qualifications; savings as a ratio of income; consumption-habits; use of natural resources, etc.

6 The working classes are contracting; the middle classes expanding; the distinction is losing its meaning.

7 The unemployed, disabled, the freelance and the part-time. Women may be under-represented.

10 A classification by gender, height, shoe-size or calorie-consumption would be objective. Most (like 'qualifications') would be subjective.

Pages 38–39

1 It argues from specific cases to generalizations. It collects data systematically in order to answer fundamental questions.

2 Perhaps it is the most comprehensive social science, but they are all interdependent – they are all about the way people behave.

5 Reform can only spring from knowledge of what needs to change and how change is brought about.

6 Not really: all scientists and all researchers, are working for improvement of some sort.

7 No. Medicine seeks a healthier society; law an ordered society; sociology an open and just society.

Pages 40–41

1 Two or more people living together, related by blood or by another commitment.

2 Formerly, families were bigger; the risk of infant mortality was greater; an extended family might live together; the father was dominant; there was little divorce; and life expectancy was lower.

3 One-person households are on the increase; the incidence of childless couples has grown; the number of children per couple has reduced; there are more single parents.

4 39.4%

5 More childless couples; more lone parents and one-person households.

Pages 42–43

2 Some children were in families with a tradition of 'good' education, books and conversation, and in schools where there was coaching for the 11+; others were not.

3 Grammar schools had graduate staff, taught languages, separate sciences, and set an academic ('middle class') tone; secondary moderns did not.

4 There was wide discontent about the 11+. Labour looked to the schools to engineer a more equal society.

5 Grammar school teachers and parents, and parents certain that their children would pass. They feared that their children would have to mix with *hoi polloi*.

6 'Brighter' children were taught together and could accelerate; whole-class teaching could assume common standards. In practice, it is invidious and difficult to draw lines, and slow learners are disadvantaged.

7 Their families were the same; expectations were still low; and they sank in low streams.

9 Children from 'poor' families are still not expected to thrive at school – and their families may want them to do paid work. Boys lack the steady motivation of girls.

Pages 44–45

1 The poor were thought to be improvident and to have big families by choice; and so they should restrain themselves. To weed out the weak was nature's way, so to help them was to thwart nature.

3 (a) 49% (b) 284% (c) 101% (d) 79%

4 Check the line graph correctly reflects the information given.

5 The expectations of their culture; the practice of their peers; their own career aspirations.

6 Pressure on land to produce food; competition for housing and industry; pollution of air and water, accumulation of waste; need for yet more energy.

7 37.2%

8 65.3%

9 The only really significant difference is in the 75 and over group.

Pages 46–47

1 Pythagoras' theorem is a rule that has no exceptions. Therefore there is no opposing argument on which to base a debate.

4 An appeal by Conservatives to Thatcherism – it is no longer relevant in its 1980s form; by US politicians to the Constitution – it can mean what they want it to mean; by communists to Marx – he was a theorist not a practical politician.

6 It seems like a close one; the truth is we do not learn a second language in the manner of the first; 'immersion' is near impossible at school.

Pages 48–49

1 (a) Create laws and you create law-breakers. The strong prevail in lawless conditions.

2 Sunday opening hours; RE teaching in schools by law; a protestant monarchy.

3 'You have the body': it is a writ to a jailer to give just cause why a prisoner is in jail. It is important since it guards against loss of freedom without a charge being brought.

4 Even kings cannot abrogate fundamental rights.

5 The most powerful and dominant criminals will usually escape getting caught, whilst the less serious offenders will be caught; laws should always represent what is true and just; the justice system is not always fair.

6 Law is force wielded with consistency; justice is law applied fairly.

7 No. It changes – but it can be assessed from the public media, from opinion polls, and from consulting key individuals and groups.

Pages 50–51

2 Competition leads to an improvement in standards, thus benefiting all.

4 Economists were tempted to think all relationships came down to financial transactions.

5 As long as economists frame hypotheses, gather relevant data systematically and draw valid conclusions from economic realities, they are behaving scientifically.

Pages 52–53

1 It discounts non-financial values; it is contemptuous of tradition and taste; it is philistine.

2 (a) Securing investment for a business proposal, and buying up competitors.
(b) Relaxing regulations on global business and finance.

3 Undoubtedly, economic enterprise will need to be ideas-driven; but excitement on stock exchanges will not trickle down to the majority. The mobile phone market will soon be saturated.

4 Percentages are fairly steady over the period. There was a marginal spread of wealth downwards from the top 1%.

5 The poor are the female manual workers, the elderly, and the sick and disabled.

6 A more progressive, redistributive tax system? Job-creation? Increased social security payments for families?

Pages 54–55

1 They are defending the theory but attacking the interpretation. Their 'economic man' is motivated by more than money. His interests are the community's.

2 He approves of its power to stimulate and regulate economic activity; he disapproves of its being applied to all human activity.

3 There is a limited supply of oil; the few producers control the flow, and everyone wants to buy it.

4 The two factors were interlinked. The computer/telecoms companies would blame the Euro; the stockmarkets would take note of a downward consumption trend.

5 All have been overcome to some extent, but i), ii) and iv) are still key issues.

6 Be more adventurous in Eastern European markets; ensure young people have relevant skills; a tax regime that favours investment in research and development.

Pages 56–57

1 A big internal market, so economics of scale; poor competition from public transport; oil resources, and a 'cheap oil' policy; long-distance travel.

2 Too many cars are being made; fierce competition calls for cost-cutting and relocation of plants; new models demand huge investment.

3 They have more power than governments, yet are not democratically accountable; they can move plants and capital as it suits them, making and breaking economies; they can exploit poor countries where there is little human rights regulation.

4 It realizes economies of scale; it makes for strong companies that can survive in the market; it brings employment to poor countries; it makes 'western' products available for all.

5 The media have raised awareness of such exploitation, and there is popular anger about it; the UN (ILO) needs to have power to curb it; the WTO must not allow near-monopolies to emerge.

Pages 58–59

1 There is still something in it: our early years are hugely formative.

2 Yes. 'Individualist' and 'collectivist' solutions spring from the deepest-rooted of all ideologies.

3 (a) Everything is in the control of the central state.
(b) As much is left to individuals to control as is consistent with a coherent society.

4 If the criteria are clear, it should be.

5 Freedom should probably be maximized, but not at the expense of the environment and the disadvantaged.

Pages 60–61

1 Yes, they both do.

2 England is; Great Britain is a constitutional construct. So is the UK.

3 It is 'good' in the way that it fosters a cultural unity; 'bad' in that it fosters enmity towards other nations.

4 England has such a great diversity of peoples that there is no real nationalism. A sense of nationalism is only good if it promotes what is good about England, and is not used as a basis for bigotry.

6 Yes. Internationalism takes account of national borders and cultures; globalization may not.

Pages 62–63

1 It is probably a factor in peoples' cynicism.

2 Government = a political unit which exercises authority over the actions and affairs of a group of people, and performs certain functions for this group of people.
Politics = the practice or study of the art and science of forming directing and administering states and other political units; the art and science of government.

Politician = someone actively engaged in politics.
Statesman = a respected political leader; a person active & influential in the formulation of high government policy. The word 'politics' in these cases means current issues.

3 He meant that much can happen in a week to change things completely.

4 For: they would master their brief, not be the mouthpieces of civil servants.
Against: they would no longer represent voters; they would *be* civil servants.

6 Conservatives favour private solutions, market economics, selection, UK 'sovereignty', NATO, strong defence; Labour favours public/private solutions, lifelong education, integrated transport, the EU, internationalism. Lib Dems favour reforms that enhance freedom and environment protection.

Pages 64–65

2 No. The executive is within the legislature, and appoints senior law officers.

3 Parliament, the media, EU and UK law.

4 It requires political maturity, an educated and sophisticated electorate, and a strong consensus.

5 Bad bills are winnowed out; there is time for support or opposition to grow in light of public opinion; but good bills may be lost, especially at the end of a session – and momentum is lost.

6 It can access the media, and MPs via pressure-groups – and it can vote.

7 Yes. It can check an arrogant government; it is relatively free from party constraint; it can subject bills to fearless scrutiny.

Pages 66–67

1 It may be seen that owners have too much influence.

3 The Conservatives are perceived to be the *laissez-faire*, deregulating party. Press owners fear EU regulation of concentration of ownership. In addition, most owners are conservatives.

4 *The Guardian*'s to repeal the Act of Succession; *The Mail*'s to 'Keep the pound', etc.

5 It is interpreting events in one's own favour. Everyone does it, has always done it, and the important thing is to be aware of it. Owners have their own agendas, which may militate against their being effective democrats.

6 It must if it is to remain credible. No government can shackle it with impunity.

Pages 68–69

1 Direct: the people themselves being involved on a day-to-day basis in government.
Representative: the people electing a few individuals to speak for them in a parliament.
The former is found at a local level only.

2 According to present standards, yes. To be democrats we must concede something to 'society'.

3 Politicians receive a bad (non-deferential and partisan) press; it all seems remote and beyond popular influence; the EU is unloved; local government seems powerless.

4 In 1, the campaign lobbied, gave evidence, organized a petition, wrote to MPs.
In 2, protesters demonstrated and so figured in the media.

5 It produces results; the media are friendly towards certain protests (Countryside March, Swampy); it is more easily understandable than politics in general; all sorts of people are seen to do it.

Pages 70–71

1 God/Gods were thought to control fertility; rites and priests sought to pleasure the gods into granting good growing conditions.

2 It is out of date, perhaps.

3 The West has often behaved as if its actions were beyond question. It has been unsympathetic to different civilizations.

7 (a) if culture is everything that nature is not, it is not too broad. It may even be too narrow.

Pages 72–73

2 Proximity, familiarity, sunshine, lots of other English-speakers at resorts, well-developed holiday industries, scenery.

6 A citizen of Europe's longest-established monarchy/democracy, with strong links with Europe, the USA and the Commonwealth; with its own currency; cradle of the international language; notable for its literature, music and fine arts tradition – but in decline as a manufacturer and progenitor of TNCs.

Pages 74–75

1 We still think of it as linear, but 'prehistory' has extended back into astronomical time.

2 Yes, but we learn less the further back we go.

3 No. Its main purpose is to help us to understand how things came to be as they are.

6 Census data, manorial rolls, letters, diaries, press reports, treaties, church records, invoices, Hansard, etc. 'Remains' and memorabilia of all sorts are of value to the social historian.

7 The sheer amount of data may overwhelm. The historian is only marginally more objective than any other commentator, from much reading.

Pages 76–77

2 Progress = movement forwards, especially towards a place or objective; satisfactory development, growth or advance; advance towards completion, maturity or perfection; increasing complexity, adaptation, etc. during the development of an individual or evolution taking place; a stately royal journey.

3 Progress = development, growth, advancement, improvement, evolution, movement, steps forward.

4 Spencer's (not Darwin's) phrase 'this survival of the fittest' was powerfully misleading. The 'fittest' may not be the most 'progressive'.

5 Both deplore progress as material accumulation: George fears its divisiveness, Froude its worship of the wrong god.

6 (a) The gas chambers, the bomb, nerve gas, propaganda.
(b) Science/knowledge is neither bad nor good; the use to which it is put may be.

7 We can believe that progress is possible in all areas (though perhaps not in the arts), but by our fertility and resource-use we may be creating as many problems as we are solving.

Pages 78–79

1 The telescope might have added to ideas about the grandeur of nature; the microscope, its intricacy and complexity. Both might have added another dimension to observing.

2 With the idea of the 'mechanical' universe; of God as a mathematician; of nature as a law-abiding system; explicable in terms of the universal law of gravitation.

3 It was no longer possible to believe in the creation of each species separately; the 'selection' of species for survival or loss seemed to be a matter of blind chance: humans had to come to terms with their animal origins.

4 An awareness of the geometry of perspective: an understanding of human anatomy; a technical capacity for rendering light and shade.

5 It had the positive effect that certain painters (Cotman, Turner, Monet) treated industrial subjects; certain painters (Blake, Ruskin, Hunt) retreated into a nostalgic naturalism or into allegory.

6 (a) Photography could represent reality with accuracy, so painters ceased to aim for photographic likeness, opting instead for impressionism or abstraction – or surrealism.
   (b) Painters like Dali (who studied abnormal psychology, and dream symbolism) expressed themselves in the language of dreams – and, sometimes, nightmares. 'Streams of unconsciousness', too, were not uncommon.

Pages 80–81

1 The media, secularization, the rise of Labour, meritocracy.

2 It is significant as 'heritage', not as a role-model for the aristocracy.

3 See page 69.

4 Soap operas and the popular press; the timing of the News. Does impact lessen as channels multiply?

5 (a) Journalists have just as much power as before. TV journalism has increased power due to increased coverage.
   (b) Sports people also have more power. They are no longer just sports people looked up for their sporting abilities, they are celebrities and style icons.
   (c) Farmers have lost almost all their power. Many have been made bankrupt by the recent BSE and foot and mouth crises, hugely depleting the numbers of farmers.
   (d) Miners have lost all of their power. There are very few working mines left, and the miners' unions have no strength.

Pages 82–83

1 He means it is unreliable, subject to sudden change, and easy to manipulate.

2 Opinion: there is no 'factual' distinction between feelings and intellect.

4 Racist chanting and literature; defamatory and offensive matter.

5 Common property; a possible ingredient in ultimate truth.

7 Opinion on homosexuality, pre-marital sex, embryo research, hanging, abortion, etc.

9 (i) There was 'immense industrial development'; smoking had been forbidden in polite society, etc.
   (ii) Albert appreciated the scientific movement; Victoria was enthusiastic about wifely fidelity, etc.

(iii) 'The final years were years of apotheosis'; Victoria should have approved of women's emancipation.

10 Strachey mostly lists Queen Victoria's beliefs, but he includes comments on them based on personal opinion.

Pages 84–85

1 The young (underweight); about half of all over-25 males, one third of females.

2 Smoking, lack of exercise, intake of saturated fats, advertising.

3 (a) Fewer criminals would be created among users; use would grow; it could be used for medicinal purposes.
   (b) Use could be taxed; control over growing use would be difficult in schools, at work, on the road.

4 Professional.

5 Ban advertising; raise price; limit and monitor sales outlets.

6 It has risen most in 16–24 age group, particularly among females.

7 Keep duties in line with income; raise them progressively on wines and spirits.

8 The resulting illness causes high NHS costs and general social distress.

Pages 86–87

1 Yes, 'true' is being used in the same way.
   Alternatives = it has been found that; we accept that.

2 Is there an afterlife? Is eugenics 'good' or 'bad'? What do we mean by 'truth'?

3 The truth would never be absolute; it would be relative to agreed definitions of 'wonderfulness' in singing, and brevity of applause in varying circumstances.

4 'Better' for whom?

Pages 88–89

1 (a) Doctors find it difficult to define what is acceptable and unacceptable in terms of treatment given and when it should stop. They find it difficult to advise relatives in life/death decisions.
   (b) It is difficult for them to know if they are doing the right thing.

3 (a) Only if human life is absolutely different from non-human life
   (b) Not at all.
   (c) Only if victims are likely to be confined to professional soldiers.

4 The sanctity of life argument believes that all life is precious and should be preserved without exception. This case and verdict illustrates a belief that living is not always better than dying. To a great extent it illustrates how out of date the 'Sanctity of Life' ethic is.

5 A being having consciousness of past and future whom we may presume to be viable, and to have a wish to live.

Pages 90–91

1 The wishes of individuals are optimally met; common sense/imagination/judgement.

2 To vote? Serve on juries? Be available for military service? Assist the police?

3 (a) Hunters, farmers, stable-owners, grooms, dog-breeders and handlers.
   (b) Residents of hunting country; animal rights activists; politicians.

4 No.

5 (a) Cannot be justified.

(b) Difficult, but not impossible, to justify.

6 Thompson's and Venables'; their families'; James's family's; everyone else's. The last is the weightiest; the boys' is next. The interest of the Bulgers has no legal standing.

7 The public must believe in the Justice System or anarchy will occur. This is why they must perceive that justice has been done. This is what is meant by 'Justice must be seen to be done'. Yes there is a potential conflict between perceived and actual justice.

Pages 92–93

1 The Thatcher government and press were anti-CND, and the public was by no means unilateralist, whereas it is anti-GM food, and is more tolerant of protest – see p. 69.

2 Second runway, Manchester Airport; hunt sabotage; 'abduction' of Elian Gonzalez by Cuban-Americans, etc.

4 The rights of others may be infringed by those claiming right of assembly.

5 It is 'democratic' when it represents public opinion, and when it does not seek to change things by force.

6 The pot-smoker seeks individual satisfaction; the poll tax protest was a principled stand against collective injustice.

7 They were trespassing.

8 Protesters are 'arrogant', presumably, if they are seeking their own good, not a perceived general good.

9 Almost. They would have done if people had been genuinely inconvenienced.

Pages 94–95

1 No. Policies affecting people cannot but be issues of value.

6 Mary's against Jodie's; Roman Catholic against secular liberal; law against 'common sense'.

7 Health? Love? Education? Justice?

Pages 96–97

1 They can help to build a public presumption in favour of equal opportunities. Some may think that the favouring of others goes too far arguing that meritocracy is threatened.

2 White heterosexual males represent much less than 50% of people; and there are more females than males.

3 Prisoners, the poor, unemployed, etc.

5 Ethnic minorities may be poor on arrival; may have modest expectations, bigger families; may suffer discrimination in job market; may find it culturally difficult to access education.

6 Black and Pakistani/Bangladeshi boys lose out; girls in these groups do not.

7 There is still inequality of opportunity at the top; women have benefited from the increase in service, white-collar jobs.

8 Grants instead of loans to the needy, for part-time as well as full-time students? Lifelong education?

Pages 98–99

1 Nature is bigger, and more awesome, than we are.

2 Waning of deference to authority; the success of science in explaining the world.

3 Religion is a matter of attitude, not worshipful behaviour.

5 Anglican (42%).

6 Muslim (280%).

7 At the hard end.

8 Knowledge and faith that God exists.

10 It has something to do with it – but the two tables measure different things.

Pages 100–101

1 It must weaken the impact of Christianity in the non-Christian world.

3 No. Religious faith is unimpressed by 'evidence'. Science is nothing without it.

4 They might be like religions; but is the word suitable for godless behaviours?

5 Could it be that the early Americans were more genuinely religious than the persecuting Europeans whom they fled? Or that religion is a badge of identity in a cultural melting-pot?

6 It does not really do either.

Pages 102–103

1 Religion has reinforced our moral code, not created it.

2 The Ten Commandments can be explained in terms of a particular time and place. They are not universal precepts, nor need their origin to be attributed to a miracle.

3 No. Religion helps people come to terms with the trauma experienced from such events, but is not the only way to explain another person's behaviour. For example, there are often medical explanations.

4 A 'God-less moral system' is very philosophical in nature, and some people do not have the level of intellect necessary to live a philosophical way of life.

5 Burrows believes that 'young Johnny' and all other young people need to learn moral guidance through example, and to build up 'good' moral behaviour habits.

6 Behave as you would have all behave; respect others' purposes, not merely for how they might serve your purposes. These axioms are the basis for all law.

8 Sin was defined by those least likely to fall into it, to keep 'inferiors' in their place.

9 Sin is not solely a religious concept. A similar atheist/humanist view of sin would be any behaviour that physically or mentally harms another individual/creature.

10 Euthanasia; offering political asylum to refugees; capital punishment; genetically modified crops; genetic engineering; cloning, etc.

12 A desire to cooperate, act in others' interests, work to long-term goals?

Pages 104–105

1 Yes. There was a mid-winter festival before there was God.

2 It encouraged them to accept their lot, and their dependence on the church.

3 See pp. 112–113.

4 It is backward-looking, illiberal, nationalistic, and inflexible.

6 Religion often refuses to accept inaccuracies in their teachings, which have been highlighted by well-structured scientific research. Science refuses to accept the teachings of the church without question, and searches for evidence to support/contradict these teachings.

7 The Roman Catholic Church, in particular, still has enormous wealth. The Anglican Church still values its liaison with the state.

8 Religion keeps people tranquil, politically comatose, and unable to fight for justice.

Pages 106–107

2 Belief in the afterlife, Providence, the possibility of sustainable 'growth', horoscopes, the wisdom of tax-cutting; these may all be examples.

3 'Miracle', like 'heaven' is a term that has meaning only for believers.

4 If you do not believe, you will go to hell and suffer eternal damnation; believers will be offered forgiveness of sins, and will be looked after by God.

5 Many people seem to be able to do so.

7 Not if we restrict 'belief' to what is rational and language-based.

9 Between a defence of UK 'sovereignty' and the possibility of pooled sovereignty within Europe? Between the freedom of an individual to run a car, and the social need for efficient transport?

Pages 108–109

I Basques and French/Spanish speakers; Northern Irish and Irish Republicans; North Welsh and English; Flemings and Walloons. There are non-linguistic factors at work in all cases.

2 Not altogether. People will use the language in which they can best give expression to their values.

3 It is naïve. Language-use will not be coerced.

5 'Goldstein' (Jews and money); 'lean' (and hungry, like the assassin Cassius); 'fuzzy' (disorderly); 'goatee' (like Lenin?); 'clever' (cunning); 'senile silliness'; 'sheep'; 'child'. He is all clever/stupid, old/young types of enemy-figure.

6 Nearly all is due to use of language.

Pages 110–111

2 The different meanings make it difficult to ascertain if all are discussing 'art' in the same context.

3 They all start with nature, because the artist is from nature, and so are his or her experiences and raw materials.

4 Of course they speak truths for the artist, the observer, in some measure – and these truths may be moral – but 'effects'? The arts may change minds; but behaviour?

5 She believes you can't rate art by popularity, and that all art is of value. She therefore believes 'Arts for Everyone' devalues the less popular arts.

Pages 112–113

I It does not seek to be art, to say something thoughtful about the human condition or to say it well.

2 Could be; but then the term 'art' is no longer very descriptive.

3 No, but they are all artefacts. Art historians have extended their territory.

4 Why does art have to 'move'? Might not design move just as much? The distinction is ultimately untenable.

Pages 114–115

I Judd is right in practice. Pointon seems to make a distinction between what is art and what is treated as such. 'Anything goes' is an abdication of critical judgement.

2 It certainly raises the question again about the magazine advertisement: see question 1 above and pp. 112–113.

3 When everything is art, only what is not yet technically feasible has not yet been done by someone, somewhere.

4 Criticisms made by the 'uncultured'.

6 To a certain extent because it has a financial value and can be an investment. Its monetary value is as much as people are willing to pay. Art also has other values, such as beauty.

Pages 116–117

I (a) 25%   (b) 152%

2 Interactivity; virtual reality; multi-sensory experiencing?

3 The total of TV, video and computer games is 3 hrs 22 mins. Music is probably concurrent with other activities.

4 60%

5 Children may be accessing the media with a family member or friend, they may be eating, they may be playing.

8 It might be a probing, thoughtful interpretation of reality, involving skilful scriptwriting, production, and acting.

9 Cinema-going has risen by nearly 60%; all other attendance has remained steady. The audiences probably overlap.

10 Special effects; boredom with TV; big-budget spectaculars; young people's need to get out of the house; multi-screen, more comfortable cinemas.

12 It is surely one of the functions of art to speak to all of us about ourselves, not to be either exclusive or trivial.

Pages 118–119

I Make relevant, significant distinctions; make distinction on irrelevant, offensive grounds.

2 (a) Critics are servants to artists, who are the real aristocrats of culture.
(b) Critics criticize without any qualification for doing so.

3 It is new; it moves; it excites; it provokes to thought; it is skilfully done; it is acknowledged to be good by critics – or by large numbers of people over time; it is fit for purpose; it is challenging.

4 Each writes its own rules. It is difficult to pin down what makes one 'better' than the other.

Pages 120–121

I It did not depend on literacy, except among actors; it poked fun at 'great ones' and did not depend on church patronage.

2 The Puritans thought it immoral and a licence to crime and irreverence.

3 Literacy was spreading; it combined art with entertainment; it gave an occupation to middle-class women.

4 The novel will endure, as will non-fiction. Drama and screenplay writing will flourish.

5 It can speak concisely, metaphorically and at different levels – but no more 'truly' than prose.

6 *Aesop's Fables*. They are engaging, accessible, universal, and critical in the best sense.

Index

Page numbers in **bold** indicate main entries.